Landscapes Past and Present: Cheshire and Beyond

Landscapes Past and Present: Cheshire and Beyond

Papers researched and written by members of
Chester Society for Landscape History
to celebrate the 30th anniversary of
the Society in 2016

Edited by
Sharon M. Varey
and **Graeme J. White**

University of Chester Press

First published 2016
by University of Chester Press
Parkgate Road
Chester CH1 4BJ

Printed and bound in the UK by the
LIS Print Unit
University of Chester
Cover designed by the LIS Graphics Team
University of Chester

Editorial Material
© Chester Society for Landscape History, 2016
The individual papers
© the respective authors, 2016
Pictures
© the respective photographers/
copyright holders

All Rights Reserved
No part of this publication may be reproduced, stored in a retrieval system or transmitted in any form or by any means without the prior permission of the copyright owner, other than as permitted by UK copyright legislation or under the terms and conditions of a recognised copyright licensing scheme

A catalogue record of this book is available
from the British Library

ISBN 978-1-908258-28-1

CONTENTS

List of Colour Plates — vii

Picture Acknowledgements — viii

Abbreviations — xi

Notes on Contributors — xii

Preface — xiv

Introduction: **Sharon M. Varey and Graeme J. White** — 1

1. Enclosure and Enclosures in Mid- and East Cheshire: **Graeme J. White** — 8

2. Medieval Moated Sites in the Cheshire–North Wales Borderland: **Ray Jones** — 47

   A Gazetteer of Moated Sites in the Cheshire–North Wales Borderland — 83

3. Ways and Meres: Pre-Turnpike Roads, Tracks, Boundaries and their Markers in the East Cheshire Peak District: **Tom Swailes** — 99

4. Keys to the Past: Unlocking the Secrets of the Landscape of Peel: **Sharon M. Varey** — 130

5. Tracing the Eighteenth-Century Landscape of Thelwall in Cheshire: **Mike Taylor** — 164

6.	When was Colwyn Bay?: **Mike Headon**	188
7.	Cheshire Airfields: A Legacy in the Landscape: **Antony Barratt**	215
8.	Landscape as History – Probing its Public Interface: **Julie Elizabeth Smalley**	239

Index of Places — 256

Index of Subjects — 268

LIST OF COLOUR PLATES

1: Mossley Moss, Congleton, from the 1992–93 Aerial Survey of Cheshire. — 87

2: Mossley Moss as it appears in the Congleton enclosure award, 1798. — 88

3: Llay Hall: the surviving arm of the moat. — 89

4: White Nancy, one of the best known landmarks in east Cheshire. — 90

5: Peel Hall Estate, 1717: map commissioned by the earl of Plymouth. — 91

6: Peel Hall: south front. — 92

7: Estate map of Thelwall Waste, 1743. — 93

8: Thelwall Waste today; with ghosts of grubbed-out hedges. — 94

9: Thelwall Estate map, 1743, showing land north of the Mersey. — 95

10: Colwyn, watercolour by David Cox, 1845. — 96

11: Aerial view of the site of HMS Blackcap, Stretton, in 2009–10. — 97

12: A 2009–10 aerial photograph of RAF Poulton showing how nature is taking back the site. — 98

PICTURE ACKNOWLEDGEMENTS

Paper 1: White, Enclosure and Enclosures
Figures 1, 3: Base map © A.D.M. Phillips and C.B. Phillips, reproduced with permission from A.D.M. Phillips and C.B. Phillips, *A New Historical Atlas of Cheshire* (Chester, 2002), 9.
Figure 4: 1992–93 Aerial Survey of Cheshire. Copyright 2009 Cheshire West & Chester Council & Cheshire East Council © All rights reserved. Flown and captured by National Remote Sensing Centre Ltd, 1992–93. Digitally converted by Bluesky International Ltd, 2009.
Figure 6: © 2006 Cheshire West & Chester Council & Cheshire East Council. All rights reserved. Flown and captured by Hunting Surveys Ltd, 1971–73. Digitally converted by Genesys International Ltd & The Aerial Surveyor Ltd, 2005/6.
Plate 1: 1992–93 Aerial Survey of Cheshire. Copyright 2009 Cheshire West & Chester Council & Cheshire East Council © All rights reserved. Flown and captured by National Remote Sensing Centre Ltd, 1992–93. Digitally converted by Bluesky International Ltd, 2009.
Plate 2: CALS, QDE 2/8: reproduced by permission of Cheshire Archives and Local Studies and the owner/depositor to whom copyright is reserved.

Paper 2: Jones, Medieval Moated Sites
Figure 15: By kind permission of Mr G. Moore, Llay Hall Farm.
Figure 16: Photograph: Derrick Gwilliam.
Figure 17: Photograph: David Roberts.
Figure 18: After J. Rigg, 'Broughton Earthwork', *[Publications of the] Flintshire Historical Society*, XIX (1961), 92–93.
Plate 3: Photograph: Derrick Gwilliam.

Picture Acknowledgements

Paper 3: Swailes, Ways and Meres
Figures 1, 4: The National Archives UK, refs. MPC1/20 and OS 26/1063, reproduced by permission.
Figure 2: Source: Earwaker, *East Cheshire, II*, 285. Figure based on an image courtesy of Hathi Trust. Available online as a permanent link: <<http://hdl.handle.net/2027/yale.39002088543229?urlappend=%3Bseq=327>>.
Figure 7: Reproduced by permission of New Mills Local History Society.
Figure 9: Photograph: Bob Langstaff.
Figure 11: 1971–73 Aerial Survey of Cheshire. Copyright 2006 Cheshire West & Chester Council & Cheshire East Council © All rights reserved. Flown and captured by Hunting Surveys Ltd, 1971–73. Digitally converted by Genesys International Ltd & The Aerial Surveyor Ltd, 2005/6.

Paper 4: Varey, Keys to the Past
Figure 4 and Plate 5: FRO, D-DM 540/7: reproduced by permission of Flintshire Record Office.
Figure 13: CALS, CPE_UK_1935_3038: reproduced by permission of Cheshire Archives and Local Studies and the owner/depositor to whom copyright is reserved.

Paper 5: Taylor, Tracing the Eighteenth-Century Landscape
Figure 6: CALS, DWW 430: reproduced by permission of Cheshire Archives and Local Studies and the owner/depositor to whom copyright is reserved.
Plate 7: CALS, DWW 431: reproduced by permission of Cheshire Archives and Local Studies and the owner/depositor to whom copyright is reserved.
Plate 8: 1992–93 Aerial Survey of Cheshire. Copyright 2009 Cheshire West & Chester Council & Cheshire East Council © All rights reserved. Flown and captured by National Remote

Sensing Centre Ltd, 1992–93. Digitally converted by Bluesky International Ltd, 2009.
Plate 9: CALS, DWW 429: reproduced by permission of Cheshire Archives and Local Studies and the owner/depositor to whom copyright is reserved.

Paper 6: Headon, When was Colwyn Bay?
Plate 10: The British Museum Collection Online © The Trustees of the British Museum.
Figures 3, 6: By permission of Conwy Archive Service.
Figure 5: By permission of the British Newspaper Archive.
Figure 9: By permission of Llyfrgell Genedlaethol Cymru/The National Library of Wales.

Paper 7: Barratt, Cheshire Airfields
Figures 2–6: Photographs: Martin Barratt.
Figures 7, 8: Photographs: Tony Barratt.
Figures 9, 10: Reproduced by permission of Historic England (RAF Photography).
Plate 11: Image captured, supplied and copyrighted by Bluesky International Ltd, 2009–10.
Plate 12: Image captured, supplied and copyrighted by Bluesky International Ltd, 2009–10.

ABBREVIATIONS

CALS: Cheshire Archives and Local Studies
Ches. Hist.: *Cheshire History*
CSLH: Chester Society for Landscape History
CHER: Cheshire Historic Environment Record
edn: edition
fos: folios
FRO: Flintshire Record Office
HER: Historic Environment Record
LHDNW: S.M. Varey and G.J. White, eds, *Landscape History Discoveries in the North West* (Chester, 2012)
Mf: microfilm
nd: not dated
NGR: National Grid Reference
Ormerod (1819): G. Ormerod, *The History of the County Palatine and City of Chester* (London, 1819)
Ormerod (1882): G. Ormerod, *The History of the County Palatine and City of Chester*, revised and enlarged edn by T. Helsby (London, 1882)
OS: Ordnance Survey
RCAHMW: *Royal Commission on the Ancient and Historical Monuments of Wales*
ser.: series
THSLC: *Transactions of the Historic Society of Lancashire and Cheshire*
TNA: The National Archives
VCH Ches.: *Victoria History of the County of Chester*, ed. B.E. Harris, C.P. Lewis and A.T. Thacker (Oxford and Woodbridge, 1979–2005)

NOTES ON CONTRIBUTORS

Graeme White is Emeritus Professor of Local History at the University of Chester and President of the Chester Society for Landscape History, having launched the Diploma in Landscape History (later to become the MA in Landscape, Heritage and Society) at what was then Chester College in 1978. Among his recent publications are *The Medieval English Landscape, 1000–1540* (2012) and *The Magna Carta of Cheshire* (2015).

Ray Jones is a retired Education Inspector, whose research interests encompass historical landscape change in the Cheshire–North Wales Borderland. His recent publications include *Gwenfro – A Landscape History of Wrexham and its River* (2012) and *Chester and the Landscape of North East Wales* (2013).

Tom Swailes is a part-time University lecturer and has published work on several aspects of civil engineering history. He is a Kerridge Ridge and Ingersley Vale volunteer carrying out historic landscape conservation and management work, as well as being a member of the Chester Society for Landscape History.

Sharon Varey is a part-time tutor and researcher. Having gained an MA in Landscape, Heritage and Society, she went on to complete a PhD on the changing landscape of Baschurch, a parish in north-west Shropshire. Co-editor, with Graeme White, of *Landscape History Discoveries in the North West* (2012), Sharon has written articles relating to aspects of the landscape history of North Shropshire and Cheshire. She is currently Chairman of CSLH.

Notes on Contributors

Mike Taylor is a retired Chartered Engineer. He has lived in Thelwall since 1986 and has published two books on its local history and another on an eighteenth-century diary that relates to the area. He also contributed to *Cheshire History* (2012) a paper on the financial problems of the Pickering family who lived at Thelwall Hall.

Mike Headon is a retired higher education lecturer. He is a graduate of the MA in Landscape, Heritage and Society and is particularly interested in place-names and the landscape history of Wales. Mike is a key member of the Planning Team for Chester Society for Landscape History, having at different times held the offices of chairman, secretary, field visits organiser and lectures co-ordinator.

Tony Barratt worked in local government, is a graduate of the MA in Landscape, Heritage and Society and is particularly interested in transport history. An active speaker to local societies, his publications include *Cheshire Shipyards* (1999), *McTay, A Wirral Shipbuilder* (2005) and *The New Life Fleet* (forthcoming).

Julie Smalley is a Business graduate, language tutor and holder of the MA in Landscape, Heritage and Society who has also published widely on the historic environment, including an article entitled 'High Street Heyday? Edwardian Retail in a Small Cheshire Market Town' in *Cheshire History* (2014). She is Lifelong Learning Co-ordinator for Chester Society for Landscape History.

PREFACE

This book celebrates the 30th anniversary of Chester Society for Landscape History (CSLH), founded in 1986 by former students of the Diploma in Landscape History and of its successor, the MA in Landscape, Heritage and Society, taught at Chester College (now the University of Chester) since 1978. Although this course is no longer delivered at the University, it continues to influence aspects of the undergraduate and postgraduate curriculum and, for its part, CSLH is one means by which the study of landscape history lives on in Chester. All the papers in this book are the work of members of the Society, and most were delivered at a well-attended and well-received Research Day organised by CSLH and held at St Mary's Centre, Chester in October 2015. Given the Society's origins, it is highly appropriate that the volume is published by University of Chester Press, as was its predecessor, *Landscape History Discoveries in the North West*, which marked CSLH's 25th anniversary.

The editors would like to place on record their gratitude for, and appreciation of, the sterling work of the University Press's Managing Editor, Dr Sarah Griffiths: herself a graduate of the MA and member of the Society. Her expert advice and determination to see the work through to publication – on schedule! – have been invaluable. The assistance of her University colleagues in Learning and Information Services, including Mark English, the Graphics Team and the Print Unit is also very much appreciated. We are also most grateful to all the contributors for their co-operation in delivering material on time, and for tolerating our editorial interventions with patience and good grace. They in turn will join us in thanking the many others whose help and expertise have been called upon, including landowners, custodians, record office staff and those family and friends who have offered encouragement and support. Special thanks are due to Gary

Preface

Duckers and Paul Varey for the production of maps and to David Matthews for his guidance in the selection and delivery of aerial photographs from various collections. The book is truly the product of a collective enterprise and it has been a pleasure and a privilege to bring it to fruition.

Sharon M. Varey and Graeme J. White (March 2016)

INTRODUCTION

Sharon M. Varey and Graeme J. White

'Landscape' is one of the buzz-words of the early twenty-first century. We frequently encounter phrases such as 'the political landscape' or 'the economic landscape' to denote an overview of conditions and prospects in our current affairs.

The word clearly has widespread appeal, embracing a sense that whatever is under review should be tackled holistically, with due regard to the connections between the component parts. It has come some way since the middle years of the twentieth century, when W.G. Hoskins introduced his pioneering book, *The Making of the English Landscape*, by assuming that every reader would understand that his subject was topography:

> What I have done is to take the landscape of England as it appears today, and to explain … how it came to assume its present form, how the details came to be inserted, and when … There is no part of England, however unpromising it may appear at first sight, that is not full of questions for those who have a sense of the past.

The present book approaches 'landscape' in Hoskins's sense of the word, and so does Chester Society for Landscape History (CSLH), whose 30th anniversary the book celebrates and whose members contributed all the papers. But it is worth stressing another phrase from Hoskins's Introduction: 'I have also chosen … to show how the pattern developed as a whole'.[1] It is this approach to the study of landscape history – a readiness to see features in a wider context, to explore developments not in isolation from but in relation to one another – which has always characterised the discipline since Hoskins's day and which has led to the present broader use of the word. We hope that the papers which follow will be seen as examples of this tradition.

Landscapes Past and Present

The origins and definition of 'landscape history' were also discussed by Dai Morgan Evans in his stimulating Introduction to CSLH's 25th anniversary book, *Landscape History Discoveries in the North West*. He saw 'landscape history' as embracing 'history, archaeology, geography, economics, botany, culture, gardening and on and on' and pointed to the value of a Society devoted to the subject in which a variety of different knowledge and experience could be shared. Indeed, in the list of some 200 lectures delivered to CSLH since its inception 30 years ago, speakers from all these disciplines can be found! We hope that the diversity of the subject is also reflected in the range of papers in this book.

Dai Morgan Evans actually looked back beyond Hoskins as the 'father of landscape history' and cited instead William Camden, whose *Britannia: Or a Chorographical Description ... from the depth of antiquity*, discussing the landscape in terms both of its past development and its present spatial arrangement, had first appeared exactly 400 years before the birth of CSLH, in 1586. As Morgan Evans pointed out, Camden had seen his account as a 'work in progress' to which others would add – as duly happened, resulting in a series of ever-expanding editions over the next two centuries.[2] There are echoes of all this in the very last paper in the present volume, 'Landscape as History: Probing its Public Interface'. Here, **Julie Smalley**, the Society's Lifelong Learning Co-ordinator, presents landscape history as a pursuit in which – from their different perspectives – almost everyone can engage, and to which – with due attention to scholarship – almost everyone can contribute. Her empirically based analysis suggests that the subject is often misunderstood and not always well presented but offers an accessibility to the past which gives it untapped potential for wider dissemination. Among several 'new markets' which she identifies for landscape history are youth

Introduction

groups, domestic tourism and the family leisure sector. There are lessons here for the future of the discipline, of the Society, and indeed for anyone who cares not only about history but also about the environment and about public education.

One of the characteristics of landscape history, as alluded to by Hoskins and as Julie Smalley's paper also emphasises, is that it involves a dialogue between the present and the past: our history informs our surroundings today, so those surroundings become part of the evidence of what has gone before. This – alongside a focus on Cheshire and places just beyond its borders – is the reason for the title of this book, *Landscapes Past and Present: Cheshire and Beyond*. All the remaining contributors have sought to explain features in the urban or rural landscape which can readily be visited and experienced today in terms of their historical development. Most have embraced the very edges of the county, some have reached beyond it, all have offered conclusions of value to any student of the landscape of England or Wales as a whole.

This is particularly well exemplified by **Ray Jones** in his paper 'Medieval Moated Sites in the Cheshire–North Wales Borderland'. The argument here is that the presence of moats to both the west and the east of the River Dee shows 'the porosity of the border' in the medieval period, although it is important to note the unevenness of distribution: in the English Maelor, for example, 'the density of moats matches those in Suffolk and Essex' while, in contrast, 'an area around Wrexham is devoid of moated sites'. This contrast, it is suggested, reflects differences in the extent to which English settlement patterns and tenurial customs had affected the districts concerned: a clear example of how the twenty-first century landscape is still influenced by twelfth-to-fourteenth-century circumstances. The paper also explores the relevance in this region of well-worn explanations for the creation of moats – status, security, food and water supply – and thus makes a significant contribution to study of the subject at a national level.

Another paper which straddles the county boundary is the study of 'Ways and Meres: Pre-Turnpike Roads, Tracks, Boundaries and their Markers in the East Cheshire Peak District' by **Tom Swailes**. Through the judicious use of maps, air photographs and surveys, allied to perceptive and energetic fieldwork, the author identifies several 'lost' way-markers – especially the remains of stone crosses – in the uplands of eastern Cheshire, a task which necessarily takes him along the relevant tracks into Derbyshire and Staffordshire as well. This is a fascinating paper, partly because of its conscious attempt to recreate the experience of earlier travellers but mainly because it brings to light features in the landscape which were largely unknown and which, in their turn, help to identify the course of abandoned routeways. It serves as an excellent illustration of how the impact of past activity on the landscape of today can often be very subtle, lying unrecognised until a well-informed, enthusiastic researcher comes along!

Tony Barratt's paper on 'Cheshire Airfields: A Legacy in the Landscape' could also be said to reach beyond the county, but only because the boundaries have changed over the years: he includes Burtonwood, which was in Lancashire when an airfield was built there in 1940, only for the place to be transferred to Cheshire in 1974. Here again, we have a study of a relatively little-known subject, but one which has left an important imprint on the landscape, whether that takes the form of distinctive field boundaries, surviving buildings or total redevelopment which would not have been envisaged but for the previous use of the site. Brief histories are provided of eleven airfields in total, with comment on what can still be seen today. Most were built in wartime but the civilian projects ranged from a private concern at Combermere (which still

Introduction

leaves clues to its former existence in the field pattern and the remains of a hangar) to Manchester Corporation's Ringway, now Manchester International Airport. There is much here to interest anyone with an eye for the landscape, in all parts of the county.

Similarly wide-ranging in its coverage of different places within Cheshire is the paper by **Graeme White** on 'Enclosure and Enclosures in Mid- and East Cheshire'. This is presented as a continuation of the same author's paper on 'The Enclosure of West Cheshire', which appeared in CSLH's twenty-fifth anniversary volume. On the whole, the conclusion is that the enclosure of both open arable and of common pasture involved very similar processes over nearly the whole of the county: that what was true of the west was also true of the rest. However, some differences are highlighted relating to the commons, notably the importance of peat mosses – and hence the distinctive field pattern associated with 'moss-rooms' – towards the east of Cheshire, and also the greater significance here of enclosure for building development. Whereas the previous paper had stressed contrasts between Cheshire's enclosure history and that of the 'champion countryside' of the midlands, this paper also offers a word of qualification about the similarities between them.

The three remaining papers in the book are reminders that landscape history does not have to cover a broad sweep of terrain extending over the whole of a county or a substantial portion thereof. Study of a specific settlement or of an individual building within its landscape, by someone who lives locally and knows it well, can be equally challenging, rewarding and informative.

A fine example is 'Tracing the Eighteenth-Century Landscape of Thelwall in Cheshire' by **Mike Taylor**. He describes this as a 'progress report' on his experience of walking through his home village, armed with documentation including a copy of a 1743 estate map, 'to see just how much of the eighteenth-century landscape survives'. We are treated to a lively account of what we would have seen in Thelwall 250–300 years ago: what is still with us, what has gone, what has changed – and, crucially, why. Few buildings remain but there is a particularly valuable account of Thelwall's common 'waste' and meadows, much of which survive in recognisable form today. The author also strikes a cautionary note by pointing out that, so far, Thelwall has largely escaped the peripheral development 'that has blighted neighbouring townships such as Lymm and Appleton'. This has made his task much more enjoyable and enlightening than it would otherwise have been, and he is right to remind anyone thinking of engaging in a similar exercise elsewhere that there may not be endless time in which to do it.

Also focusing on a particular locality is **Sharon Varey**'s paper, 'Keys to the Past: Unlocking the Secrets of the Landscape of Peel'. The central feature here is the seventeenth-century Peel Hall, surrounded by gardens and fields, and the paper shows how the development of the building and of its accompanying landscape can be elucidated through maps, plans, prints, air photographs, hearth tax returns, diaries, rentals, probate inventories and descriptions by earlier writers: a range of sources which others engaged on similar projects might well find a helpful guide. Above all, the paper is a celebration of what can be learned from the landscape itself, especially in a context – as here – where there is a good deal of continuity over the past four centuries. Here again, however, as in Mike Taylor's paper, there is a word of warning about the vulnerability of the landscape, with a concluding reminder about the role of various parties in saving Peel Hall, a building which seemed ripe for demolition in the 1960s.

Introduction

Finally, we cross the county boundary once more in **Mike Headon's** illuminating paper, 'When was Colwyn Bay?' This is the only one in the collection whose subject matter lies entirely outside Cheshire, although, as a seaside resort on the North Wales coast about 40 miles from Chester, it is familiar to many residents of the county. The paper traces the growth of the settlement, especially following the arrival of the main railway line to Holyhead, but its chief fascination lies in the analysis of how variants of the place-name were applied to different features in turn – to a sea bay, to a recreational area along the coastal strip, to the principal hotel and ultimately to the resort itself and its accompanying railway station. Acrimonious disputes arising largely from the development of the new resort – over tollgates and ecclesiastical jurisdiction – add spice to the account, reminding us that landscape historians, like all who study any branch of history, must ultimately engage with the human ambitions, conflicts, decisions and disappointments which have gone into the making of our collective story.

One outstanding feature of all the papers in this volume is the sheer enjoyment which the authors have had in researching their material. We believe this enjoyment shines through. We hope that the papers will inspire others to take up the challenge of exploring the historical background to features in the landscape which excite their interest. If that proves to be the case, this book will indeed be a fitting celebration of the 30th anniversary of Chester Society for Landscape History.

Endnotes
1. W.G. Hoskins, *The Making of the English Landscape* (Harmondsworth, 1970), 15. The book was first published in 1955.
2. D. Morgan Evans, 'Introduction' in *LHDNW*, 2-3.

1

ENCLOSURE AND ENCLOSURES IN MID- AND EAST CHESHIRE

Graeme J. White

Introduction

In 1654, a pamphleteer called Joseph Lee published *Considerations Concerning Common Fields and Inclosures*. His intention was to refute the arguments set out in a previous pamphlet by a Leicestershire minister, John Moor, under the title *The Crying Sinne of England of not Caring for the Poor*. Lee was in favour of the enclosure of the common fields and his basic argument anticipated the fundamental contest of capitalism versus socialism: that, while the old communal regime might be thought to benefit the poor by giving everyone a stake in the land, enclosed fields in the hands of the few could be farmed more efficiently to the ultimate benefit of the poor.

In the course of his argument, Lee listed various alleged abuses associated with common fields, such as a tendency to encroach on one's neighbour's all-too-accessible holdings, and aired what he implied was a fairly widespread belief at the time, that William the Conqueror had deliberately imposed the practice of farming in strips distributed across open fields as a means of distracting the English people from turning against him and his regime.

> It was a practice of policy in King William the Conqueror ['s time] to have men's land laid scattered as they are in common fields, of purpose to minister unto them so much occasion of contention with one another, that they might not have opportunity and leisure to unite against him, in consideration whereof it hath been called the Conqueror's curse.[1]

Enclosure and Enclosures

Needless to say, twenty-first century students of the origins of open fields offer an alternative explanation! Stress is normally laid on such factors as a commitment to sharing out the most fertile parts of a community's land as arable leaving the less favoured areas as pasture; the convenience of ploughing in long narrow strips without obstructions between them; and the need to draw on different individuals' beasts to make up a plough-team (so encouraging co-operative enterprise). Opinions differ on the extent to which decisions to farm communally were taken by the lords or by the peasant-farmers themselves.

The seventeenth-century understanding of how and why open field farming was introduced was wrong, but at least it had a basis in a presumption that the experience was one familiar to much of the conquered country. It seems clear that a commitment to utilising at least some of the available land – the pasture, the woodland and often the meadow and the arable as well – as a shared, communal enterprise was widespread across medieval England, despite differences in soils, terrain and climate.[2] Versions of open- and common-field farming were being adopted nearly everywhere in England between the ninth and the twelfth centuries, albeit with considerable variation in the extent to which communal regulation governed the diverse farming activities. The great midland belt of 'champion countryside', where by the twelfth century, in a typical settlement, most of the available land was laid out in open arable fields and there was tight control of crop rotation and common pasturage, represented one end of a spectrum, with communal regulation prevailing over individual initiative. However, this was not the case everywhere, even in central England, and to the west and east of the midland belt, throughout the Middle Ages, a good deal of farming was conducted in individually held enclosed fields, interspersed with pockets of open arable divided into strips. Within these western and eastern zones, there was almost certainly shared access to the common pasture and woodland, but there is rarely any evidence of the extent to which some form of communal regulation governed the working of the arable strips. Medieval Cheshire, with its mixture of enclosed and relatively small open fields, allied to a lack of information about how they were worked, is generally seen as belonging to the 'western' zone.[3]

There is room for debate, however, over how far Cheshire – the historic county from Wirral to the panhandle – should be regarded as a single entity in discussions of this subject. At the Chester Society for Landscape History's 25th anniversary conference in 2011, a paper on 'The Enclosure of West Cheshire', focusing on Wirral and the lowlands watered by the Dee, Gowy and their tributary streams, with occasional straying onto the mid-Cheshire ridge, contributed to this sense of disunity.[4] In doing so, it had a respectable pedigree, dating back to Vera Chapman's pioneering article on 'Open Fields in West Cheshire', published in 1953, and sustained through books such as *The Domesday Geography of Northern England* (which divided Cheshire into eight sub-sections), Nicholas Higham's *The Origins of Cheshire* (five) and Lancaster University's survey of *The Wetlands of Cheshire* (four: 'the uplands of the Pennine fringe ... the Wirral, a low-lying peninsula bounded by the Dee and Mersey estuaries ... the mid-Cheshire ridge which divides the western and eastern portions of the Cheshire Plain' and 'the Cheshire Plain' itself).[5]

However, while we cannot argue about the distinctiveness of the Pennine edge which forms the eastern frontier of the county, it is easy to exaggerate the diversity of Cheshire. The section on 'Physique' in the *Victoria County History* presents the county as a whole as 'a representative part of western lowland

Enclosure and Enclosures

England', marked by 'cohesion and a distinct identity' within boundaries clearly defined by natural features:

> the county consists essentially of an eastern and a western lowland, divided by a north-south sandstone ridge which, as it approaches the Mersey valley, turns east to Alderley Edge where it abuts upon the Pennine foothills.[6]

Maps in the *New Historical Atlas of Cheshire* depict terrain which, apart from in the eastern uplands, hardly anywhere rises beyond 180 metres above sea level; drift geology which was dominated nearly everywhere, except in the eastern margins, by glacial till, sand or gravel; and – most relevant for present purposes – a bioclimatic classification which makes virtually the whole of the county just as suitable for both arable and pastoral farming as the 'champion' lands of the midlands.

> Apart from the upland areas in the county, which are colder and wetter, Cheshire exhibits much uniformity in environmental warmth and soil moisture. The majority of the county may be classed as possessing a slightly cool, slightly moist climate for agriculture. Cheshire shares these climatic characteristics with much of the central and eastern parts of the country, being warmer and drier for agricultural activities than counties to its north and west. The emphasis on grassland farming in Cheshire in physical terms is likely to owe more to the presence of wide areas of heavy soils than the possession of a distinctively wet climate.[7]

Comparison of data from early seventeenth-century *Inquisitions Post Mortem*, on the one hand, and from agricultural returns of 1875, on the other, suggest that the relative percentages of tillage (arable) and cultivated grassland changed in the intervening period from 45:55 to 24:76, indicative of a shift in the county's agricultural activity in favour of pastoral farming, mainly during the eighteenth century. But the key point for our purposes is that this shift applied over nearly the whole of the county. There were of course some exceptions but, in broad terms, nearly all parts of Cheshire behaved as one.[8]

In any study of enclosure, therefore, our expectation ought to be that the experience of west Cheshire would differ little, if at all, from that of the rest of the county. The 2011 conference was presented with a picture of a rural landscape which in the medieval period had largely been composed of small pockets of open arable field divided into strips, interspersed with closes – individually held enclosed fields which might be arable, pasture or meadow – and with areas of communally accessed land, typically woodland, common pasture ('waste') or meadow. Over some seven centuries, from the thirteenth to the nineteenth, the land not already enclosed was gradually taken into individual occupation and hedged about, so that the open arable strips disappeared and most of the common pasture, meadow and woodland ceased to be generally accessible and could if their proprietor wished be put to other uses. This was a piecemeal process mostly unrecorded, and largely accomplished by a series of private agreements, not always amicable. That said, for surviving tracts of common pasture, there was sometimes resort in the late eighteenth and nineteenth centuries to a formal enclosure award, whether or not initiated by Act of Parliament, and in these cases we do have some documentary evidence of enclosure taking place. However, compared to 'champion England', open arable fields in medieval west Cheshire were far less dominant in the landscape – individually held closes always seem to have been important complementary features – and the precocity of the piecemeal enclosure movement meant that there was far less reliance on parliamentary enclosure or other authoritarian processes leading to a formal enclosure award. The west Cheshire landscape, therefore, tends not to be one of straight-sided fields with right-angled corners, the product of the drawing boards of the surveyors employed by enclosure commissioners, although examples of such fields can certainly be found where formal awards were granted. The purpose of this paper is to explore how far this description of west Cheshire applies also to the rest of the county – and in so doing, present some thoughts on the nature of the Cheshire landscape as a whole which may serve as a useful prelude to the other studies in this book.[9]

The Open Fields
For the open arable fields of mid- and east Cheshire, the story is indeed a familiar one. One of the messages of Domesday Book is that Cheshire was a very sparsely populated county, but within that context Wirral and the Dee valley had more people per square mile than elsewhere. By the sixteenth century, this imbalance in the distribution of population was no longer apparent[10] but it helps to explain why, in general, townships and parishes – mostly the product of the tenth and eleventh centuries – were smaller in area in the better-resourced west than those in the centre and east of the county. This partly accounts for the greater abundance of open-field evidence in the west noted in previous studies of this subject:[11] there was a higher density of townships within which to find them. If one produces a rather different map, one which shows the full extent of each township where there were one or more 'Town Fields' in the early-Victorian Tithe Awards, the distribution across the county is rather more evenly spread, even extending to Tintwistle in the southern Pennines or High Peak (Figure 1). The name 'Town Field' is a fairly reliable – though not infallible – indicator of a field which, though it may

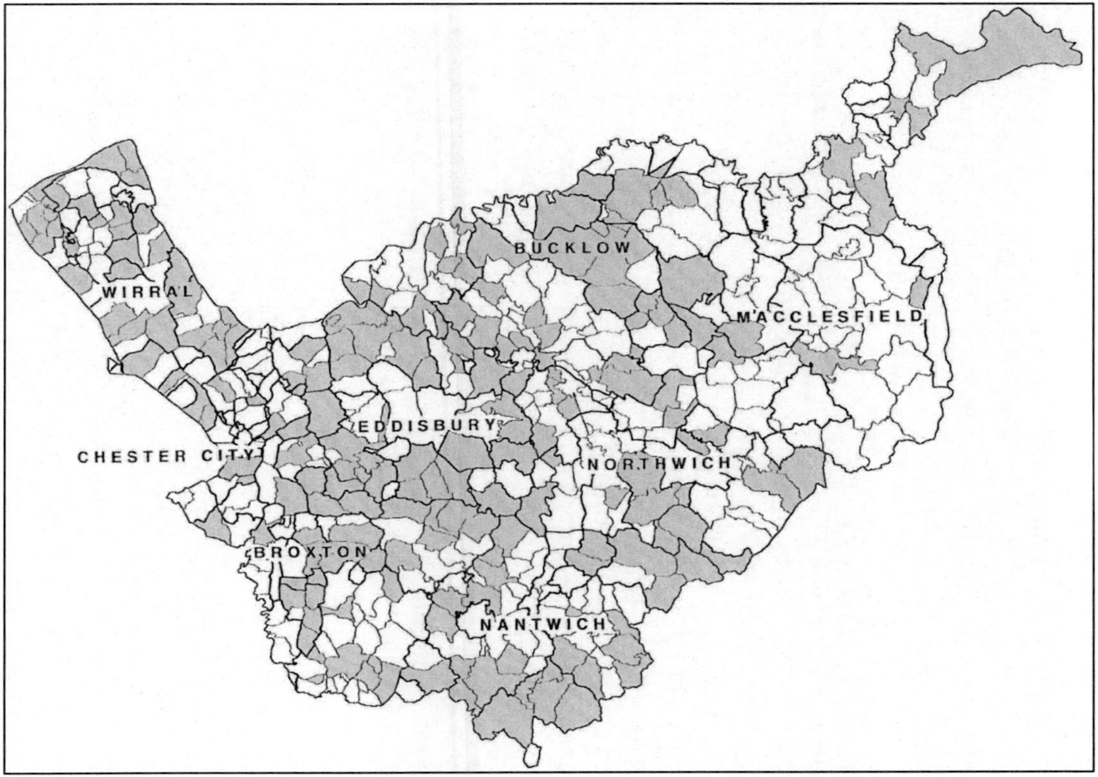

Figure 1: Cheshire townships with one or more fields called 'Town Field' or a variant thereof in the Tithe Award. (Base map © A.D.M. Phillips and C.B. Phillips, reproduced with permission from A.D.M. Phillips and C.B. Phillips, *A New Historical Atlas of Cheshire*, Chester, 2002, 9).

now be enclosed, was once part of the local township or community's principal (or only) open arable field, so to find it occurring in all parts of Cheshire is testimony to the former presence of open field farming right across the county.[12]

As explained in the 2011 paper, it is possible to attempt a reconstruction of former open 'Town Fields' by adding together neighbouring enclosures which, in the Tithe Award, bear some derivative of the name – 'Near Town Field', 'Further Town Field', 'Higher Town Field' and so on.[13] On this basis, some of the Town Fields in the middle and east of the county had been – by Cheshire standards – of considerable size. At Wettenhall the various 'Town Field' closes added up to over 100 acres, at Hurleston to about 67 acres, at both Swettenham and Tabley Superior around 46, at Checkley cum Wrinehill some 38: totals which bear comparison with (and in the first case exceeds) any of those in the west. And as in the west, so in the rest of the county, the fact that several different owners are often recorded in the Tithe Awards as in possession of former portions of the 'Town Field' is a further pointer to the origin of these fields as tracts of land in which a multiplicity of people once had a stake: eight different owners of fields or plots whose names derived from 'Town Field' in the Tithe Awards for both Barnton and Weston (near Runcorn), for example, seven in that for Altrincham, six in each of those for Church Coppenhall, Mobberley, Over and Wybunbury, to set alongside similar numbers in the west: eight at Horton (near Tilston), Tranmere and Wallasey, six in Kelsall, though as many as twelve at Frodsham Lordship and Tattenhall.

Occasionally, unenclosed strips survived to be recorded in the Tithe Awards, usually under an acre in size and bearing the name of 'quillet' or 'loont'. There was a half-acre unenclosed 'quillet' entered in the Tithe Award for Lymm, and a series of unhedged 'loonts' in the 'Lower', 'Higher', 'Near' or 'Further'

Figure 2: Part of the former Town Field of Over, adjacent to the medieval St Chad's church.

Town Fields of Barnton, mostly between a half and a full acre in size. Similarly, at Over, ten 'Loonts in Town Field' (or a variant thereof) were recorded, all less than an acre in extent, and although these have now been enclosed part of the area is still farmland with the 'Town Fields' name preserved on the modern OS map (Figure 2). Lower Walton, Great Budworth, Rostherne and Shurlach are other townships where Tithe Awards showed the survival of unenclosed loonts.[14]

However, these were oddities by the early-Victorian period. Thomas Wedge's *General View of the Agriculture of the County Palatine of Chester*, of 1794, reckoned that there were 'not so much as 1,000 acres of common field' (by which he meant unenclosed strips) remaining in Cheshire and a *Return Relating to Common and Common Field Lands*, produced for the House of Commons in 1874 but based largely on the Tithe Awards over a generation earlier, gave an estimated acreage for the county of 715. This looks to be far too high, but it still left Cheshire

Enclosure and Enclosures

with a smaller area of surviving open strips than all but three counties in England.[15] The more typical story is not the persistence of these isolated remnants of a former farming regime but – as we saw in west Cheshire – a gradual process of piecemeal consolidation and enclosure. This can be traced back to the thirteenth century, usually through references to strips – selions, butts, doles, loons or loonts – or blocks of strips – flatts or furlongs – ceasing to be left open.

So we find, for example, that, sometime between 1265 and 1291, what were described as 'the heads of five butts' against the abbot of Chester's houses in Church Lawton – in the extreme south-east of Cheshire – were conveyed to the abbot by Ranulf of Lawton, 'to be ditched and enclosed ... with full right ... in all the land enclosed within the said ditch.[16] This reads as if the abbot was seeking to extend the land immediately attached to his buildings by encroaching on to the open arable strips – probably through a negotiated purchase from Ranulf as lord of the manor[17] – and it parallels similar acts of consolidation and enclosure under the same abbot identified at Manley and Poulton in the west of the county.[18] A similar image of enclosures and open strips in juxtaposition emerges from an apparently thirteenth-century grant in Peover by Robert son of Meylor to Cecilin his sister of 'a piece of land called Heycroft enclosed by a hedge' and 'another piece ... serving a selion which Richard son of Arurit held'.[19]

A highly formal procedure is recorded from 25 April 1274, when in a court held at Northampton before the chief steward to Edward I's Queen Eleanor – lordship of the county having passed into royal hands in 1237 – and also before eight witnesses from neighbouring townships, Thomas the clerk of Macclesfield surrendered 6 acres in 'Halleghfield', an open field to the east of the town, to be used by the burgesses to pay for the repair of roads; in return, the borough gave him permission to enclose the rest of his holding in the field, albeit with some residual rights which allowed the burgesses to pasture their beasts on his land.[20] This may be a case where all or most of a complete furlong – one of the blocks of parallel strips which made up the open fields – had been consolidated into the hands of an individual landholder who then proceeded to hedge it about. If so, we encounter a similar phenomenon in 1303, when Richard of Cranage and his mother Christiana, 'in our necessity', sold to Thomas Craket and his wife Matilda two salthouses in Middlewich and a 'plot of land called Sheep furlong' in neighbouring Newton for £10. Fifty years later, on Christmas Day 1353, Hugh de Venables lord of Kinderton, conveyed to Richard le Page a plot in Kinderton for building ('ad superedificandum'), to be held for a term of 49 years, describing it as lying in one direction between the high road and the 'land of the said Hugh called Wychefurlonge' and in the other between two existing messuages.[21] In the immediate aftermath of the Black Death, with vacant holdings increasing the opportunities to acquire additional land, it is no surprise to find a whole furlong in individual occupation; to encounter building activity is more unusual.

The evidence continues through the sixteenth and seventeenth centuries. In 1549, a lease in Radnor near Somerford (again not far from the south-east county boundary) by James Pygot of Somerford, yeoman, to Ralph Deyne of Newbolde, husbandman, included 'butts of ground in a close called Over Rinstones between the ground of William Somerford on the south and north'.[22] The phraseology suggests an interim phase in the enclosure process in which some open strips remained (as 'butts') but a block of them had come to be held by the same individual and had already been hedged about within a 'close'. Several other plots of land were identified in the lease, with William Somerford appearing so often as holding adjacent property as to imply that he had by this time consolidated a good deal of Radnor in his own hands. Half a century or so later, among the published *Inquisitions Post Mortem* for Cheshire detailing the landholdings of recently deceased tenants of the crown, we find several field-names which imply that former strips, blocks of strips or portions of the Town Field itself had already been consolidated into individual occupation and enclosed: closes 'called Longley Flatte' in Alderley in 1594, 'called ... Betlebutt' in Sproston in 1595, 'called ... the Ball Flatte' in (Church) Lawton in 1604, 'Little Town Field' and 'Pease Flatt Field' in Wincham in 1604, 'two closes called the Pease Flatt' in Acton in 1613 and 'the Townfield in Hurleston called Willmon Field' in 1614.[23] By contrast, at Cheadle near the north Cheshire boundary in 1631 the rector reached agreement with one of his parishioners over oats due as tithe from 'Worthing croft', described as 'being part of the town field and is not inclosed and not hedged about only distinguished one from the other by Meares and boundaries':[24] again, it seems, a glimpse of an interim phase in the enclosure process, where there had been consolidation of strips in the Town Field into an identifiable 'croft', but not yet the hedging which clearly separated them from their neighbours.

Moving into the eighteenth century, we have a survey of Appleton (also in north Cheshire) to determine entitlements to a stake in the common, prior to its enclosure under an Act of Parliament of 1765. This gives the impression of a Town Field partly enclosed, partly still open as 'loonts' or strips. Among the claimants were Peter Harrison who held the apparently enclosed 'Big Town Field' (just over three and a half acres) and the evidently open 'Town Field Loont' (little more than half an acre); Ann Dutton and John Peacock, both of whom held plots of about one acre each called 'Town Field'; and five other people who held 'Town Field Loonts' each of about a quarter of an acre in size.[25]

Glebe terriers, the periodic surveys of land held by the incumbents of parish churches, have long been recognised as a good means of tracing ongoing piecemeal enclosure[26] and there are indeed a few glimpses within some of them of the slow demise of open field farming in mid- and east Cheshire. At Northenden (between Cheadle and Sale) in 1735, the priest held as his glebe no less than eight strips, variously described as doles, loonts or (in one case) a butt, generally a quarter of an acre or less in size, one in a plot adjoining his orchard, three in 'the close of common ground nearer Swinorth', one in a field called Coppocks Eye, one in the Bell Croft, another in 'the little Salterbank ... now exchanged with John Sumner ... for a part of the Dobb Ridding', and finally 'another lying in great Salterbank ... now exchanged with John Lingard for ... land lying in the middle of Swinorth to the south side of the further new erected hedge and to the advantage of the Rectory and with the Rector's consent'. He also held 'the Maggots Field now enclosed'. We cannot know the precise disposition of these various holdings, but the message is clearly one of active exchange and consolidation leading to the enclosure of land; even the strips which had not been exchanged seem to have lain in small closes or crofts, making them liable to be swapped and effectively swallowed up into larger units. A later terrier, of 1754, shows the rector with only three loonts or butts left, among holdings which were otherwise enclosed. Similarly at Marbury in the south of the county, to take one other example, a terrier of 1701 mentions closes of arable or pasture totalling about seven acres along with 'two little doles or loonds of glebe ground', one of which seems to have been an isolated survivor within an otherwise-enclosed former open field: 'the ... loond lyeth in ... certain field lands anciently called the Bridgefield, now enclosed'. By 1778, the terrier lists only three holdings, all enclosed fields totalling about nine and a half acres, the product presumably of the last few strips having been sold or exchanged in the meantime.[27]

So, to summarise thus far, we have a picture of open arable fields widespread across the county, at least into the eighteenth century. It is too much to claim that they were once found in every Cheshire township, and most of them probably never approached the acreage commonly found in the midlands, but they were familiar features in the landscape. And so was their gradual piecemeal enclosure, leaving only tiny pockets of strips by the time of the Tithe Awards.

Common Pastures
If we turn now to the enclosure of the common pastures, the story is again one of broad similarity between the west of Cheshire and the rest – a story largely of opportunistic encroachment and hedging about, a nibbling away at the rough pastures, by lords of the manor and others with a stake in them, mostly unrecorded for as long as there was more than enough for everyone. And as in the west, enclosure might also provide an opportunity to fix township boundaries, where these had previously been left undefined in tracts of rough pasture to which more than one community had access.[28] Only a minority of townships required a formal enclosure award to complete the process sometime in the eighteenth or nineteenth century, although such awards were to be found in most parts of the county: under the divisions of the county into west, mid- and east outlined above, there were 35 enclosure awards in the west of Cheshire, compared to 27 in mid-Cheshire and 11 in the east, all focused on the common pastures with the exception of two dealing with open arable in the west (Figure 3).[29] Nineteen of these 73 awards pre-dated 1800, the earliest being Cuddington

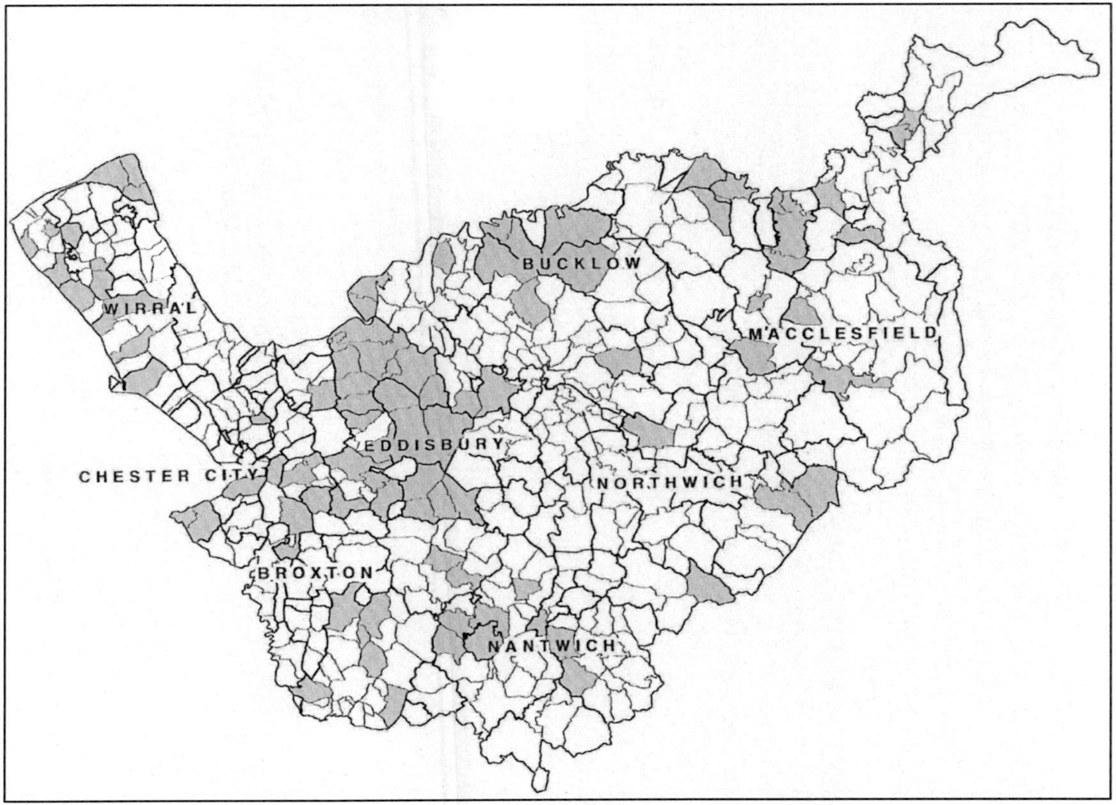

Figure 3: Cheshire townships with enclosure awards (Base map © A.D.M. Phillips and C.B. Phillips, reproduced with permission from A.D.M. Phillips and C.B. Phillips, *A New Historical Atlas of Cheshire*, Chester, 2002, 9).

Enclosure and Enclosures

in Weaverham in 1767 and Appleton and Lymm in 1768. Eighteen post-dated 1850, the last being Runcorn and Weston in 1898.

Under the so-called Statute of Merton of 1236, a series of measures passed for 'the common good of the realm' at what may be regarded as an early meeting of parliament, lords of the manor were entitled to enclose portions of the commons without restriction, provided that they left sufficient grazing for local freeholders who enjoyed common rights. If the freeholders:

> have as much pasture as suffices for their tenements and ... have free access and egress from their tenements to their pasture, then they are to be content with it and they of whom they have complained may go quit for having profited from the lands, wastes, woods and pasture. If, however, they say that they have not sufficient pasture or sufficient access or egress as belongs to their tenements, then the truth is to be enquired into ... .[30]

Despite the claims of Cheshire's medieval baronial community to be governed by laws and customs distinct from those in the rest of the kingdom,[31] there is ample evidence that this stipulation was seen as applying within the county. 'According to the Provision of Merton it was lawful to raise the hedge in dispute' was the successful defence in a plea in the Cheshire county court in 1260 which, despite the sketchy details, appears to relate to enclosure in Budworth. Some 28 years later, Richard son of Hugh of Calveley challenged John de St Pierre over the latter's enclosure and cultivation of former woodland in Beeston; St Pierre replied that as chief lord he was entitled to act as he had, citing the latest legislation and claiming that he had left sufficient estovers (wood for collection) for his neighbours and tenants. In the following year, 1289, William de Brereton and Margery his mother also referred to the statute when challenged by Adam de Halhulm over their encroachment on the waste of Brereton.[32]

The principle was still being cited in the nineteenth century. In 1815 Randle Wilbraham of Rode Hall, who wanted to take in some of the Odd Rode commons for the purpose of extending the plantations and improving the view from his house, duly obtained legal opinion on the matter. One lawyer offered the following:

> After looking into this case which refers to common rights, it appears that the lord of a manor may inclose and approve part of the commons leaving sufficient for the tenants – the question rests on sufficiency ... which is left? Evidence of enjoyment must be shown, which few if any can prove. The inclosing and improving does not apply only to planting as many have suggested. There appears no restriction as to the mode of improvement by the lord – and if the parts intended to be inclosed are barren and do not produce pasture or a small quantity only, there seems little risk in inclosing and improving such parts.

Another noted that the 'amount proposed is much less than he is entitled to as lord of the manor, leaving sufficient to those tenants entitled to common', so:

> I am of opinion that Mr Wilbraham may inclose as against the common of pasture if he leave sufficient common for all who have a right to enjoy it – but if there be any right to dig turves or gravel he cannot enclose as against them. Mr Wilbraham will have a right of action against such persons as throw down his inclosure for the sake of common of pasture, but the persons of any who have a right to common of turbary or to dig gravel may enter the inclosure for these purposes.

However, the proposal aroused the wrath of many of the freeholders of Odd Rode. Their concern was one frequently encountered when it came to the enclosing of common pastures: faced with a lord intent on reducing the commons, it might be best to press for a full enclosure by formal agreement or award, so that all stakeholders could benefit before it was too late. Accordingly, some thirteen years later, at a meeting in the Golden Lion Inn on 17 September 1828, the Odd Rode freeholders decided to make representations to Wilbraham and the other lord of the manor, Revd Moreton Moreton, calling for the remaining commons to be apportioned between them: 'such an invasion of their just Rights and Privileges calls upon them to step forward to prevent the sacrifice of such Rights altogether'. In the course of the correspondence a paper was produced citing enclosures from the common for which 1,000-year leases had been agreed with the lord of the manor as far back as 1668, like 'the Moss Croft upon Rode Heath, 2 acres' and a 'cottage upon little moss and an enclosure of above a statute acre'. Although Moreton Moreton agreed to the full enclosure, Wilbraham did not and our record of the case peters out amid claims and counter-claims – by Wilbraham that not all the freeholders were present at the meeting, by the freeholders that those who were absent were under his influence, and that his attitude as lord was such 'as to put an end to the idea of an amicable agreement'.[33] Whatever the outcome, no formal enclosure award for Odd Rode ensued.

The lawyers' interpretation that rights of turbary – to dig peat – were excluded from the provisions of the Statute of Merton is relevant to mid- and east Cheshire because the presence of substantial wetland mosses as a source of peat was a feature which did distinguish this part of the county from the west. There was no presumption in law that, provided sufficient was left for others, lords were free to enclose as much common peatland as they wanted – a circumstance which may well have contributed to the survival of mosses as a particular type of commons in Cheshire into the eighteenth century and often much later. Burdett's map of 1777 showed several extensive common mosses such as Carrington Moss north-west of Altrincham, Danes Moss near Macclesfield, Featherbed Moss in Longdendale and that at Lindow south-west of Wilmslow: a distribution weighted heavily towards the middle and east of the county, as was the *Wetlands of Cheshire* survey over 200 years later.[34] In medieval times, peat seems to have been regarded as a readily available resource, access to which required little or no regulation: until the middle of the fourteenth century, peat-digging was evidently permitted in Delamere Forest without any supervision by the foresters.[35] However, as the population increased, each landholder with common rights was allocated his or her own strip, or 'moss-room', marked out from its neighbours, a process attributed to the seventeenth century in the case of Lindow Moss near Wilmslow. Here, a moss which had once extended to 1,500 acres was steadily reduced to a quarter of this size by the late nineteenth century through various encroachments and agreements, but a series of long narrow paddocks in the southern part of the moss preserves the pattern of the former (unenclosed) moss-rooms (Figure 4). As late as 1808, Henry Holland in his *General View of the Agriculture of Cheshire* wrote that 'each farm, where there was a peat moss in the township, had its moss-rooms allocated to it, from which peat was procured'. He admitted, however, that by then peat as a fuel was giving way to 'pit-coal' as he called it, and this trend was exacerbated after the coming of the railways made cheap coal readily available, with peat-digging tending to survive longest in the east of the county where the commodity was seen as good bedding for livestock.[36]

Enclosure and Enclosures

Figure 4: Aerial view of former moss-rooms of Lindow Moss close to the suburbs of Wilmslow. The moss-rooms are now represented by long narrow fields in the lower part of the picture but in the medieval period the unenclosed moss extended over most of the area further north. The photograph was taken on 31 October 1992. (1992–93 Aerial Survey of Cheshire. Copyright 2009 Cheshire West & Chester Council & Cheshire East Council © All rights reserved. Flown and captured by National Remote Sensing Centre Ltd 1992–93. Digitally converted by Bluesky International Ltd 2009.)

The distinctive field pattern associated with moss-rooms, with their tendency to taper inwards towards the best peat in the centre of the moss, only survives where they were individually enclosed by their respective proprietors. Leighton Moss north-west of Crewe is recalled today by a farm name, the name of a lane, and even a bridge on the West Coast main line, but there are no traces of the former moss-rooms because an enterprising landowner, James France France of Bostock Hall near Middlewich, bought out the local farmers so that he could enclose the whole of the moss in the winter of 1826–27; the result was the obliteration of the narrow plots.[37] Conversely, the moss-rooms were specifically protected in the Congleton Enclosure Act of 1795 – a measure to which we shall return. This guaranteed that 'all Mossrooms and Rights of Turbary which shall have been claimed, and the Claims thereto allowed and confirmed ... shall be vested in the Owners and Proprietors thereof respectively, freed and exonerated from all Rights of Common and other Rights whatsoever'.[38] It has left us today with the singular group of fields to the south of the built-up area of Congleton, looking towards Congleton Edge, now enclosed by hedges when prior to the award they were separated one from the other by markers depicted on the enclosure map by dotted lines (Plates 1–2 and Figure 5).

One major enclosing enterprise affecting a Cheshire peat bog was that at Carrington Moss, to the south of the River Mersey, which in the early-Victorian period was the largest lowland moss in the county.[39] According to Tithe Awards of around 1840, this covered some 917 acres in the ownership of the earl of Stamford and Warrington, not counting the moss-rooms which abutted onto its northern, north-western and north-eastern sides; at that time, it was mostly being used as a grouse moor. By 1880, the moss had been reduced to around 600 acres through encroachments on the edges and through

Figure 5: Mossley Moss, with Congleton Edge in the background.

reclamation schemes associated on the one hand with the construction of a railway line between Timperley and Glazebrook, opened in 1873, and on the other with farming initiatives undertaken by the earl of Stamford in the vicinity of the line. However, pressure was building for the complete reclamation of the moss,[40] and Manchester Corporation duly responded in 1886, buying from the trustees of the late earl of Stamford the remaining unenclosed moss, along with some tenant farms and moss-rooms on its margins, as a dump for night-soil and other refuse; the intention was to convert the moss into fertile arable land to feed the city. Tenants were given notice to quit, rectilinear fields were laid out, drains were inserted, roads and a light railway were built across the moss, and by 1899 the area was in full cultivation, with seventeen new tenant farmers producing market garden crops and also animal fodder for the horses of Manchester. In the preceding decade some 591,000 tons of night-soil had been brought here from Manchester, initially almost all by rail but latterly mostly via the Ship Canal after this had opened in 1894.

The success of the scheme, in terms both of helping to solve Manchester's refuse disposal problem and of yielding a profit from the agricultural enterprise, led the Corporation to purchase the larger Chat Moss in south Lancashire for the same purpose in 1895. However, with the advance of the water closet, the need for night-soil dumping fell away in the interwar period and although farming continued at Carrington, and still does, the old moss was destined for a varied future – as host to a Starfish site diverting enemy aircraft during the Second World War, as a base for a large petrochemical works for half a century from the 1950s, and nowadays as home to several nature reserves and two professional football clubs' training grounds. For our purposes, it offers one of the clearest examples in the county of rural landscape planning on a grand scale, a comparatively rare case within Cheshire of an extensive area of straight-sided fields with right-angled corners (Figure 6).

This excursion into the problems of servicing Manchester – where the population within the municipal limits (including Salford) increased from 94,000 in 1801 to 476,000 in 1871, and the number of greengrocer and fruiterer retail outlets rose from 14 to 741 in the same period[41] – has led us to another area where some contrast can be drawn between mid- and east Cheshire and the zone to the west: differential growth in population. We have noted already that Domesday Cheshire was a sparsely populated county in national terms, but that the greatest densities were in the west, in Wirral and the lowland watered by the Dee. By the seventeenth century there had been a shift towards the middle of the county, and by the nineteenth to the east: in the 1851 census, six of the eight towns in Cheshire with populations over 10,000 were in the east.[42] Not only did these large urban populations have to be fed (alongside those of Manchester and south Lancashire), they also had to be provided with houses and workplaces. The incentive to enclose common land for property development did of course apply in

Enclosure and Enclosures

Figure 6: Aerial view of the former Carrington Moss, as it appeared in 1973, from 1971–73 Aerial Survey of Cheshire. The reclaimed moss is clearly shown by the rectilinear pattern of fields, despite industrial development in the northern part. The Timperley-Glazebrook railway line crosses diagonally in the south-west, the Manchester Ship Canal can be seen in the north-western corner and the River Mersey meanders across the top of the picture. © 2006 Cheshire West & Chester Council & Cheshire East Council. All rights reserved. Flown and captured by Hunting Surveys Ltd 1971–73. Digitally converted by Genesys International Ltd & The Aerial Surveyor Ltd 2005/6.

the west of the county as well, but it was particularly strong further east.

In Stockport, for example, where the total population is reckoned to have grown almost fivefold (to 15,000) during the second half of the eighteenth century,[43] there were a series of deals struck by the Warren family as lords of the manor which allowed buildings to appear on the former common pastures. In 1712, Edward Warren and 42 of the principal burgesses, 'having taken into consideration the affairs of the town of Stockport, and especially the great increase of poor therein', agreed to the enclosure and sale of so much of the commons on Stockport Moor, Shaw Heath and Heap Ridings as would yield an annual rent of £60, two-thirds of which would be spent on poor relief (so reducing the poor rates) and the remainder on mayoral expenses and the master of the free school – although significantly the moss-rooms on Stockport Moor, which dated back to at least 1559, were not to be touched, with no enclosure to be made within 15 roods of any of them without the owner's permission. Piecemeal sales followed, especially of commons close to the River Mersey which were ripe for industrial development, such as one by John Warren in 1716 whereby Thomas Siddall, wheelwright, bought:

> all that piece or parcel of waste ground ... in a certain place ... called the Petty Carr [close to the River Mersey] ... being 102 square yards in measure; and liberty for the said Thomas Siddall to erect, build or run up one or more chimneys at the side of the Rock or Bank adjoining to the said piece of waste ground.

By the 1760s, Sir George Warren, who continued to sell off portions of the common for the building of mills near the river, had antagonised the burgesses who felt that they were entitled to a share of the profits; towards the end of the century, he yielded to the extent of donating free of charge plots for the building of a new prison and dispensary.

However, it was only after his death in 1801, to be succeeded by an absentee daughter, that the burgesses were able to reassert their entitlements to the dwindling commons by securing an Enclosure Act, passed in 1805 and covering the remaining 125 acres, this time including the moss-rooms on the moor. With 267 burgesses who could claim a stake in the common land, the reallocation of these 125 acres would have created very small plots, so the arrangement was that the plots set out by the commissioners – 100 were eventually created – would be sold off or leased out at auction, the proceeds being applied:

> for the benefit of the … Town of Stockport, and in defraying the Expenses of erecting and building a Poor House or House of Industry within and for the Use of the poor of and belonging to the said township of Stockport and in Aid of the Poor Rates thereof.

Trustees including the lord and lady of the manor, the mayor, the rector and all £50 freeholders of the town, were identified as responsible for putting the Act into effect, and the auctioning process duly took place, eventually being completed in stages down to 1812.

Later nineteenth-century OS maps show housing development as a result over much of the former common – mainly at Petty Carr, Cale Green and Shaw Heath (next to the industrial suburb of Edgeley) – and the enclosure was successful insofar as just over £7,000 was raised from the auctioning of the plots. The sting in the tail is that, although the Act specified that up to £4,000 of this total was supposed to be spent on a new 'good and commodious' workhouse, only £1,000 appears to have been accounted for, and there is no reference in the overseers of the poor's accounts to any income from the enclosed land. The Act made provision for trustees' meetings to be publicly advertised and for a record of proceedings to be kept, but details of their activities seem to have disappeared. No original of the enclosure award survives and all the papers of the solicitor who kept a copy of it were burned after his death. Suspicion fell on the trustees and in 1836 a radical journalist, James Acland, called on the mayor to institute an enquiry 'for the vindication of gentlemen suspected of a misappropriation of the fund'. But the enquiry never happened and nothing untoward can be proved!

A much more transparent outcome to the enclosure of the commons can be found at Congleton, where some 600 acres remained unenclosed when a broadly similar Act of Parliament – possibly a model for that at Stockport – was passed in 1795. As at Stockport, it arose from concerns among the freeholders of the town about the activities of the lord of the manor, Charles Shakerley, in enclosing and building on portions of the commons without consulting them, which had led to a meeting being called in the Town Hall at the beginning of 1793 to take matters into their own hands. And, just as at Stockport, there was provision in the Act for the commons to be apportioned into lots to be held by trustees and sold at auction, the income to be administered by the trustees named in the Act:

> in the Relief and Maintenance of the Poor of the said Borough and Township of Congleton, and in aid or ease and in discharge (so far as the same will extend) of the Poor's Rates within the same.

There was additional discretion in this case to spend any surplus on the highways or other public benefit.

These auctions duly went ahead in 1796 and 1797, prior to the formal award in 1798, although, as we saw above, an exception was made of the moss-rooms, which were preserved for their existing holders. The original leases on the various lots were for 21 years, too short to make them attractive for building investment, so in 1849 an Amendment Act was passed, acknowledging that 'it would be advantageous if leases could be long leases for building upon' and empowering the trustees to rearrange the lots into the most advantageous portions and lease them for more than 21 years – for anything up to 999 years – if there was an intention to build on them. The principal outcome, at least before the end of the nineteenth century, was to encourage the development of a new suburb on Mossley Moss called High Town, north of the surviving moss-rooms, close to the railway station opened in 1848 at a point where the Stoke to Manchester line intersected with the Macclesfield canal of 1831 and a road giving access to the Congleton to Biddulph turnpike (Figure 7). The construction in 1810 of a workhouse on one of the plots in High Town retained by the trustees – a building which still survives despite being superseded by the Union workhouse at Arclid following the Poor Law Amendment Act of 1834 – is one tangible result of development in this area[44] (Figure 8).

Congleton was fortunate in that the trust set up to administer the enclosed commons – leasing some plots by auction, retaining others, disbursing the income so as to relieve the poor, ease the poor rate and support other beneficial causes – appears to have been above corruption. Unlike in Stockport, where the trustees acted by virtue of their offices or £50 freeholds, the original Congleton trustees were individuals specifically named in the Act, although whether this had any bearing on the way they conducted their affairs is impossible to say. The Congleton Trust is still in existence, still holding some former common pasture at Lower Heath to the north of the town but now governed by a Charity Commission scheme of 1994 which allows it to use its investments and property portfolio to make:

Figure 7: Intersection of road, rail and canal at High Town, Congleton, in an area of former common developed following enclosure. Until the bridge was opened in 1965 the road was served by a level crossing.

grants towards projects that benefit the areas of Congleton, together with the parishes of Astbury and Hulme Walfield, for the relief of poverty or sickness, the provision of support for recreational leisure or educational facilities or a charitable purpose which is helpful to residents in the area.

As a trust which can trace a continuous history since its establishment by an Enclosure Act, still holds land allotted by the award and still disburses income for good causes broadly related to its original purpose, the Congleton Inclosure Trust is a very rare survivor of its type in England.[45]

Figure 8: Congleton's parish workhouse of 1810, occupying an allotment following the Enclosure Act of 1795.

Conclusion

Setting this brief account of enclosure in Cheshire into a wider context, it is worth reflecting on the extent to which the process contributed to agricultural improvement. Enclosure often appears in the literature as a key aspect of 'progress', promoting efficiency and encouraging investment and innovation; Joseph Lee's pamphlet, with which this paper began, pursued this theme in the seventeenth century and the plea that farmland could not be improved unless it was enclosed became a standard preamble to enclosure acts in the eighteenth and nineteenth. However, several commentators either side of 1800 remarked upon the failure of farmers in different parts of England to take advantage of the potential offered by enclosure.[46] Locally, Thomas Wedge's *General View of the Agriculture of the County Palatine of Chester* (1794) was certainly in favour of enclosure and bemoaned what he saw as its exorbitant cost, but focused instead on short leases, high rents and the lack of under-draining as the main barriers to agricultural advance.[47]

Half a century later, William Palin took farming within enclosed fields for granted as he discussed crop rotation and stock breeding, but criticised poor maintenance of hedges and ditches. Indeed, he considered Cheshire's agriculture to be: 'not of so high a character generally as that of some other counties in England; and perhaps it exhibits as great a variety of methods, and as bad specimens of farming, as can possibly be conceived'.[48]

His low opinion of Cheshire's farmers, despite the apparent advantage of working in an almost entirely enclosed environment, was echoed by others around the middle of the nineteenth century. In a paper to the Manchester Statistical Society in 1851, another commentator declared:

> Look at Lancashire and Cheshire: considering the immense breadth of fine arable land and the unequalled markets for all kinds of produce, what has yet been done for the improvement of the soil? With a few notable exceptions very little. In general, cultivation is slovenly and wasteful, much as it was a century ago.

In a report on *English Agriculture in 1850–51*, published the following year, James Caird endorsed this: 'Improvements in agriculture have made very slow progress in Cheshire'.[49]

The story changed dramatically in the second half of the nineteenth century, a period of severe challenge for some of the traditionally more prosperous agricultural regions of England, when Cheshire's farmers must be regarded as among the most successful in the country. Loans from all sources for investment in under-drainage between 1847 and 1899 were higher in Cheshire than in all but four English counties.[50] Cheshire was the only county in England where rents for farmland increased between 1872–73 and 1910–11 (by 0.1%) at a time when they fell nationally by over a quarter. The farm labour force in Cheshire between the census years of 1871 and 1911 fell by only 16%, the third lowest percentage of any English county, while the national farm labour force was dropping by 28%. Real farm output between 1873 and 1911, measured at constant 1911 prices, remained static for England as a whole but grew by 22% in Cheshire – the highest percentage of any county, moving Cheshire from fifteenth to eighth in absolute terms.[51] All this is a reflection not of the impact of enclosure in Cheshire, since we have seen that the process was virtually complete before the middle of the century, but of buoyant demand from the industrial conurbations for fruit and vegetables, meat and dairy products, serviced by a well-developed railway network. But the long-drawn-out disappearance of open and common land did of course help individuals to respond to that demand when it eventually took off. And the consequence of all this enclosing activity over seven centuries, mostly piecemeal and mostly unrecorded, is that present-day Cheshire has less common land left than about two-thirds of the historic counties in England.[52]

Reflecting over half a century ago on the paucity of surviving common land in Cheshire, those titans of post-war geography and landscape history, L. Dudley Stamp and W.G. Hoskins – who had sat together on the Royal Commission on Common Land from 1955 to 1958 – placed the county in the 'Lowland Heart of England' in their map of English regions, alongside Derbyshire, Nottinghamshire, Leicestershire, Northamptonshire and other counties where there was little common left.[53] Strange as it is to see Cheshire grouped for this purpose among counties associated with 'champion England', noted for their rather different medieval farming regimes and enclosure histories, this classification reminds us that if the sharing out of arable and pasture was a widespread phenomenon in early medieval England, so in later centuries was the urge to enclose the land and gain individual control over it. The processes differed, and indeed the resultant rural landscape differed, with significantly less regularity to field boundaries in Cheshire than may be found in counties where there was heavier reliance on enclosure by award, based on the work of commissioners and surveyors. But while it is right to stress the contrasts between Cheshire's farming experience and rural landscape and those of 'champion England' to its southeast, we ought to find room to acknowledge some similarities as well.

Endnotes
1. J. Lee, *Considerations Concerning Common Fields and Inclosures* (London, 1654), quotation on 38-39.
2. For a summary of these points, with references to further reading, see G.J. White, *The Medieval English Landscape, 1000-1540* (London, 2012), 14-29, 56-62 and (more recently) T. Williamson, R. Liddiard and T. Pardida, *Champion: The Making and Unmaking of the English Midland Landscape* (Exeter, 2013).
3. G. Elliott, 'Field Systems of Northwest England' in A.R.H. Baker and R.A. Butlin, eds., *Studies of Field Systems in the British Isles* (Cambridge, 1973), 41-92; B.K. Roberts and S. Wrathmell, *Atlas of Rural Settlement in England* (London, 2000), 54; A.D.M. Phillips and C.D. Phillips, *A New Historical Atlas of Cheshire* (Chester, 2002), 52-53. Although the terms 'open field' and 'common field' are often found without a clear distinction being made between the two, strictly speaking the former applies to a field in which different farmers worked their individual holdings without hedges or fences separating them, the latter to a field worked to some extent as a communal enterprise. A given field might fit one or both descriptions.
4. G.J. White, 'The Enclosure of West Cheshire: Keeping Ahead of "Champion England"', in *LHDNW*, 101-34. I am grateful to Jonathan Pepler, former County Archivist, for his comments on one point made in this paper. He observes that the enclosure of Upton Heath was almost certainly later than the implied date of 1735 (115); this was the date of a map of the heath, to which the new enclosed fields and accompanying table of reference were

added in a different hand, sometime before 1801 (CALS, DEO 1/7 and cf. DEO 1/18).
5. V. Chapman, 'Open Fields in West Cheshire', *THSLC*, CIV (1953), 35–59; H.C. Darby and I.S. Maxwell, eds, *The Domesday Geography of Northern England* (Cambridge, 1962), 380–83 (by I.B. Terrett); N.J. Higham, *The Origins of Cheshire* (Manchester, 1993), 8–10; M.D. Leah, C.E. Wells, C. Appleby and E. Huckerby, *The Wetlands of Cheshire* (Lancaster, 1997), 10.
6. *VCH Ches.*, I, 1, 3.
7. Phillips and Phillips, *New Historical Atlas*, 4–5, 52–53 (quotation on 52).
8. Phillips and Phillips, *New Historical Atlas*, 56–57; for *Inquisitions Post Mortem*, see below note 23.
9. White, 'Enclosure of West Cheshire', esp. 101–8. For the purposes of the present paper, 'east Cheshire' is defined as lying between the county boundary and an imaginary line running due south of the point where the Micker Brook enters the River Mersey (at Cheadle, close to the junction of the M56 and M60); 'mid-Cheshire' runs from here to an imaginary line due south from the mouth of the River Weaver. A judgement has been made over where to place townships which straddle these lines.
10. Phillips and Phillips, *New Historical Atlas*, 28–29, 42–43.
11. Summarised in Phillips and Phillips, *New Historical Atlas*, 52–53.
12. For examples which caution against assuming that the name 'Town Field' necessarily indicates a former open field, see Elliott, 'Field Systems', 91 and (in Shropshire) S.M. Varey, 'Society and the Land – the changing landscape of Baschurch, North Shropshire, c.1550–2000' (Univ. of Liverpool PhD thesis, 2008), 114. It is tempting to seek explanations for the blank areas in Figure 1, such as Delamere Forest in Eddisbury hundred, but the exercise is of doubtful value since much depends on how consistently the name 'Town Field' survived into the Tithe Awards. Cheadle and Runcorn are examples of townships whose Tithe Awards make no mention of a 'Town Field', but for which there is seventeenth- or eighteenth-century evidence of fields of this name still at least partly unenclosed: CALS, EDC

5/1631/59 and CALS, DBN A/3/15. Although Macclesfield hundred is blank on the map, other names indicative of former open fields – such as 'Black Butts', 'Crow Butts' and 'Far Bridge Flatt' in Bollington, 'High Flatt' and 'Sour Butts' in Bosley, and 'Big' and 'Little Hill Flatt' in Butley – occur in the Tithe Awards for this part of the county.

13. This paragraph is based on the data on tithe awards presented online by Cheshire Archives and Local Studies at <<http://maps.cheshire.gov.uk/tithemaps>>, but see also G.J. White, 'Open Fields and Rural Settlement in Medieval West Cheshire' in T. Scott and P.M. Starkey, eds, *The Middle Ages in the North West* (Oxford, 1995), 15–35.
14. <<http://maps.cheshire.gov.uk/tithemaps>>; cf. C.S. Davies, *The Agricultural History of Cheshire, 1750–1850* (Manchester, 1960), 54–58.
15. T. Wedge, *General View of the Agriculture of the County Palatine of Chester* (London, 1794), 8; *Return Relating to Common and Common Field Lands* (House of Commons Paper 85 of 1874), 21–30; W.G. Hoskins and L. Dudley Stamp, *The Common Lands of England and Wales* (London, 1963), 89–94. The three English counties with smaller areas of open strips ('common fields') were Northumberland, Leicestershire and Shropshire.
16. *Chartulary or Register of the Abbey of St Werburgh, Chester*, ed. J. Tait (Chetham Society, 1920–23), II, no. 815.
17. Cf. the manorial descent in Ormerod (1882), III, 11–17.
18. *Chartulary of the Abbey of St Werburgh*, ed. Tait, I, no. 387, II, no. 718; White, 'Enclosure of West Cheshire', 108.
19. Charter of Robert son of Meylor of Peover, nd: CALS, DLT/A 8/61.
20. History of the Commons (MS.): CALS, D 2489/3.
21. *A Middlewich Chartulary*, ed. J. Varley (Chetham Society, 1941), 141, 85.
22. Lease for six years by James Pygot of Somerford, 1 May 1549: CALS, D 181/45.
23. *Cheshire Inquisitions Post Mortem, 1603–1660*, ed. R. Stewart-Brown (Record Society of Lancashire and Cheshire, LXXIV,

LXXVI, XCI, 1934-38), III, 65, 129, 24; II, 60; III, 179, 175. Cf. the 'Yate Flat' and the 'Long Butts' in Butley in 1610 (I, 161), the 'Poole Flatt' ('where the clay pits are made') in Heywood near Alderley in 1641 (II, 79), the 'Hauxflatt' in Dernhall in 1611 (II, 118), 'Breretons Flatt' and the 'Lesser' and 'Greater Flatts' in High Legh and Rostherne in 1627 (II, 146).

24. Diocesan Consistory Court papers, 1631: CALS, EDC 5/1631/59. Compare the examples in 1466 of enclosures using markers rather than hedges at Lyme Overhanley and Netherhanley, and of consolidated blocks of selions 'lying together' at Grappenhall in *The Legh of Lyme Survey*, eds J. and B. Fothergill et al., (Ranulf Higden Society, 2011), 218-23, 233-37.
25. Survey of the manor of Appleton, 1765: CALS, D 6022/1.
26. Thus, a pioneering paper by M.W. Beresford, 'Glebe Terriers and Open Field Leicestershire' in W.G. Hoskins, ed., *Studies in Leicestershire Agrarian History* (Leicester, 1949), 77-126 and, as an example of recent work, S.M. Varey, 'Illuminating the Silent Enclosure Process: Evidence from North West Shropshire', *Transactions of the Shropshire Archaeological and Historical Society*, LXXXVII (2014 for 2012), 81-94.
27. Glebe terriers for Northenden, 1705-54 (CALS, EDV 8/65) and for Marbury, 1698-1778 (CALS, EDV 8/58).
28. Cf. the fixing of the Clotton-Duddon boundary in 1819 (White, 'Enclosure of West Cheshire', 126) with the determination of the boundary between Kettleshulme and Taxal at the time of enclosure, some years before 1738, although we learn of this case because a failure to complete the fencing left part of the common in dispute (CALS, DDS 20/15).
29. These two were Frodsham Townfields and St Mary on the Hill, Chester: see White, 'Enclosure of West Cheshire', 118, 123 (where the figure of 'around a hundred examples' refers to the total number of townships covered by these awards, some of which were composite). Comparison of Figures 1 and 3 in the present paper shows several townships which had both 'townfields' and enclosure awards and several others which had neither, a contrast possibly arising from the extent to which a communal

approach to farming had been adopted or eradicated over previous centuries. The issue merits further investigation but cannot be pursued here. The regional divisions of the county for the purpose of this paper are set out in note 9, above.

30. *English Historical Documents, III, 1189–1327*, ed. H. Rothwell (London, 1975), 352. The 1236 measure provided for sufficient common pasture to be left for the lord's tenants; the Statute of Westminster of 1285 extended this protection to others with rights of pasture (the 'neighbours' of John de St Pierre in the next paragraph).
31. G. Barraclough, 'The Earldom and County Palatine of Chester', *THSLC*, CIII (1951), 23–57; *VCH Cheshire*, II, 1–35; G.J. White and J. Pepler, *The Magna Carta of Cheshire* (Chester, 2015).
32. *Calendar of County Court, City Court and Eyre Rolls of Chester, 1259–1297*, ed. R. Stewart-Brown (Chetham Society, 1925), 101, 142, 6; cf. for the west of the county, 15–16, 20.
33. Baker Wilbraham papers: bundle on enclosure of Rode Heath, 1815–28: CALS, DBW M/4/A/1–18.
34. P.P. Burdett, *A Survey of the County Palatine of Cheshire of 1777*, eds J.B. Harley and P. Laxton (Hist. Soc. of Lancs. and Ches. occasional series I, 1974), plates X, XI, XIII; Leah et al., *Wetlands*, 14–15.
35. B.M.C. Husain, 'Delamere Forest in Later Medieval Times', *THSLC*, CVII (1955), 23–39, at 33.
36. Leah et al., *Wetlands*, 156; M. Hyde and C. Pemberton, *Lindow and the Bog Warriors* (Wilmslow, 2002), 7, 14–16; 'Peat Reek', *Cheshire Life*, XLIII, no. 6, Jun. 1977, 50–51.
37. Papers regarding enclosure of Leighton Moss, 1826–45: CALS, LBCr 4755/7.
38. *Acts Local & Personal [L & P] 35 Geo III, c.56*, clause 14, reprinted in K.P. Boon and D.A. Daniel, *History of the Congleton Inclosure Trust* (2011), 133–34.
39. This paragraph is based on A.D.M. Phillips, 'Mossland Reclamation in Nineteenth Century Cheshire', *THSLC*, CXXIX (1979), 93–107.

40. E.g. *Manchester Guardian*, 23 Aug. 1884, cited in Phillips, 'Mossland Reclamation', 97: 'the idea does not seem a bad one to convert a thousand acres [sic] of barren morass into the most fertile cropping or market garden land ... and although a thousand acres of first-class ground would not meet all our demands, it would be as well for the citizens of Manchester as the same area 200 miles distant.'
41. R. Scola, *Feeding the Victorian City: The Food Supply of Manchester, 1770–1870* (Manchester, 1992), 19, 190.
42. Darby and Maxwell, eds, *Domesday Geography of Northern England*, 348; Phillips and Phillips, *New Historical Atlas*, 28–29, 44–47, 82–83. (The six towns were Congleton, Macclesfield, Stockport, Hyde, Dukinfield and Stalybridge; the other two were Birkenhead and Chester.)
43. P.M. Giles, 'The Enclosure of the Common Lands in Stockport', *Transactions of the Lancashire and Cheshire Antiquarian Society*, LXII (1953), 73–110, at 84. This and the next paragraph are based partly on the Enclosure Act, *Acts L&P, 45 Geo. III, c.91*, and partly on this article, which includes a map of the former commons on 90–91. On the subject of enclosure for urban development generally, see G.E. Mingay, *Parliamentary Enclosure in England* (London, 1997), 42–44.
44. Correspondence, 1792, prior to Congleton Enclosure Award: CALS, DSS 3991/12/1; Congleton Enclosure Award: CALS, QDE 2/8; Congleton Enclosure Papers: CALS, DCB 1716/10/2; *Acts L&P 35 Geo. III, c.56*; Boon and Daniel, *Congleton Inclosure Trust*, esp. 9, 11–17, 25–31, 53–56, 127–226.
45. Boon and Daniel, *Congleton Inclosure Trust*, 241–50; Congleton Inclosure Trust website: <<http://www.congleton inclosure trust.org.uk/congletoninclosd.html>>, accessed 30 Sep. 2015. Hopesay (Shropshire) also had an Inclosure Trust from 1858 to 1998, but this is now incorporated into the Hopesay Parish Trust: <<http://www.2shrop.net/live/welcome.asp?id=3167>>, accessed 30 Sep. 2015. See also the Town Estate charity, formerly the Embankment Enclosure Trust, based near Doncaster, which

traces its origins to an enclosure award of 1762 (<<http://opencharities.org/charities/259585>>, accessed 14 Mar. 2016).
46. J.D. Chambers and G.E. Mingay, *The Agricultural Revolution, 1750–1880* (London, 1966), 95–96.
47. Wedge, *General View*, 25, 62–63.
48. W. Palin, *Cheshire Farming: A Report on the Agriculture of Cheshire* (London, 1845), 4, 45–46; in fairness, Palin did acknowledge that 'many of [Cheshire's] farmers approximate very closely to an excellent state of cultivation'.
49. Scola, *Feeding the Victorian City*, 35.
50. A.D.M. Phillips, *The Underdraining of Farmland in England during the Nineteenth Century* (Cambridge, 1989), 76–79; the four counties above Cheshire were Northumberland, Yorkshire, Shropshire and Durham.
51. F.M.L. Thompson, 'An Anatomy of English Agriculture, 1870–1914' in B.A. Holderness and M. Turner, eds, *Land, Labour and Agriculture, 1700–1920: Essays for Gordon Mingay* (London, 1991), 211–40, esp. 223–40; cf. Phillips and Phillips, *New Historical Atlas*, 62–63.
52. Hoskins and Stamp, *The Common Lands*, 102–10, 256–57. Among the better-known Cheshire commons listed here are Thurstaston Common on Wirral, Knutsford Heath and Gresty's Waste, Delamere.
53. Hoskins and Stamp, *The Common Lands*, 107.

2

MEDIEVAL MOATED SITES IN THE CHESHIRE–NORTH WALES BORDERLAND

Ray Jones

Introduction

Moated sites have been defined as 'an area of ground, often occupied by a dwelling or associated structure, bounded or partly bounded by a wide ditch, which in most cases was intended to be filled with water.'[1] Research using aerial photography, field walking and field-name evidence has identified a great number of previously unrecognised moated sites in England and Wales over the past four decades and it is now clear that far more existed than was previously thought.

In 2015, a new database was created which included 6,350 probable moated sites in England together with 2,103 possible moated sites.[2] Wales as a whole has around 150 such sites mostly located in the eastern borderlands and the South Wales coastal strip. They are the second most common earthworks found in England and Wales (after tumuli) and should not be confused with motte and bailey structures that are generally of an earlier date. Jean le Patourel and Brian Roberts showed that moated sites were found in Europe at least 50 years before their first appearance in England from around 1150.[3] The apogee of construction of moated sites was the period 1200–1325.

For England and Wales as a whole, the distribution pattern is uneven with a high density of such sites in four main areas of concentration: the Essex/Suffolk/Hertfordshire region, the West Midlands, Norfolk/Lincolnshire and Yorkshire.[4] W.G. Hoskins noted the proliferation of moated sites on the heavy boulder clays of central Suffolk where he believed the houses

Landscapes Past and Present

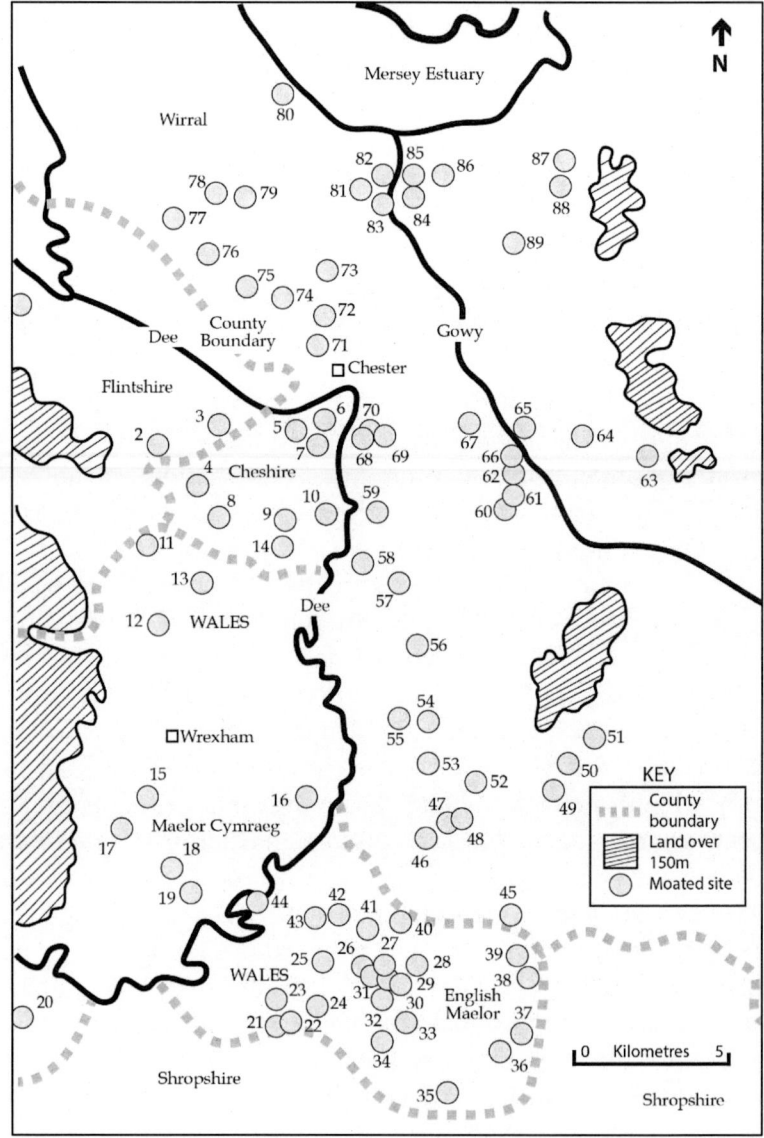

Figure 1: The distribution of moated sites in the Cheshire–North Wales borderlands. (See Gazetteer at the end of the chapter.)

were moated from the outset following clearance of dense woodland in the twelfth and thirteenth centuries.[5]

Figure 1 shows the distribution of moated sites in the Cheshire–North Wales borderlands. As is the case nationally, the distribution in the borderlands is patchy with a very dense occurrence of moated sites in the English Maelor (Maelor Saesneg), where the density of moats matches those in Suffolk and Essex. In the 1530s, Leland noted that in the Hanmer area, 'every gentleman has his attractive pool'.[6]

In contrast, an area around Wrexham is devoid of moated sites. In Cheshire there are small concentrations in the triangular area lying west of the Dee to the south of Chester, in the mid-Gowy valley, in south Wirral and in an area near the mouth of the Gowy. In south Cheshire there is a fairly even distribution of moated sites but the density is markedly lower than those further south across the Welsh border in English Maelor.

Location and Drainage

What Hoskins had noted in Suffolk was also true of moated sites in west Cheshire and the adjacent North Wales borderlands where such sites are most numerous in areas of water-retaining glacial boulder clay soils rather than sands, sandstones or limestone. Thus researchers concluded that most moated sites originated from a need for either a dry site to erect buildings or a need to preserve water supplies through dry seasons[7] which records show prevailed during the last decades of the thirteenth century when many moated sites were founded in this region.

Both water supplies and drainage were more accessible close to watercourses where leats from the stream fed the moat as at Emral Hall (Figure 2) and Foulk Stapleford that lies

Figure 2: Emral Hall. The foreground shows Emral Brook; this fed and formed the fourth arm of the moat. The seventeenth-century hall was demolished in 1936 and the rubble was used to infill the moat.

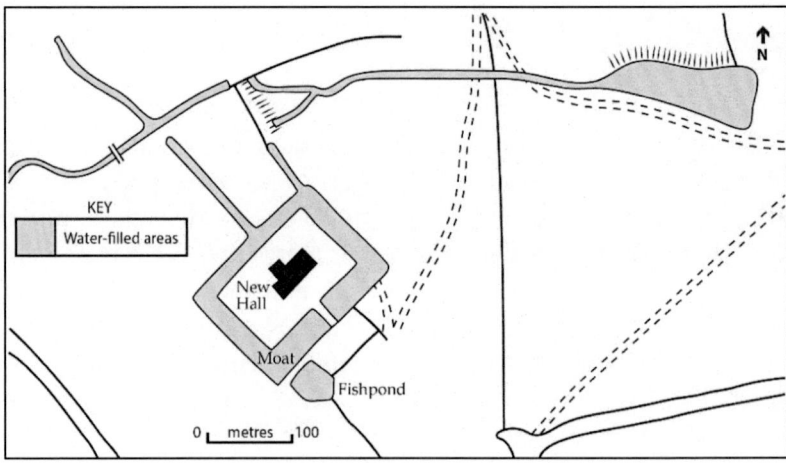

Figure 3: New Hall, Chirk. This site, located in the marcher lordship of Chirkland, was occupied in the late medieval period by the Edwards family. The moat is linked by a leat to a small stream to the north.

Medieval Moated Sites in the Borderland

adjacent to the now canalised River Gowy. Sometimes a channel from the moat also supplied fishponds as at Elton and New Hall, Chirk (Figure 3). Water supply could also be from springs in areas with a high water table, with moated sites located along spring lines marking the boundary between permeable and impermeable underlying rocks as at Haulton Ring in English Maelor.

Drainage was an important factor in the choice of site. At times it was necessary to drain the moat and thus most moats had sluice gates that could also control the water level in times of flood. The sluice gates fed a water channel connected to a field drainage ditch or small stream as at Llyn Tro, Wrexham (Figure 4). Aerial photographs have revealed a similar channel at Rake Lane moat, Eccleston, fed by a sluice gate in the south-west corner of the moat; while at Iddinshall a drainage channel

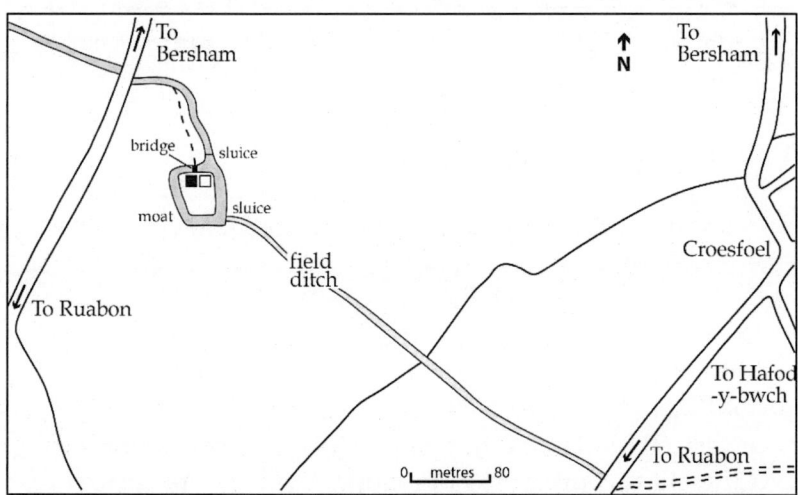

Figure 4: Llyn Tro, Pentre Bychan, Wrexham. Dating to the fourteenth century, Llyn Tro was occupied by the Roberts family who also held the nearby late medieval estates of Croesfoel and Hafod-y-bwch. A timber-framed cruck building remained on the site until the second half of the twentieth century.

is identifiable on the south-west corner of the moat linked to nearby Waterless Brook (Figure 5).

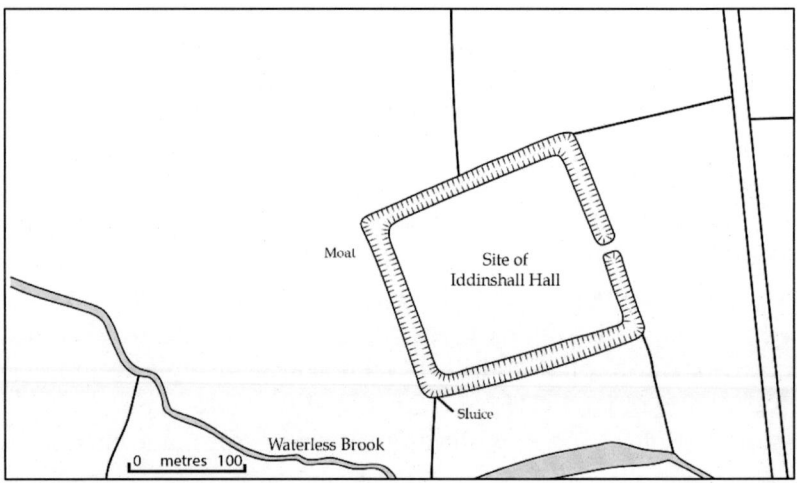

Figure 5: Iddinshall Hall – an ecclesiastical estate of the Benedictine monks of St Werburgh's Abbey, Chester.

Settlement Patterns

On the national scale, the distribution of moated sites gives us an insight into the distribution of dispersed settlement patterns in medieval England and Wales since this is the context in which most of the 6,500 known sites were created.[8] These developments took place in a period of warmer and drier climatic conditions that had begun from around AD 900,[9] contributing to better harvests. This was a factor in stimulating a rise in population from the late Anglo-Saxon period until the late thirteenth century.[10] Population growth stimulated a greater demand for food and a consequent rise in prices for agricultural products. This encouraged the opening up of more marginal lands for food production.

Medieval Moated Sites in the Borderland

In the borderland, which shared in these trends, there was a considerable amount of available land to expand the amount of arable and pastoral land in production. These lands included uncleared woodland, damp oak-alder woodland on often waterlogged soils and considerable expanses of undrained marshland. The rise in population triggered the building of new farmsteads, particularly moated houses, not only as symbols of status and wealth, but as a means of defending moveable wealth such as cattle and horses; hence many moated sites included stables and cattle pens. The original occupants were usually important local landowners and many manor houses occupied such sites. Others were messuages of freeholders or prosperous tenants without manorial status.[11]

In many cases status played a part with the occupiers of moated houses mimicking the castle moats of the highest tier in medieval society. The moated dwellings occupied by lords of the manor are known as 'seignorial' sites. These sites were generally located close to the centre of a parish or township, often close to the nucleus of a settlement and have been described as 'the central places of a landed estate'.[12] It seems likely that larger moats found closer to centres of settlement reflect the higher social status of their occupants.

The moated site at Old Beachin, Coddington (Figure 6), may have been a manor house of the Boteler family of Warrington who held the nearby manors of Clutton, Coddington and Beachin during the fourteenth century.[13] In south Wirral, it is also possible to identify the families who created moated sites. Close to the ancient ford across the River Dee at Shotwick lies an abandoned moated site created by the Hockenhull family who moved from the medieval moated house in favour of the newly built Shotwick Hall in 1662 (Figure 7). In the adjacent township of Puddington, the Massey family created a moated manor house at Old Puddington Hall.[14]

Dodleston moated site (Figure 8) was owned by the Grosvenor family in the sixteenth century until Sir Richard Grosvenor sold it to Sir Thomas Egerton (later Lord Chancellor) in 1582. The sixteenth-century house that stood in the centre of this large platform was demolished in 1785 when a farmhouse replaced it.[15]

A further type of moated house has been designated 'sub-manorial'. These sites were generally smaller and of lower social status than those of the seignorial classes and included merchants, lawyers, franklins and the cadet branches of seignorial families. It seems likely that in this sub-manorial class of homestead, the moat may be seen as a means of emulating the homes of the leaders of local society. Sometimes it is possible to suggest the early occupants of these sub-manorial moated sites. Edge Hall stands close to the site of a medieval moated house that can be attributed to the Dodd family who occupied the site for centuries after the marriage of Hova Dot (presumably a Welshman) to the heiress of Edge in the reign of Henry II (1154–89).[16]

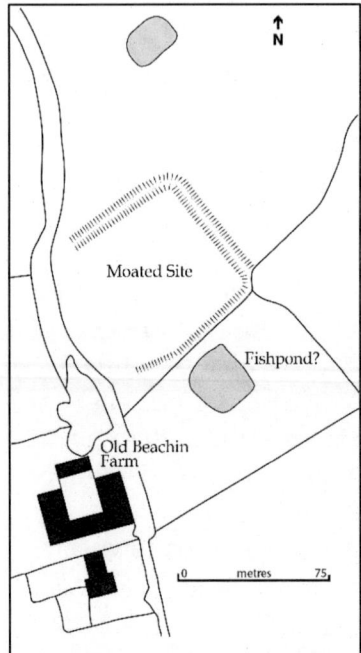

Figure 6: Old Beachin, Coddington.

Medieval Moated Sites in the Borderland

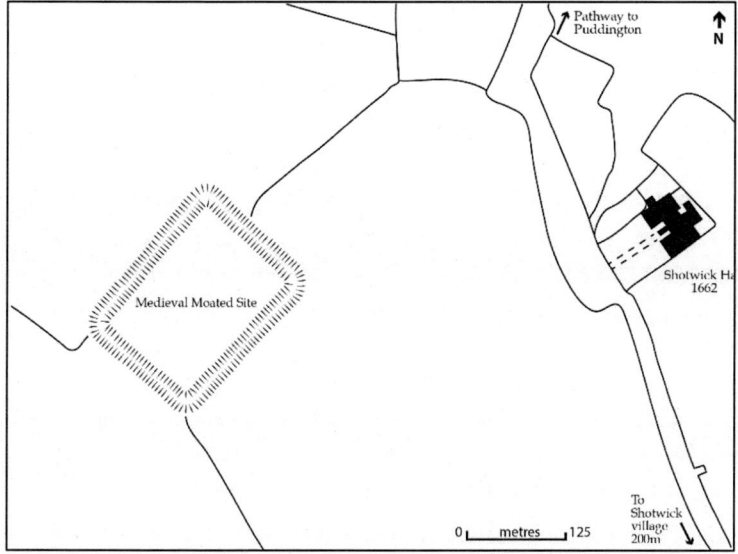

Figure 7: Shotwick Hall lies close to an ancient ford over the River Dee.

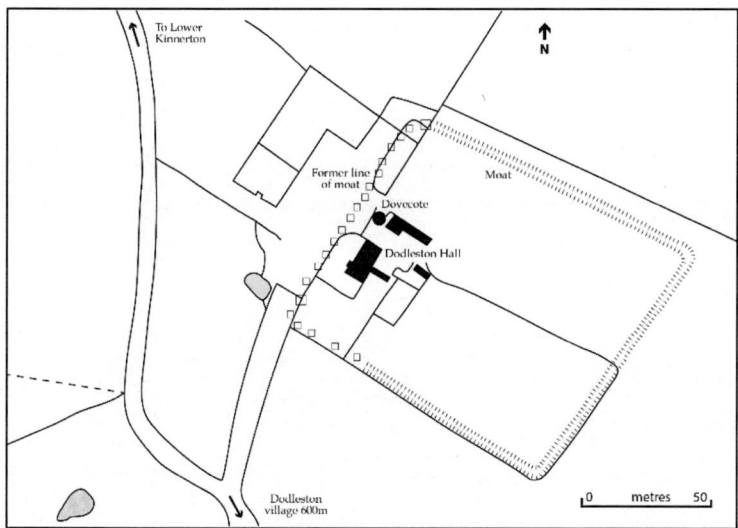

Figure 8: Dodleston Hall, located on the edge of Dodleston Moor close to the Welsh border.

Landscapes Past and Present

To the south of Chester, Belgrave moated site (Figure 9) lies close to the present Eaton Hall; this was the site of a small manor from the 1280s when it was occupied by Richard the Engineer, a military architect of Edward I. It is possible that these lands were granted to him by the king (who also held the former earldom of Chester) for services rendered during the conquest of Wales in 1277 to 1282. There is documentary evidence that Richard was involved in the construction of Flint Castle and its adjacent bastide town from 1277 to 1286.[17] Richard also occupied a house and business premises in what is now Lower Bridge Street in Chester on a site that lay adjacent to St Olave's church. There is documentary evidence that Richard was acquiring lands to the south of the city in Eccleston and Pulford from 1284,[18] giving a possible date for the construction of the Belgrave site.

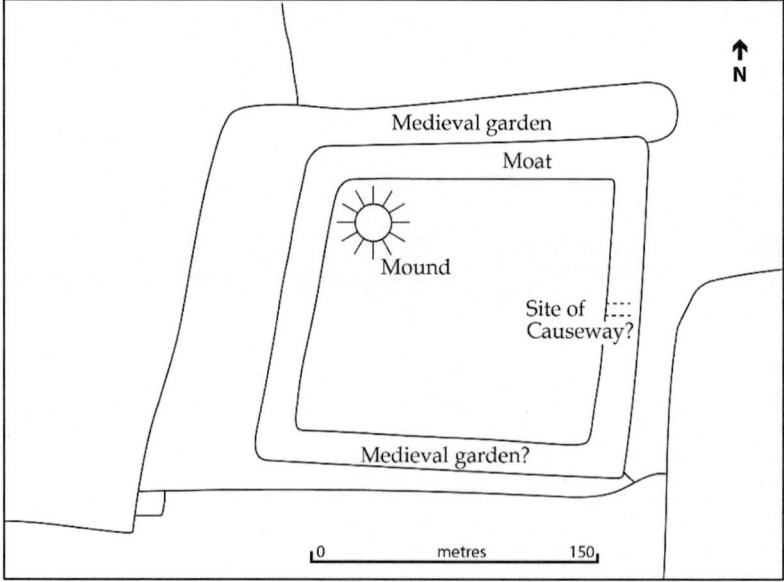

Figure 9: Belgrave, owned and possibly constructed in the late thirteenth century by Richard the Engineer, a key figure in the construction of Edward I's castle and bastide town at Flint.

Medieval Moated Sites in the Borderland

A further eminent Chester family who were the possible owners of a small (0.29 hectare) moated site to the south of the city at Marlston-cum-Lache were the Blunds, wealthy Chester merchants trading in luxury imports during the first half of the fourteenth century (Figure 10). The moated site may have been the lost Marlston Manor which was possibly abandoned before the end of the medieval period.

Also to the south of Chester, off the Eccleston road, lay the moated site known as Netherleigh Hall. The exact site of this moated settlement is unknown but it probably lay at the centre of a small extramural estate and was possibly constructed by Adam of Dutton who held it until 1270. A farmhouse known as Netherleigh Hall was in existence in the early nineteenth century.[19]

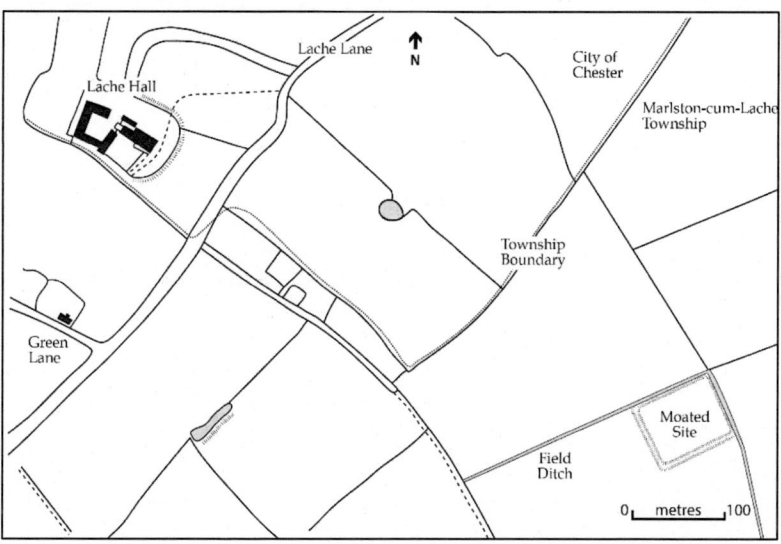

Figure 10: Marlston-cum-Lache, located close to the boundary between this township and the city of Chester. The site was probably abandoned in the late medieval period.

Landscapes Past and Present

Sometimes the small freehold or leased estates of this sub-manorial class had been built following the breakup of large landed estates in the later medieval period. Their isolated position within a township or parish probably suggests locations on assarted land. Other sub-manorial moated homesteads and their estate lands were linked to lands purchased, leased or granted on the fringes of parishes or on township boundaries. These areas were often made up of common woodland[20] or marsh where it was possible to create new farmland by assarting or draining marshland such as the large tract of marsh that lay between the rivers Gowy and Weaver containing the moated sites at Ince and Elton.

In neighbouring Shropshire, 71 out of 107 moated sites were in isolated locations more than 800 metres from a settlement.[21] It is clear that in the Cheshire–North Wales borderlands too, most moated sites are to be found in areas of

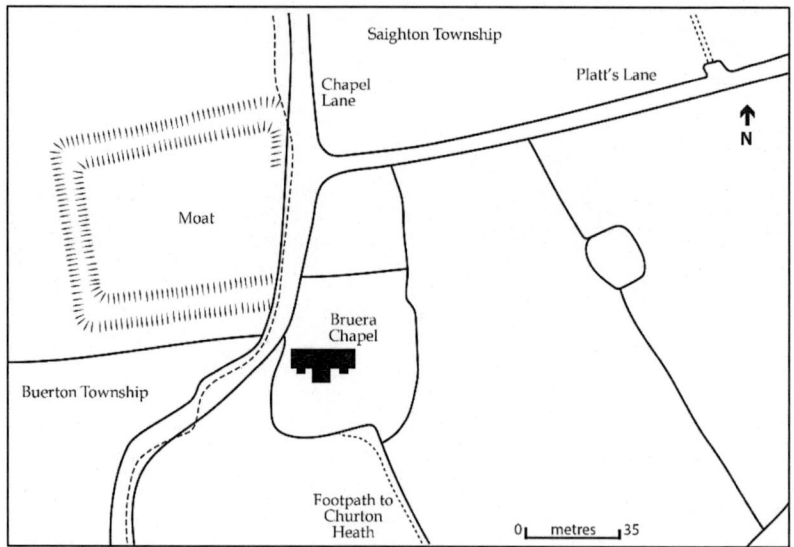

Figure 11: Bruera, a monastic moated site located close to the boundaries of three townships: Buerton, Saighton and Churton Heath.

dispersed settlement in a medieval landscape of hamlets and farmsteads.

The moated site at Bruera (Figure 11) lies at the junction of the three medieval townships of Buerton, Saighton and Churton Heath.[22] In many areas, moated sites represent the first, pioneering, settlement in this part of a township. This created a pattern of satellite farmsteads on the fringes of parishes and townships where marginal lands were available for clearance. Foulk Stapleford moat was located in the Gowy marshes close to the township boundary. The moat platform may have been the site of a now lost house: Foulk Stapleford Hall. A new hall in the neighbouring township of Bruen Stapleford, 750 metres to the east, may have replaced the original moated hall.[23]

During the thirteenth century, many manor houses moved to the periphery of villages as the settlements grew in size limiting the opportunity for expansion. Thus more grandiose moated sites were built where there was more space at the edge of the built-up area as in the large (1.6 hectare) site at Dodleston Hall, Shotwick and Old Beachin at Coddington.

Rhys Williams concluded that moats in Cheshire 'tend to occur on the basis of no more than one per township'.[24] This is largely true in west Cheshire as a whole but there are exceptions: Capenhurst, Huntington, and Chorlton near Malpas. In English Maelor, there were often several moats in a township.

Further north, in the area surrounding Wrexham and Marford, moated sites are few. This may be attributed to Welsh systems of land tenure existing at the time of conquest and surviving in Bromfield and Yale into the sixteenth century. The townships of Wrexham Fawr, Wrexham Fechan, Wrexham Abbot, Marford and Hoseley were bonded townships in which the majority of the inhabitants were bondmen (taeogion) who farmed the lands within these townships on behalf of their lord.[25] Both Wrexham and Marford had twelfth-century Norman motte and bailey castles sited on former Iron Age hill forts. By 1191, both sites and their adjacent hunting parks were in the hands of the princes of Powys who used the motte sites as centres of local administration[26] and possibly hunting lodges. After 1282, these townships remained as unfree bailiwicks of the lordship of Bromfield and Yale each administered by an official known as a raglot. The lack of wealthy freeholders or tenants may explain why no moated sites were constructed here in the later medieval period. In contrast, adjacent free townships such as Burton, Llay, Bersham, Esclusham and Is-y-coed all possessed moated sites.

Monastic/Ecclesiastical Sites
The availability of considerable amounts of unimproved land in the borderland region made it possible for lands to be granted to ecclesiastical establishments. These estates were created from the late Anglo-Saxon period and especially to the reformed monastic orders, with the period from 1075 until 1225 seeing monastic houses being formed at a rate unsurpassed in history.[27]

The presence of monastic lands was often associated with the establishment of moated sites on granges and tenanted farms. These are more prolific on the Cheshire side of the border. On the east bank of the Dee, in the Anglo-Norman period, St Werburgh's Abbey in Chester founded in 1092 was endowed with the townships of Huntington-cum-Cheaveley, Saighton and Lea Newbold. A chapel of St Oswald's parish (formerly the parish of St Werburgh's), Chester, located at Bruera, 8 kilometres to the south-east of Chester, served the area which contained the three moated sites at Huntington together with those at Bruera and Lea Newbold.[28] The Norman

Medieval Moated Sites in the Borderland

earls of Chester also bestowed the manor of Upton, 3 kilometres to the north of Chester, upon the abbey of St Werburgh's. Moated sites were established on these lands at Upton Grange and Bache Hall. Twelve kilometres east-south-east of Chester, Iddinshall Hall moated site was also the property of the Benedictine monks of St Werburgh's and, like most others under the same ownership, passed to the Dean and Chapter of the new cathedral at Chester following the Dissolution. In Wirral, St Werburgh's was very much a part of the peninsula's monastic history[29] and no doubt was responsible for the establishment of a number of moated sites on abbey lands as at Ince, Irby and Bromborough.

In Wirral, there is plenty of evidence of clearance of the Forest to make way for moated homesteads. The abbey of St Werburgh's lands in Wirral benefited from exemption from the strict laws of the Forest from around the mid-twelfth century until Wirral was disafforested by Edward III in 1376.[30] During the time of abbot Simon of Whitchurch (1261–91), 140 acres of waste on Wirral was enclosed from the forest while in the period 1324–30, abbot William of Bebington was reported to have assarted 400 acres of waste in Wirral without a licence.[31] Given the fashion for moated homesteads in this period, it is possible that a number of the abbey's new tenants created such sites in the south of the peninsula such as those at Lea and Capenhurst East (Figure 12).

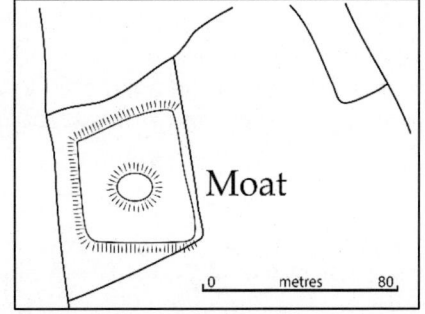

Figure 12: Capenhurst (East). The first edition OS map shows 'Site of ancient manor house'. A round mound is shown in the centre, possibly the site of a tower.

Landscapes Past and Present

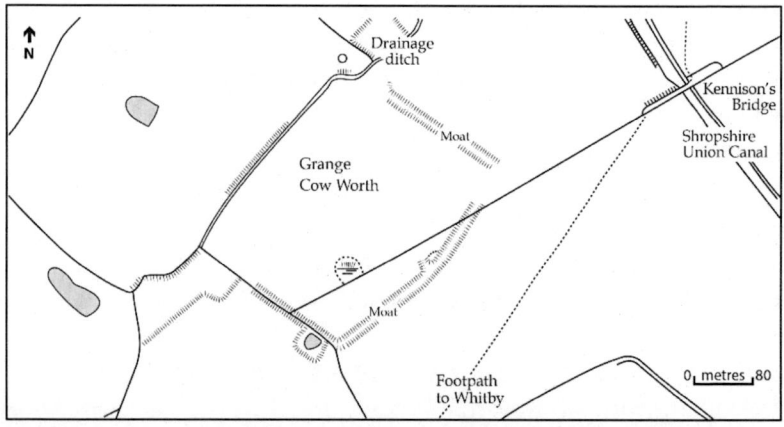

Figure 13: Cow Worth, Ellesmere Port – a grange of the Cistercian abbey at Stanlow to which it was linked by a causeway.

The Cistercians too brought about significant changes to the landscape of the borderland. The Cistercian system of land management, particularly the establishment of granges, was a model subsequently copied by other monastic orders. A monastic grange is a farm complex owned by a religious house. St Werburgh's Abbey, Chester, (Benedictine) eventually owned five granges, as did Vale Royal Abbey (Cistercian, 1270). Other monastic houses in the northern borderlands included Stanlow Abbey (Cistercian, 1172), Combermere (Savigniac, 1133, later transferred to the Cistercians), Valle Crucis (Cistercian, 1201) and the lost abbey at Poulton (Cistercian, c.1150). Stanlow Abbey, although relatively short-lived, maintained a moated grange known as Cow Worth at Stanney (Figure 13), linked to Stanlow by a causeway across the marshes. The monks of Stanlow also held the vill of Aston where a moated manor house was located. After the movement of the Cistercians from Stanlow to Whalley in Lancashire, in 1296, a cell for four or five monks was left behind at Stanlow presumably farming the grange at Stanney.[32] The Augustinian canons of Norton Priory,

62

Runcorn (1115, moving to Norton 1134) also held lands in Stanney.

Thus it is clear that, especially through their establishment of granges, monastic orders played an active part in the clearance of woodland in west Cheshire. This may account for the number of monastic granges and tenanted farmsteads; many of them moated sites within the newly cleared lands. During the first half of the thirteenth century, the abbot of St Werburgh's Abbey was given extensive rights to clear land within his manors in the forest.[33] Ince Manor was one of the five granges of the Benedictine Abbey at Chester and is a moated site dating from the thirteenth century. A licence to crenellate was granted in 1398 perhaps indicating that the buildings on the moat platform were of stone. To the north-west of Ince, the abbey at Chester had a further moated manor house at Irby Hall.

The Cistercian abbey at Poulton, close to the Welsh border at Pulford Brook, only survived for a little over half a century following its foundation in 1146–53 but was retained as a grange following the move to Dieulacres in Staffordshire in 1214. The Dieulacres Chronicle records that the move followed continuous incursions by the Welsh.[34] The grange at Poulton was listed as the most valuable asset of Dieulacres Abbey at the Dissolution in 1538. It is possible that the grange at Poulton was a moated site, for an inquisition dated 1598 refers to 'the pool moat'.[35]

In north-east Wales ecclesiastical sites are few. However, Llys Farm in Prestatyn, now vanished, was a moated seignorial farmstead of the bishops of St Asaph. In English Maelor, Vicarage Meadow moated site located adjacent to Hanmer Church is a possible former parsonage and is believed to have been part of the estates of Haughmond Abbey in Shropshire until the Dissolution.

Landscapes Past and Present

Frontier/Defensive Sites
In the Cheshire borderlands seignorial manor houses or the houses of free yeoman farmers occupied most moated sites. As in Ireland, the distribution of moated sites in the Cheshire–North Wales borderlands tends to relate to the area of Anglo-Norman colonisation. This must be set against the fact that it took 200 years for the Norman Conquest to be consolidated in its entirety and during the period 1066–1277, parts of the northern borderlands were alternately in either Norman or Welsh control for long periods.[36]

Husain defined the Marches as 'the ill-defined zone which separated England from the Wales of the princes and yet was part of neither'.[37] Nevertheless, the North Wales border commotes of English Maelor, Marford and Hoseley, Welsh Maelor (Maelor Cymraeg) and Yale, with the latter two forming the core of the marcher lordship of Bromfield and Yale after 1282, were, until the wars of 1277–82, part of the principality of Powys Fadog. This Welsh principality had, from the closing years of the twelfth century, regained control of most of the area lying west of the River Dee that had been part of Domesday Cheshire in 1086. The inhabitants shared strong linguistic, legal and cultural bonds. They were frequently hostile towards the English and raided the Cheshire Plain to supplement their food supplies, making it possible that some moated homesteads on the Cheshire–North Wales border fulfilled a defensive need. There was nevertheless some cross-border contact for we learn that on the death of the last effective prince of Powys Fadog, Madog ap Grufydd, in 1236, he left his wife Emma d'Audley, a Staffordshire woman, his park at Eyton and the enclosure therein,[38] probably Eyton Old Hall, a moated site.

The creation of the Marcher lordships of Denbigh, Ruthin, Chirkland plus Bromfield and Yale following the final conquest

Medieval Moated Sites in the Borderland

of Wales in 1282 may well have been as important a part of Edward I's plans to control the Welsh as the great castles that he built along the coast and it is following their creation that the first 'Welsh' moated sites appeared.

With the possible exception of Llys Edwin near Northop, there is no evidence that moated sites existed in Powys Fadog and it seems that the earliest moated sites on the Welsh side of the border postdate the Edwardian conquest of 1277-82. Many of the moated sites followed woodland clearance and colonisation of lands especially in areas close to the present Welsh border. In these areas forfeited lands of the descendants of the prince of Powys Fadog were awarded to lesser lords as a reward for military service in the newly conquered lands after the 1277-82 wars.[39]

A considerable amount of land clearance took place as part of the strategic plan to invade Wales in 1277. In April of that year an 'army of woodcutters' under the direction of William Beauchamp, earl of Warwick and commander of the king's army in Cheshire, descended upon the 'pass of Pulford' that lay between the River Alyn and the Cheshire border at Pulford Brook. Their intention was to widen significantly the area surrounding a route from Chester into Bromfield. This action offset the risk of a Welsh ambush in a wooded area as had befallen Henry II near Ewloe in 1157. Records of the time reveal that the cleared land had never been previously cut. To the north of Pulford lay the now lost 'Swerdewood' (Black Forest). These lands lay on the border between the Lordship of Hawarden and Cheshire in the townships of Dodleston and Bretton. The felled timber was offered free of charge to the men of Chester and Wirral.[40] It is significant that these cleared areas subsequently became the sites of several moated houses, possibly after the close of the initial phase of hostilities in 1277. Other instances of woodland clearance to improve the passage of English forces took place at Redbrook on the border between Whitchurch and English Maelor in 1282. This area also became the site of several medieval moated settlements. The place-name 'Trench' is also associated with military clearance of woodland to provide access into north-east Wales. Such place-names exist close to the Shropshire border to the south of Overton and Penley and may be linked to the moated sites at Penley, Lightwood Green and the possible site at Nant Climbers which lies very close to the cleared area.[41]

The forfeited Manor of Banconbury (Bangor Is-y-coed) was granted to Queen Eleanor in 1283; she subsequently acquired most of the other land in English Maelor by exchange. Thus there was a significant change of land ownership in the area where moated sites have their highest density on the borderland. She was also granted Hope manor, together with Marford and Hoseley which became detached parts of the new county of Flintshire, part of the holdings attached to the earldom of Chester. Following the death of Eleanor in 1290, the lands of Hopedale were farmed out to John de Warenne, lord of Bromfield and Yale. During this period there were widespread complaints from the residents of Hopedale (which then included the townships of Burton, Llay, Honkley and parts of Allington) that de Warenne's bailiffs were exploiting the woods: assarting, hedging and ditching.[42] There is a possibility that the cluster of moated sites at Llay Hall farm, Town Ditch, Llyn Tro and possibly Burton Hall date from this period of assarting and enclosure.

These anglicised forms of land settlement are particularly thick on the ground in English Maelor (Figure 14).[43] This area had a significant expanse of sparsely settled uncleared woodland, ideal for settlement by Edward I's supporters. One of these, Roger de Puleston, was granted what became of the moated site of Emral Hall. A deed of sale of land in nearby

Medieval Moated Sites in the Borderland

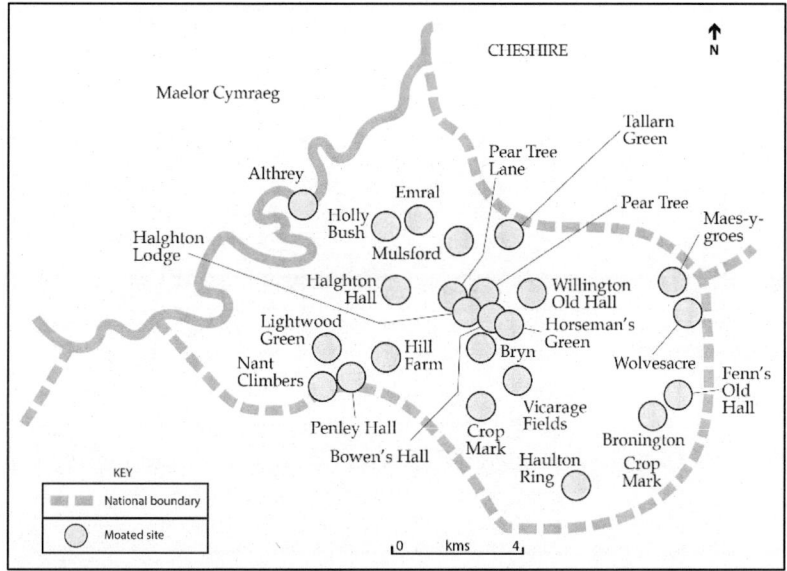

Figure 14: The distribution of moated sites in English Maelor (Maelor Saesneg).

Willington in 1284 mentions the 'forest domain' of Roger de Puleston as a boundary,[44] supporting the probability that extensive parts of English Maelor were still wooded at the time of the English conquest of 1277–82, and that woodland clearance provided land for new moated settlements in this part of the Welsh borderland such as the seignorial moats at Willington, Penley and Althrey Hall.

English Maelor has the greatest density of moated sites in the whole of the northern borderlands. This may reflect local families adopting the fashionable trend in the early fourteenth century of surrounding country manor houses with moats. It is interesting to note that when a younger son of the Puleston family of the moated Emral Hall acquired an estate in neighbouring Welsh Maelor at Lower Berse this site was also moated, perhaps by their new owners. The Hanmer family also acquired the moated farmhouse and estate at Llay Hall through marriage in 1391 (Figure 15). Here, the moated site was probably already in existence before 1391 since it was the property of Dafydd ap Grono ap Iorweth, the chief forester of Bromfield and Yale.[45] This indicates that before the end of the fourteenth century, some Welsh families held key administrative roles, owned moated properties in the marcher lordship and were intermarrying with English families. Several families, established in early moated sites, came to dominate land tenure in English Maelor: the Hanmers, a Macclesfield family, occupied moated dwellings in Hanmer, Bronington and Haulton Ring; the Puleston (a Shropshire family) seat was in the moated Emral Hall, the Dymocks occupied moated sites in

Figure 15: Llay Hall. (By kind permission of Mr G. Moore, Llay Hall Farm.)

Penley, Halghton and Pear Tree Farm while a surviving Welsh family, the Lloyds, were based at Willington.[46]

Even after the final conquest of Wales, cross-border raids and high levels of criminal activity persisted in the border areas. It seems clear that the most obvious reason for constructing a moat is to offer the occupants a degree of safety and security against groups of determined ne'er-do-wells. The need for protection is supported by judicial records in Cheshire, which indicate that in

Figure 16: Llay Hall surviving arm of moat. Photograph: Derrick Gwilliam.)

the thirteenth and fourteenth centuries, crime was common. There is evidence of bands of marauders sheltering in the forest of Wirral and in 1318, bands of armed men threatened the approaches to Chester itself and 'terrorised the people of those parts'.[47] It is likely that a number of these criminals had seen military service in Wales, Scotland and France. It is therefore not surprising that those who could afford it built moats around their houses in the rural areas surrounding Chester (Figure 16 and Plate 3).

Despite this, it is now considered that most moats were not built solely as defensive structures. One writer has described the defensive capabilities of moated sites as 'negligible';[48] another has expressed the opinion that a typical moated house 'would scarcely deter a determined sheep'.[49] This was hardly the case in the Welsh borderlands where some moats were over two metres deep and up to twenty metres wide (Figure 17).

The moated site at Llys Edwin, Northop, was strongly defensive and had an external wooden palisade and corner towers. Excavation revealed that part of the charred remains of the palisade was found in the moat.[50] But even here, the moat

Figure 17: Llyn Tro, Pentre Bychan, Wrexham, showing the moat, platform and bridge abutment. (Photograph: David Roberts.)

also provided the household with fish, waterfowl and the domestic animals with drinking water.

In a few locations, the defensive character of moated sites is enhanced by the presence of a tower house. At Brimstage Hall, Wirral, a medieval moated site had its defences enhanced by a stone tower possibly added in the late fourteenth century, a time of rural dissent and cross-border cattle raids from Wales, which continued until the stronger control of the Tudor monarchs. The moated sites at Capenhurst (East), Green Lane, Broughton (Figure 18) and Belgrave also contain mounds that may have once held defensive towers. In the borderlands of North Wales other defensive towers existed on non-moated

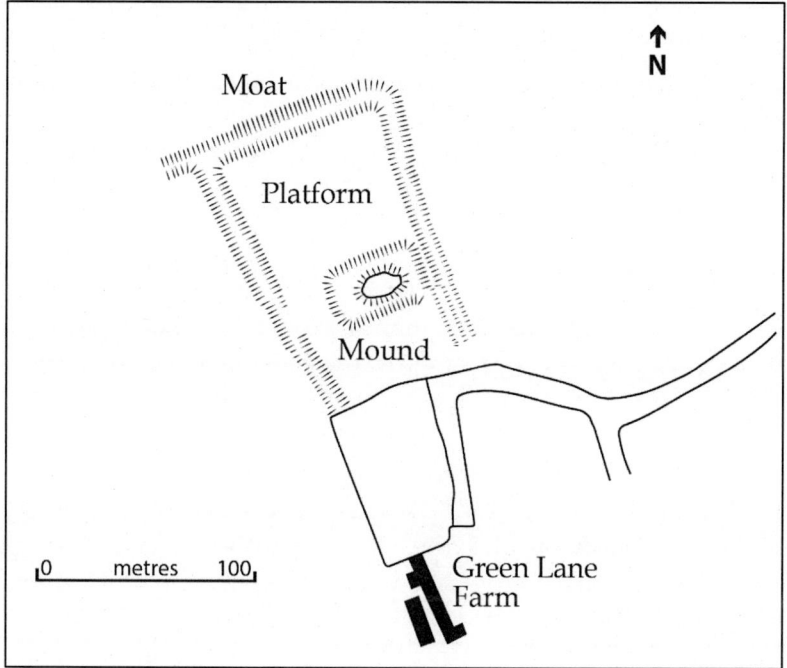

Figure 18: Moated site at Green Lane Farm, Broughton (after J. Rigg, 'Broughton Earthwork', *[Publications of the] Flintshire Historical Society*, XIX (1961), 92–93).

sites at Saighton Grange and at The Tower at Nerquis near Mold. It may be concluded that defence was not the only factor in the development of moated sites although in the Welsh borderlands it may have had more significance than elsewhere in England and Wales.

Status Symbol v Economic Function
Most recent researchers see moats as symbols of local power and prestige.[51] Nevertheless, the moat was a psychological barrier and a means of lessening the risk of damage by fire. In addition, they offered security against cattle raiders (a frequent problem in late medieval Cheshire and the Welsh borderlands), bands of armed robbers, local feuds and occasional civil unrest. It may be the case that in the borderlands,[52] high levels of crime may have rendered the defensive function of moats more important. Rhys Williams concluded that most moated sites in west Cheshire were 'working' moats and that 'few seem to have become status symbols'.[53] Nevertheless, there are a number of examples in west Cheshire of moats that were relatively shallow (one metre or less in depth), or with only three arms such as the moated sites at Dodleston, Lower Huxley, Hampton Heath, Eccleston and Marlston-cum-Lache, which may suggest that appearance was more important than defence in many cases.

The range of other working functions suggested for moated sites include swan and fish keeping and the protection of farm products from deer.[54] In 1327 Edward III ordered the creation of a park around the site of Shotwick Castle. The keeper of this royal hunting park was housed in a moated lodge on the site of the present-day farmhouse of Shotwick Lodge Farm. When visiting the site in 1955, Ellison noted that traces of the moat still remained.[55] Elsewhere in England the islands within the moats were sometimes occupied by other features[56] such as orchards or even haystacks, as was the case on a site at Frodsham[57] where, in 1316, a moat was created to protect the hay from Mersey floods.[58] In Cheshire and north-east Wales, the moats were sometimes surrounded by an outer bank that may have once been topped by a palisade as a means of excluding cattle from the moat. Examples of such a feature have been identified at Hafod Wood, Halkyn and at Foulk Stapleford moated site where the counterscarp bank is 2 metres high and 10 metres in width.[59] In west Cheshire, a 0.3 metre bank exists at Marlston-cum-Lache to the south of Chester while Iddinshall had an inner bank 0.5 metres high and six metres wide with an outer bank one metre high.[60]

Abandonment and Rebuilding
When their usefulness as a defensive or dry point domestic site came to an end most moated sites were abandoned and the moats themselves were allowed to silt up. However, a minority continued to be occupied as dwellings. Field surveys and limited archaeological evidence suggests that in the North Wales–Cheshire borderlands most of the original platforms contained timber-framed buildings. Today, few moated sites retain their original medieval houses but elements of late medieval aisle-trussed moated halls have survived on the Welsh side of the border at Horseman's Green Farm (Willington), Lower Berse (Wrexham), Althrey Hall (Bangor Is-y-coed) and Llay Hall farm. A number of second generation buildings still exist on moated platforms; many, particularly in English Maelor, dating back to the Restoration period in the 1660s as at Emral Hall and Llay Hall. A number of these were rebuilt again in the eighteenth and nineteenth centuries, as at Dodleston Hall and The Plassey (Figure 19).

Many of the replacement houses were located away from the original moated site leaving the platforms as empty relict

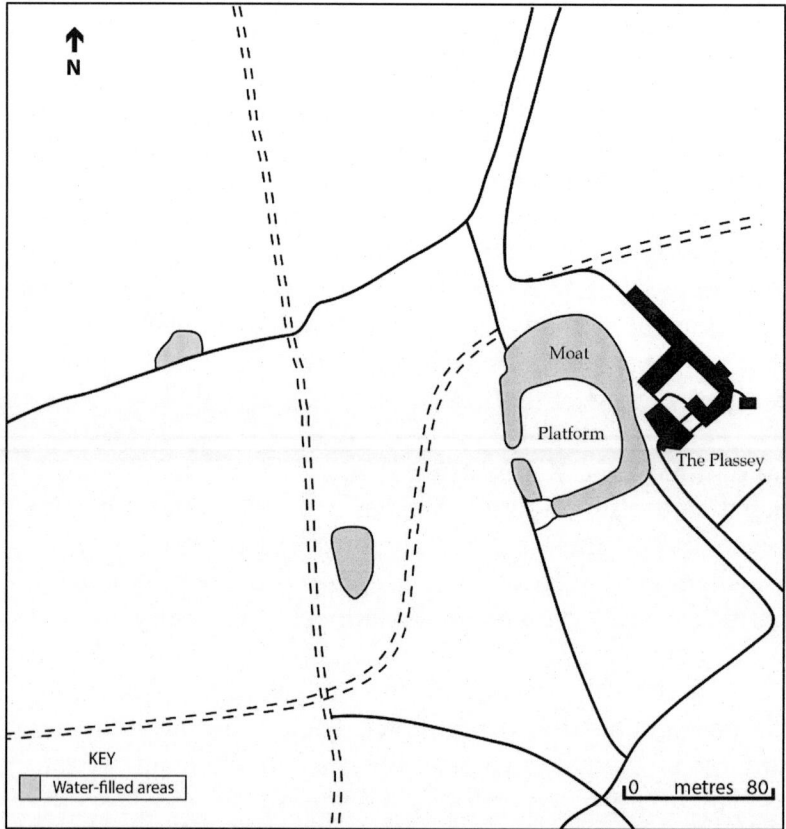

Figure 19: The Plassey, Eyton, c.1870. The map shows the site before infilling and rebuilding destroyed the moated site in the late nineteenth century.

features. At Lea Newbold Hall, Aldford, the moated platform lies 100 metres to the east of the present farm house. The medieval site lay on the old road linking Coddington to Aldford, which takes a sharp bend around the moated site. At Cholmondeley Castle (Figure 20), the original moated site lies a short distance from the nineteenth century 'castle'. The site is described by Leland in the late 1530s as 'a fine timber building with a moat watered by a pool.'[61] Whether or not the house

Medieval Moated Sites in the Borderland

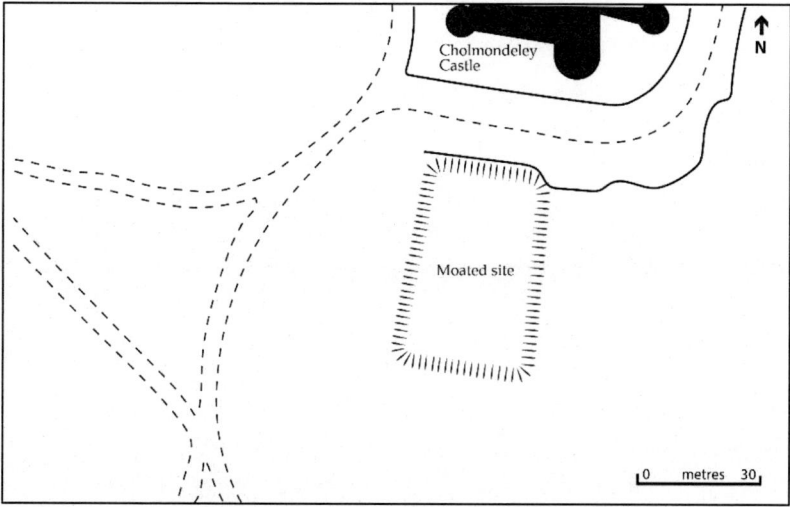

Figure 20: Cholmondeley. The medieval building on the platform was replaced by a half-timbered house in the sixteenth century and the present 'castle' to the north in the nineteenth century.

described by Leland is the medieval original on the site cannot be verified but a medieval chapel located close to the moat dates from at least 1285. The moats at Llyn Tro, Burton, Tallarn Green and Willington have been filled in by farmers in the post-medieval period. In some cases, where there is no documentary evidence or remaining earthworks, field-names may indicate the presence of a possible site as is the case at 'Cae Moat Well Field' south-west of Penley[62] and at Kiln Farm, Marchwiel.

The abandonment of moated sites began towards the end of the fourteenth century as was probably the case at Marlston-cum-Lache and Belgrave. Occasionally, the date of abandonment is recorded in contemporary documents as at Haulton Ring in English Maelor. The house on the site was demolished and the site was abandoned following the death of the last occupant, Lady Dorothy Hanmer in 1656. The Civil War saw the destruction of the houses on several moated sites in

English Maelor. In 1645, Penley Hall, home of the royalist Dymock family was burned down by Parliamentary troops. In some cases the royalist occupants of some moated houses in English Maelor burned down their own houses in the face of Parliamentary forces approaching from Whitchurch and Malpas. This was the case at Wolvesacre (Figure 21) and Maes-y-groes.[63] In the Chester area too, the Civil War siege of the city brought about the destruction of the timbered house that occupied the medieval moated site at Bache Hall. Although the house was later rebuilt, the medieval moat disappeared, although it is labelled on the 1910 OS map of the area. In addition, the mid-nineteenth-century Tithe Map names a 'Moat Field' close to the site.[64]

In the nineteenth century many moats were infilled and platforms levelled to create land for agricultural purposes. This

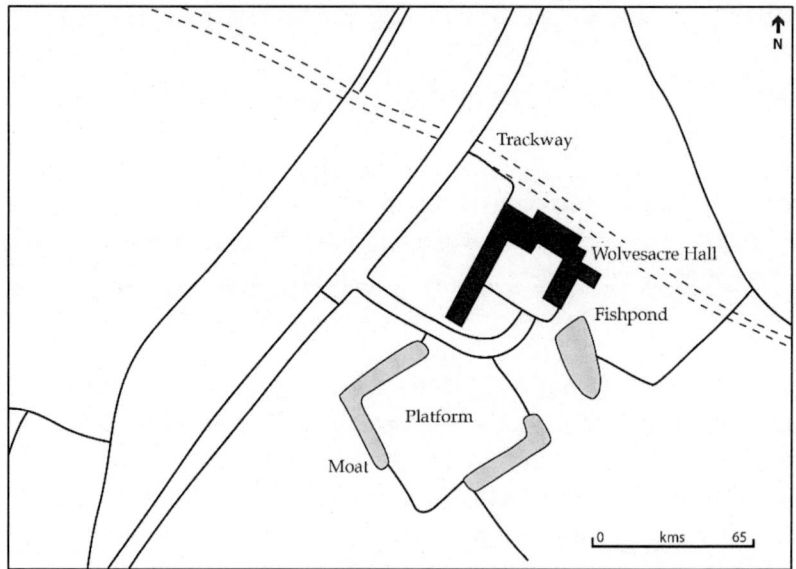

Figure 21: Wolvesacre Hall, English Maelor. Buildings on the platform were destroyed during the Civil War. The present hall to the north dates from the post Restoration period after 1660.

was the case at Emral Hall, Worthenbury which was demolished in 1936 and the rubble used to infill the moat. A moated site in Burton, Wrexham, known as Talant Cottage, Town Ditch, was destroyed between 1963 (when it was well preserved) and 1985.[65] The moated site at Yew Tree Farm, Willington, has lost three of its arms to twentieth-century gravel working. At New Hall, Chirk, the moat has been partly infilled but the well-preserved south-western part is still water-filled and has survived as a garden feature.[66]

Recent Discoveries
There may be still a significant number of moated sites that remain undiscovered or wrongly identified.[67] In the last 40 years aerial photography has increased the number of known moated sites. These include the Bowen's Hall moated site at Willington in the English Maelor and Nant Climbers, near Penley identified by aerial photographs taken by Clwyd-Powys Archaeological Trust (CPAT)[68] while in nearby Bronington, a rectangular cropmark visible only from the air has been identified as a likely moated site. In Cheshire, the moat at Old Hall Heyes in Edge is visible from the air but is only just visible on the ground. Likewise, aerial photography helps to support the identification of suspected moats when site and documentary evidence is meagre. This was the case at Althrey Hall, Bangor Is-y-coed, where aerial photographic evidence supplied by CPAT in 1989 helped confirm the existence of a moated site. In rare cases, lost moated sites have been identified through field walking. This was the case at Little Bryn Farm, Is-y-coed, where in 1986 a raised platform was discovered possibly indicating the presence of a moated site. Sometimes, the exact location of a moated site referred to in medieval manuscripts has been lost as at Netherleigh Hall, Chester, and Redbrook Upper House, south of Wrexham.

Concluding Comments

The late Dorothy Sylvester described the Welsh borderland as 'a contact area',[69] and since moated sites have been described as 'a characteristically English medieval institution',[70] and thus a feature of the English sphere of influence in north-east Wales, they can be seen as an example of the porosity of the border and an indicator of how aspects of rural settlement can be influenced by the flow of ideas and fashion across a frontier which displayed a lasting ethnic, linguistic and cultural characteristic throughout the late medieval period. Jack Spurgeon believes that the moated sites of the Welsh borderlands represent an extension of the Midlands moated area where densities of moated sites are amongst the highest in England and Wales.[71] It is significant that the greatest density of moated sites in the northern borderlands are found in the English Maelor close to the Shropshire border, lending some support to Spurgeon's conclusion.

Most of the moated sites in the Cheshire–North Wales borderlands occupy sites reclaimed from woodland or marshland. One notable exception to this was the moated site at Upton Grange near Chester that occupied the site of a Roman practice camp. This site, like a number of others on the Cheshire side of the border, was located on lands reclaimed from wastes or forests following grants of lands to monastic foundations by the earls of Chester. A number of these ecclesiastical moated sites, as well as many secular sites located close to the Welsh border such as those at Poulton Grange and Llay Hall probably had a partly protective function since cross-border raids and rural crime are well documented in the late medieval period. A number of moated sites in the North Wales borderland also functioned as symbols of prestige and status. This may account for the high density of moats in some areas such as English Maelor where the addition of a moat around the houses of

Medieval Moated Sites in the Borderland

wealthy local landowners or tenants may have been a fashion trend.

Regardless of their function, moated sites are of great significance for they represent a class of medieval monument that give insights into the medieval settlement pattern and the distribution of wealth and status within the rural borderlands of west Cheshire and North Wales.

Endnotes
1. C. Taylor, 'Moated sites: their distribution, form and classification' in F.A. Aberg, ed., *Medieval Moated Sites, CBA Research Report,* 17 (London, 1978), 5.
2. N. Coveney, 'Moated Sites in Medieval England: A Reassessment' (Univ. of Leicester, PhD thesis, 2015), 73. << https://lra.le.ac.uk/bitstream/2381/33361/1/2015COVENEYNPhD.pdf>>, accessed 26 Oct. 2015.
3. H.E.J. Le Patourel and B.K. Roberts, 'The Significance of Moated Sites' in *Medieval Moated Sites,* 46.
4. F.A. Aberg, 'Introduction' in *Medieval Moated Sites,* 3.
5. W.G. Hoskins, *English Landscapes* (London, 1973), 31.
6. D. Williams, *The Epic Tudor Journey* (Pwllheli, 2008), 29.
7. I.H. Adams, *Agrarian Landscape Terms: a Glossary for Historical Geography,* Institute of British Geographers, Special Publication, IX (London, 1976), 55.
8. G.J. White, *The Medieval English Landscape, 1000–1540* (London 2012), 79.
9. H.H. Lamb, 'Climate and Landscape in the British Isles' in S.R.J. Woodell, ed., *The English Landscape: Past, Present and Future* (Oxford, 1985), 153-63.
10. C. Dyer, 'The Retreat from Marginal Land' in M. Aston, D. Austin and C. Dyer, eds, *The Rural Settlements of Medieval England* (Oxford, 1989), 46.
11. J.M. Steane, *The Archaeology of Medieval England and Wales* (London, 1985), 59.
12. Le Patourel and Roberts, 'Significance of Moated Sites', 48.

13. S. Reynolds, 'A Survey of Two Moated Sites in West Cheshire' in *Cheshire Past* (Chester, 1993), 19.
14. N. Ellison, *The Wirral Peninsula* (London, 1955), 132.
15. Dodleston Hall moated site, CHER 1978/3/1, <<rcp.cheshire.gov.uk/singleResult.aspx?uid=MCH1358>>, accessed 17 Sep. 2014.
16. P. de Figueiredo and J. Treuherz, *Cheshire Country Houses* (Chichester, 1988), 97.
17. S.R. Williams, *West Cheshire from the Air* (Chester, 1997), 63.
18. A.T. Thacker, 'Later Medieval Chester, 1230–1500' in *VCH Ches.:* V, 53.
19. A.T. Thacker, 'Manors and Estates in and near the City', in *VCH Ches.:* V, part 2 (London, 2005), available online <<http://www.british-history.ac.uk/vch/ches/vol5/pt2/pp322-330>>, accessed 13 Apr. 2015.
20. A.N. Palmer and E. Owen, *A History of Ancient Tenures of Land in North Wales and the Marches* (2nd edn, Wrexham, 1910), 95.
21. D. Wilson, *Moated Sites* (Aylesbury, 1985), 29.
22. Bruera moated site, CHER 1951 <<rcp.cheshire.gov.uk/SibgleResult.aspx?uid=MCH1442>>, accessed 15 Sep. 2014.
23. Williams, *West Cheshire from the Air*, 61.
24. Williams, *West Cheshire from the Air*, 58.
25. G.R.J. Jones, 'The Distribution of Bond Settlement in North West Wales', *Welsh History Review*, II (1964), 262.
26. D. Pratt, 'Fourteenth-century Wrexham', *Transactions of the Denbighshire Historical Society*, LIV (Wrexham, 2006), 34.
27. R. Bartlett, *England under the Norman and Angevin Kings, 1075–1225* (Oxford, 2000), 412, 417.
28. Bruera Chapel, CHER, 1951. <<rcp.cheshire.gov.uk/SibgleResult.aspx?uid=MCH1442>>, accessed 15 Sep. 2014.
29. N. Blake, 'The Monastic and Religious Orders in the Hundred of Wirral from the Saxons to the Dissolution of the Monasteries,' <<www/roydenhistory.co.uk/monasticwirral.htm>>, accessed 5 Apr. 2015.
30. J.A. Green, 'The Forests', in *VCH Ches.:* II, 187.
31. H. J. Hewitt, *Cheshire Under the Three Edwards* (Chester, 1967), 15.

32. R.W. Morant, *Monastic and Collegiate Cheshire* (Braunton, 1996), 84.
33. B.M. Husain, *Cheshire under the Norman Earls 1066-1237* (Chester, 1973), 83.
34. Wessex Archaeology, *Poulton Hall, Pulford, Cheshire – Archaeological Evaluation and Assessment of Results*, Report 62507.01 (Salisbury, 2007), paragraph 1.3.4.
35. Wessex Archaeology, *Poulton Hall*, 1.3.7, 1.3.9.
36. M. Richards, 'The Population of the Welsh Border', *Transactions of the Honourable Society of Cymrodorion*, part 1 (London, 1972), 83.
37. Husain, *Cheshire under the Norman Earls*, 98.
38. A.N. Palmer and E. Owen, *A History of Ancient Tenures of Land in North Wales and the Marches*, 92-93.
39. J. Spurgeon, 'Mottes and Moated Sites', in J. Manley, S. Grenter and F. Gale, eds, *The Archaeology of Clwyd* (Mold, 1991), 167.
40. D. Pratt, 'Bromfield and Yale 1277-84', *Transactions of the Denbighshire Historical Society*, LVI (2008), 24-25.
41 Nant Climbers moated site, Clwyd-Powys Archaeological Trust (CPAT) Regional HER, <<http://archaeologydataservice.ac.uk/archsearch/record.jsf?titleId=830308>>, accessed 12 May 2015.
42. D. Pratt, 'A Local Border Dispute', *Journal of the Flintshire Historical Society*, XXI (1964), 46-55.
43. F.V. Emery, *Wales* (London, 1969), 54.
44. Rev. Canon M.H. Lee, 'Emral and its Occupants', *Archaeologia Cambrensis*, V (1888), 283.
45. A. Rogers, 'Caer Alyn: A Border Landscape', *Monograph of the Caer Alyn Archaeological and Heritage Project* (Gresford, 2009), 68.
46. D. Pratt, 'Moated Settlements in Maelor' *Journal of the Flintshire Historical Society*, XXI (1964), 110.
47. Hewitt, *Cheshire Under the Three Edwards*, 105-6.
48. J. Spurgeon, 'Mottes and Moated Sites', 165.
49. R. Muir, *Reading the Landscape* (London, 1981), 185.
50. T.A. Glenn, 'Llys Edwin', *Bulletin of the Board of Celtic Studies*, VI (1933), 96-98.
51. C. Taylor, *The Cambridgeshire Landscape* (London, 1973), 127.
52. Hewitt, *Cheshire Under the Three Edwards*, 106.

53. Williams, *West Cheshire from the Air*, 60.
54. L. Cantor, ed., 'Castles, Fortified Houses, Moated Homesteads and Monastic Settlements', in *The English Medieval Landscape* (London, 1982), 139.
55. Ellison, *Wirral Peninsula*, 145.
56. J.C. Bond, *Moated Site Research Group*, VIII (1981), 4.
57. J.P. Green, 'Medieval Haystacks', *Landscape Archaeology*, IV (1972), 69.
58. Hewitt, *Cheshire Under the Three Edwards*, 21.
59. Foulk Stapleford moated site, CHER 1885, <<rcp.Cheshire.gov.uk/SingleResult.aspx?uid=MCH1351>>, accessed 9 Sep. 2014.
60. Iddinshall moated site, CHER 1846, <<www.heritagegateway.org.uk/gateway/chr/hrtdetail.aspx?grit=>>, accessed 15 Oct. 2013.
61. J. Chandler, *John Leland's Itinerary – Travels in Tudor England* (Stroud, 1993), 51.
62. CPAT *List of scheduled monuments in Wrexham C.B.C.*, <<http://archaeologydataservice.ac.uk/archsearch/record.jsf?titleId=82576 5>>, accessed 8 Aug. 2015.
63. Pratt, 'Moated Settlements in Maelor', 119.
64. K. Roberts, 'Bache Hall', in *Upton-by-Chester – A People's History* (Chester, 2005), 33.
65. Spurgeon, 'Mottes and Moated Sites', 169.
66. D. Pratt, 'New Hall Moated Site, Chirk', *Transactions of the Denbighshire Historical Society*, XXXXV (1996), 7–20.
67. R. Muir, *The NEW Reading the Landscape* (Exeter, 2000), 239.
68. R.J. Silvester, C.H. Martin and S. Watson, *Historic Settlements in Wrexham County Borough Council*, CPAT Report 1186, (Welshpool, 2013), <<http://archaeologydataservice.ac.uk/archsearch/record.jsf?titleId=830311>>, accessed 8 Aug. 2015, on which most of this paragraph is based.
69. D. Sylvester, *The Rural Landscape of the Welsh Borderland* (London, 1969), 23.
70. Pratt, 'Moated Settlements in Maelor', 112.
71. Spurgeon, 'Mottes and Moated Sites', 165.

Medieval Moated Sites in the Borderland

A Gazetteer of Moated Sites in the Cheshire-North Wales Borderland

Map No.	Name of Moated Site	Location (Parish/Township)	OS Grid Ref.
1	Llys Edwin	Northop (Flints.)	237693
2	Green Lane Farm	Broughton (Flints.)	334638
3	Bretton Hall	Bretton (Flints.)	336637
4	Moor End	Lower Kinnerton	351619
5	Marlston (Manor?)	Marlston-cum-Lache	393635
6	Netherleigh Hall	Netherleigh, Chester	4064[1]
7	Mill Hill, Rake Lane	Eccleston	401626
8	Dodleston Hall	Dodleston	361614
9	Belgrave Moat Farm	Eaton	390605
10	Eaton Hall	Eaton	413605
11	Town Ditch	Burton	326590
12	Llay Hall	Llay, Wrexham	326557
13	Llyn Tro	Burton, Rossett	346577
14	Poulton Hall	Poulton	396597
15	Lower Berse	Bersham, Wrexham	312501
16	Little Bryn Farm	Isycoed	381498
17	Llyn Tro	Pentre Bychan, Wrexham	304482
18	The Plassey	Eyton	350452
19	Eyton Old Hall	Eyton	349437
20	New Hall	Chirk	275390
21	Nant Climbers	Penley	392390
22	Penley Hall	Penley	417405

---

[1] Precise location is unknown.

Landscapes Past and Present

23	Lightwood Green	Overton	389410
24	Hill Farm	Penley	400400
25	Halghton Hall	Halghton, English Maelor	416424
26	Pear Tree Lane	Halghton	437417
27	Pear Tree House	Halghton	433418
28	Willington Old Hall	Willington	456424
29	Horseman's Green	Willington	447415
30	Buwen's Hall	Willington	442420
31	Halghton Lodge	Halghton	418432
32	Bryn Moat	Hanmer	427401
33	Vicarage Fields	Hanmer	458398
34	Crop mark	Hanmer	447392
35	Haulton Ring	Hanmer	469373
36	Bronington Crop Mark	Hanmer	447393
37	Fenn's Old Hall	Bronington	505396
38	Wolvesacre Hall	Iscoyd	506424
39	Maes-y-groes	Iscoyd	498431
40	Tallarn Green	Willington	447439
41	Mulsford Hall	Worthenbury	431438
42	Emral Hall	Worthenbury	419442
43	Holly Bush Farm	Worthenbury	409439
44	Althrey Hall	Bangor Is-y-coed	379441
45	Wigland	Wigland, Malpas	493448
46	Overton Hall	Overton, Malpas	471483
47	Chorlton Old Hall	Chorlton, Malpas	459482
48	Chorlton (north)	Chorlton	461484
49	Hampton Manor	Hampton, Malpas	511505
50	Egerton Hall	Egerton	518505
51	Cholmondeley Castle	Cholmondeley	546517

Medieval Moated Sites in the Borderland

52	Edge Hall	Edge	494491
53	Grafton	Grafton	449513
54	Lower Stretton Hall	Stretton	449531
55	Wetreins Green	Stretton	442532
56	Old Beachin	Coddington	445574
57	Lea Newbold	Lea Newbold	432588
58	Bruera	Buerton	437606
59	Huntington South	Huntington	429620
60	Golborne New Hall	Golborne David	459593
61	Golborne Old Hall	Golborne David	462598
62	Rushall Hall	Golborne Bellow	466603
63	Beeston Moat House	Beeston	534584
64	Iddinshall	Iddinshall	534627
65	Foulk Stapleford	Foulk Stapleford	484640
66	Lower Huxley Hall	Huxley	498623
67	Hatton Hall	Hatton	472611
68	Huntington Old Hall	Huntington	418634
69	Saighton Camp (south)	Huntington	433640
70	Huntington north	Huntington	419640
71	Bache Hall	Bache, Upton-by-Chester	403682
72	Upton Grange	Upton-by-Chester	424691
73	Lea Old Hall	Lea-by-Backford	393713
74	Little Mollington	Little Mollington	387695
75	Shotwick Park Lodge	Shotwick Park	353714
76	Shotwick Hall	Shotwick	335720

Landscapes Past and Present

77	Puddington Old Hall	Puddington	326733
78	Capenhurst Old Hall	Capenhurst	367738
79	Capenhurst (east)	Capenhurst	377736
80	Poole Hall	Netherpool, Ellesmere Port	391785
81	Little Stanney Old Hall	Little Stanney	413742
82	Cow Worth Grange	Great Stanney	411754
83	Stoke Hall	Stoke	421738
84	Ince Manor	Ince	448765
85	Thornton-le-Moors	Thornton-le-Moors	443746
86	Elton	Elton	455748
87	Alvanley Hall	Alvanley	504738
88	Manley Hall	Manley	504726
89	Horton Hall	Horton-cum-Peel	495688

Colour Plates

Plate 1: Mossley Moss, Congleton, 31 October 1992, from 1992–93 Aerial Survey of Cheshire. Copyright 2009 Cheshire West & Chester Council & Cheshire East Council ©. All rights reserved. Flown and captured by National Remote Sensing Centre Ltd 1992–93. Digitally converted by Bluesky International Ltd 2009. See Paper 1: *Enclosure and Enclosures in Mid- and East Cheshire.*

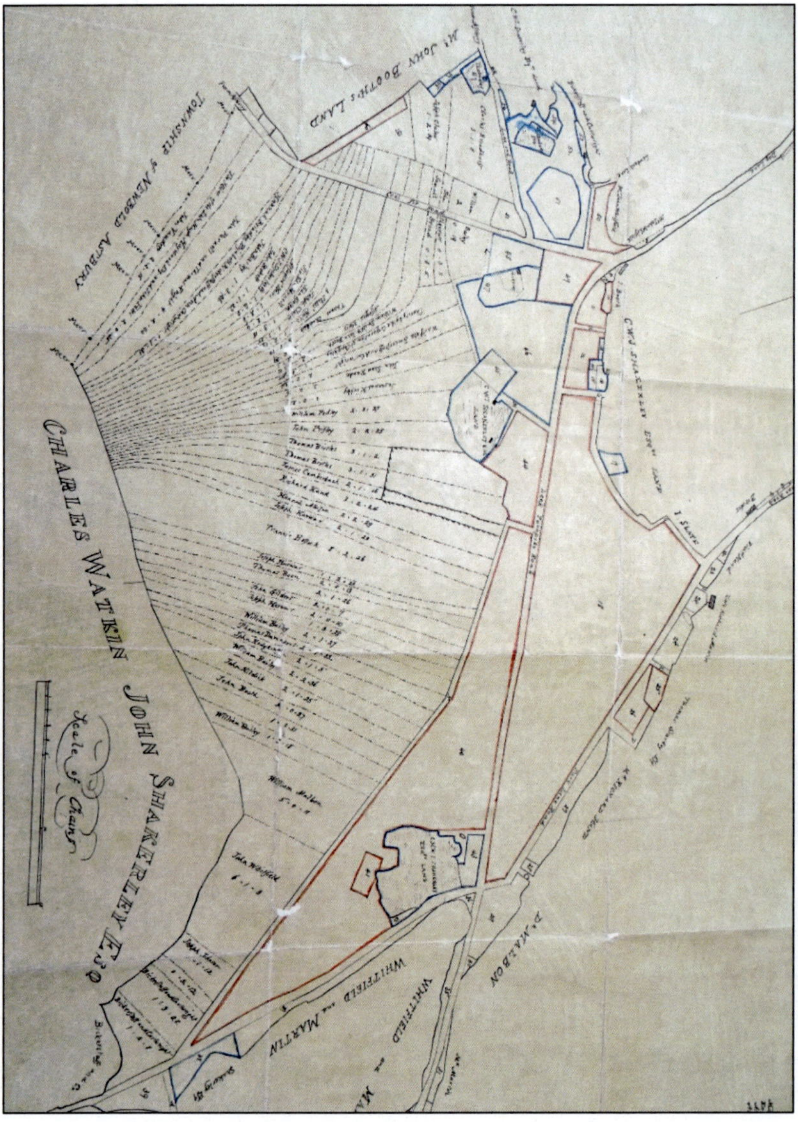

Plate 2: Mossley Moss as it appears in the Congleton enclosure award, 1798 (CALS, QDE 2/8: reproduced by permission of Cheshire Archives and Local Studies and the owner/depositor to whom copyright is reserved.) See Paper 1: *Enclosure and Enclosures in Mid- and East Cheshire*.

Colour Plates

Plate 3: Llay Hall: the surviving arm of the moat. (Photograph: Derrick Gwilliam). See Paper 2: *Medieval Moated Sites in the Cheshire–North Wales Borderland*.

Landscapes Past and Present

Plate 4: White Nancy, viewed from the south. This former summer house on Kerridge Hill is named Northern Nancy in Robert Hidey's notebook (1869). The origin of the name of the monument is uncertain but one possibility is that it stands at the former site of the northernmost Ordnance Survey marker in a pair. The other marker in the pair would have been at the site of an OS concrete pillar about a kilometre further south along Kerridge Hill. See Paper 3: *Ways and Meres: Pre-Turnpike Roads, Tracks, Boundaries and their Markers in the East Cheshire Peak District*.

Colour Plates

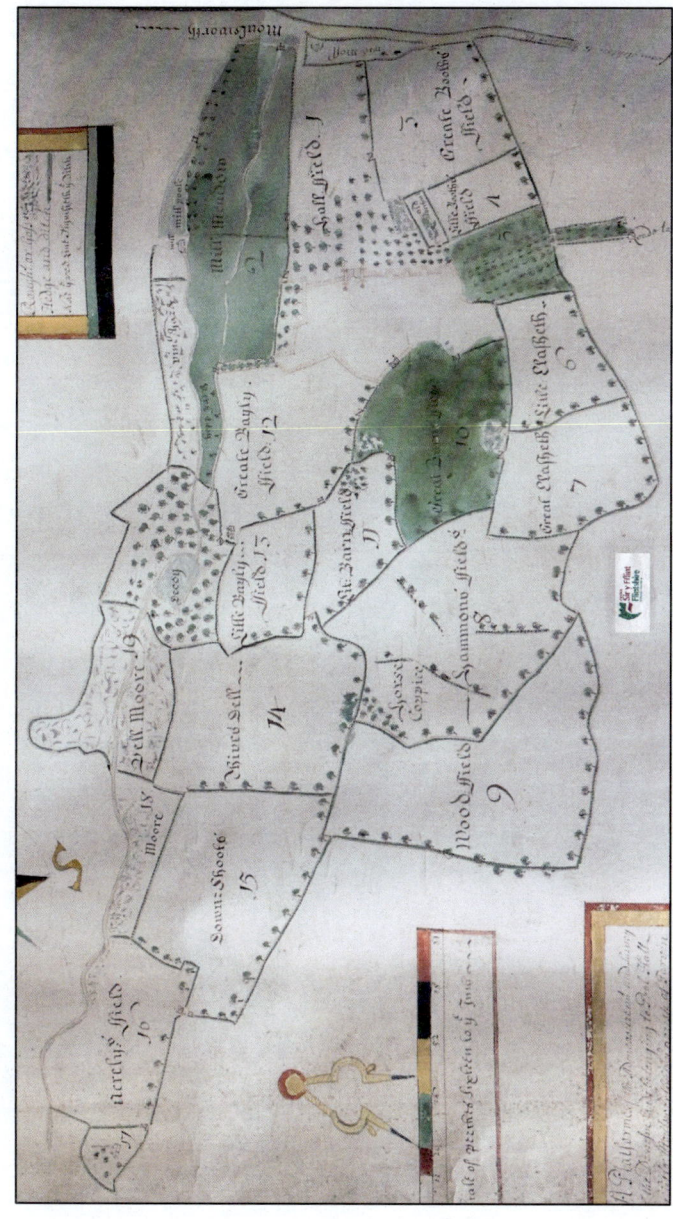

Plate 5: Peel Hall Estate, 1717: map commissioned by the earl of Plymouth, 1717 (FRO, D-DM 540/7, reproduced by permission of Flintshire Record Office). See Paper 4: *Keys to the Past: Unlocking the Secrets of the Landscape of Peel*.

Landscapes Past and Present

Plate 6: Peel Hall: south front. See Paper 4: *Keys to the Past: Unlocking the Secrets of the Landscape of Peel*.

Colour Plates

Plate 7: Estate map of Thelwall Waste, 1743. North is at the bottom. (CALS, DWW 431: reproduced by permission of Cheshire Archives and Local Studies and the owner/depositor to whom copyright is reserved.) See Paper 5: *Tracing the Eighteenth-Century Landscape of Thelwall in Cheshire*.

Plate 8: Thelwall Waste today; with ghosts of grubbed-out hedges. Isolated trees mark courses of earlier field boundaries. (1992–93 Aerial Survey of Cheshire. Copyright 2009 Cheshire West & Chester Council & Cheshire East Council © All rights reserved. Flown and captured by National Remote Sensing Centre Ltd 1992–93. Digitally converted by Bluesky International Ltd, 2009.) See Paper 5: *Tracing the Eighteenth-Century Landscape of Thelwall in Cheshire*.

Colour Plates

Plate 9: Thelwall estate map 1743, showing land north of the Mersey. North is at the bottom. Strips in Town Field can also be seen (at top). Two fords, labelled 'upper' and 'lower', are marked on this map. (CALS, DWW 429: reproduced by permission of Cheshire Archives and Local Studies and the owner/depositor to whom copyright is reserved.) See Paper 5: *Tracing the Eighteenth-Century Landscape. of Thelwall in Cheshire.*

Plate 10: Colwyn, watercolour by David Cox, 1845. The British Museum Collection Online © The Trustees of the British Museum. See Paper 6: *When was Colwyn Bay?*

Colour Plates

Plate 11: Aerial view of the site of HMS Blackcap, Stretton, in 2009–10. Virtually the whole site north of the M56 has been redeveloped, including the airyard. The buildings to the left of the picture include part of the prison, while to the right and south of the motorway are the two hangars built for Fairy Aviation (the large white roofed building is a relatively new warehouse). It is reasonably safe to assume that if the airfield had not been built the site would still be largely undeveloped, and reflect the landscape of the surrounding fields. Image captured, supplied and copyrighted by Bluesky International Ltd. See Paper 7: *Cheshire Airfields: A Legacy in the Landscape*.

Landscapes Past and Present

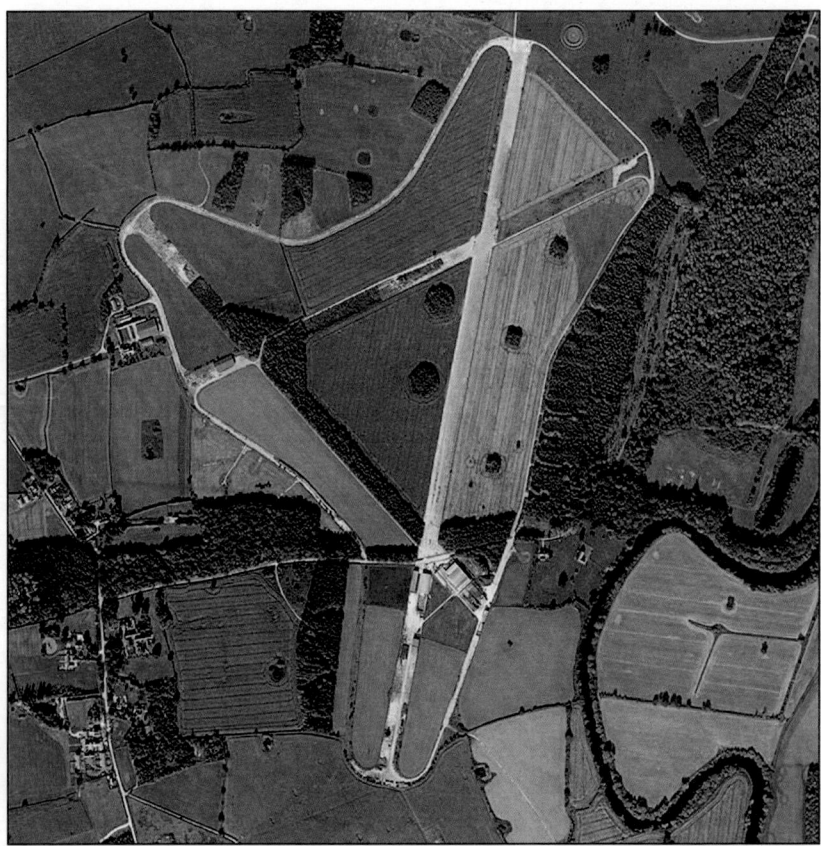

Plate 12: A 2009–10 aerial photograph of RAF Poulton showing how nature is taking back the site. The former hard standings appear to be 'decaying' back into the landscape, and there are indications that farming has returned. Interestingly it appears that the bulk of one of the three runways has been removed for probable use in a building project. Later reports are that this is now happening to the northern runway. Eaton Hall is just off the top right corner of the picture. Image captured, supplied and copyrighted by Bluesky International Ltd. See Paper 7: *Cheshire Airfields: A Legacy in the Landscape*.

3

WAYS AND MERES:
PRE-TURNPIKE ROADS, TRACKS, BOUNDARIES AND THEIR MARKERS IN THE EAST CHESHIRE PEAK DISTRICT

Tom Swailes

This paper first revisits a pioneering use of maps over a century ago in an investigation of the Peak District landscape. Next, an example is given to illustrate the work of the surveyors who produced maps of east Cheshire for different purposes from the early seventeenth century onwards. Evidence from maps and aerial photography has been used alongside historical research and field survey to explore landscape associations between landmark stones, pre-turnpike roads and tracks and historic boundaries. Some 'lost' stone monuments have been rediscovered and the probable former locations of others identified. In particular, some suggestions are made about the siting of stone crosses and about the origins of some surviving monuments in which parts of the shafts of broken crosses were recycled.

Discoveries with a Map

In summer 1904 the Revd J. Charles Cox walked the moors of the Derbyshire High Peak with his friend W.J. Andrew looking for stone crosses and cross remains.[1] Crosses and guide stones were often at a junction or crossing of ways. Cox obtained tracings of seventeenth-century pre-enclosure plans from the Public Record Office in London to use as finding aids alongside the printed 6 inches to 1 mile Ordnance Survey (OS) maps.[2] The pre-enclosure plan for Mellor Old Moor promised most, with illustrations of several crosses and of intriguing

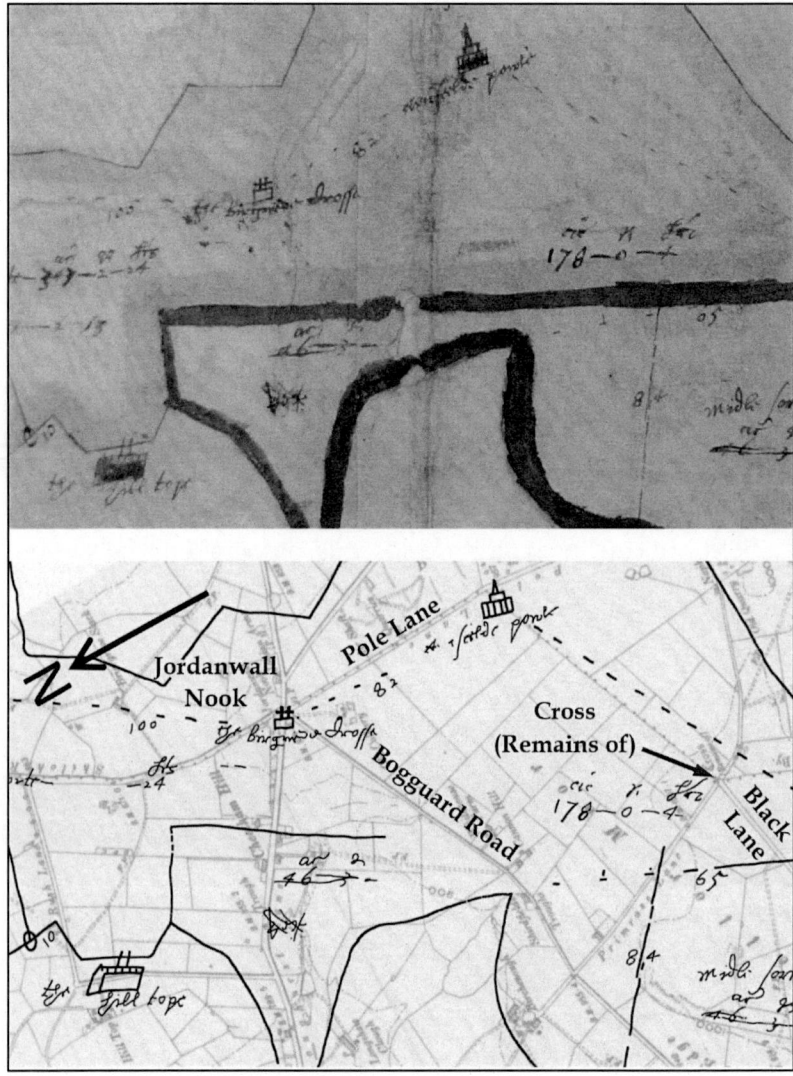

Figure 1: Crosses on Mellor Old Moor. Above: an extract from a pre-enclosure map of *c*.1640 (The National Archives UK, ref. MPC1/20, reproduced by permission). Below: a tracing of the extract overlain on the first edition 6 inch to 1 mile OS map, with additional place-names added.

monuments that might once have been crosses.³ Figure 1 shows an extract of the pre-enclosure map and a tracing of the extract overlaid on the 1899 OS map. In 1635 landowners and inhabitants of the Forest of the High Peak had petitioned Charles I for disafforestation, after which a commission of inquiry determined that the king should retain a third or half share of the commons and wastes and that the rest should be made available for enclosure by others.⁴ Surveys were made, the open land was marked on the plans according to its quality (as the best, middle or worst sort) and the king's share was staked out on the ground. The best sort of land would provide upland summer grazing for cattle and the remainder would be suitable for sheep. The deer were either killed or moved but the plans for enclosure were stalled on the outbreak of civil war and not completed until after the restoration of the monarchy.⁵

The two friends started at the junction of Primrose Lane with Black Lane where 'Cross, Remains of' is marked on the OS map sheet of 1899. This monument survives as a large stone cube with a socket in the top, set in the corner of a dry stone wall.⁶ According to Cox, half a mile to the north-west was a place called Jordanwall Nook, but this is a misdirection as the place of that name is to the north-east of the starting point for the walk. The older map is plotted with east at the top and any rambler will appreciate the mental and physical struggle of trying, whilst out of doors, to refer simultaneously to two large map sheets at different scales and with different orientations. Cox believed that Arnfielde powle had stood at Jordanwall Nook, but the large pieces of stone base or bases that he found there (and which are there still, built into the dry stone walls) are at the site of Birgrieve Cross. The name Birgrieve on the pre-enclosure map can be read with perhaps 80% confidence, but it might be read instead as Birgirde. A struggle with seventeenth-century secretary hand might be the origin of the present-day name of Bogguard Road, one of the lanes meeting at Jordanwall Nook.

Walking north along Shiloh Road, Cox found pieces of another cross base at the junction of Chatterton Lane, probably part of the 'Mishawe Cross in Bradshaw Head', but there is no sign of this now. Further north still are Robin Hood's Picking Rods or, as they were called c.1640, 'the two standing stones called maiden stones'.[7] Abots Chere is marked as the most north-easterly feature on the old map. The Anglo Saxon word 'cerre' means bend or corner and the abbot was of Basingwerk, a house of the Cistercian order with lands near Glossop.[8] Robin Hood's Picking Rods are a very similar monument to one that stands next to a track near the eastern boundary of Lyme Park

Figure 2: Engraving of the Bowstones at Lyme. Source: Earwaker, *East Cheshire, II*, 285. Figure based on an image courtesy of Hathi Trust. Available online as a permanent link: <<http://hdl.handle.net/2027/yale.39002088543229?urlappend=%3Bseq=327>>.

called Bowstones; a pair of round stone shafts set into a double-socketed stone base (Figure 2). These belong to a large group of round-shaft sandstone cross pieces believed to date from the late tenth or eleventh century found in the Peak District fringe of east Cheshire and extending into neighbouring counties.[9]

The vicar of Disley had gone exploring in 1809 but with a stone mason's tools rather than with a map; he found the socketed bases to the Bowstones and Robin Hood's Picking Rods monuments to be of stone found fairly near where they stand but the shafts to be a of a different sandstone, more 'fit for the chisel'.[10] The Revd Marriott also examined a stone base on Whaley Moor that has two sockets for rectangular shafts, now called the Dipping Stone (Figure 3). He saw pieces of cross shaft there but there is no sign of these now. The 1466 survey of the lands of Sir Peter Legh in Lyme Hanley refers to 'Le Borestone', and places the monument at a junction of ways and at a meeting place of the boundaries of four tenanted properties.[11] The Borestone was at or close to the present day Bowstones monument and, along the highway to the south, the present-day footpath called the Gritstone Trail, was the 'Jordanlawecrosse'. Renaud incorrectly placed the site of this cross towards Disley and it seems likely he confused it with cross pieces found near Badger Clough as described later in the present paper.[12] The place-name elements 'low' or 'law' are commonly linked with the old English *hlæw*, a rounded hill often associated with a burial mound,[13] which points to a quite likely site for the Jordan Law Cross as being near the bowl barrow in Ox Close, just south of the Bakestonedale Road. Another boundary marker in 1466 was the Whytebor stone on Shrigley Moor. A plausible meaning for borestone is a stone with a hole bored in it to receive a wooden post or standing stone as a boundary marker. The Mellor Old Moor map lends weight to this theory as another 'hole bored stone' is shown on a boundary.

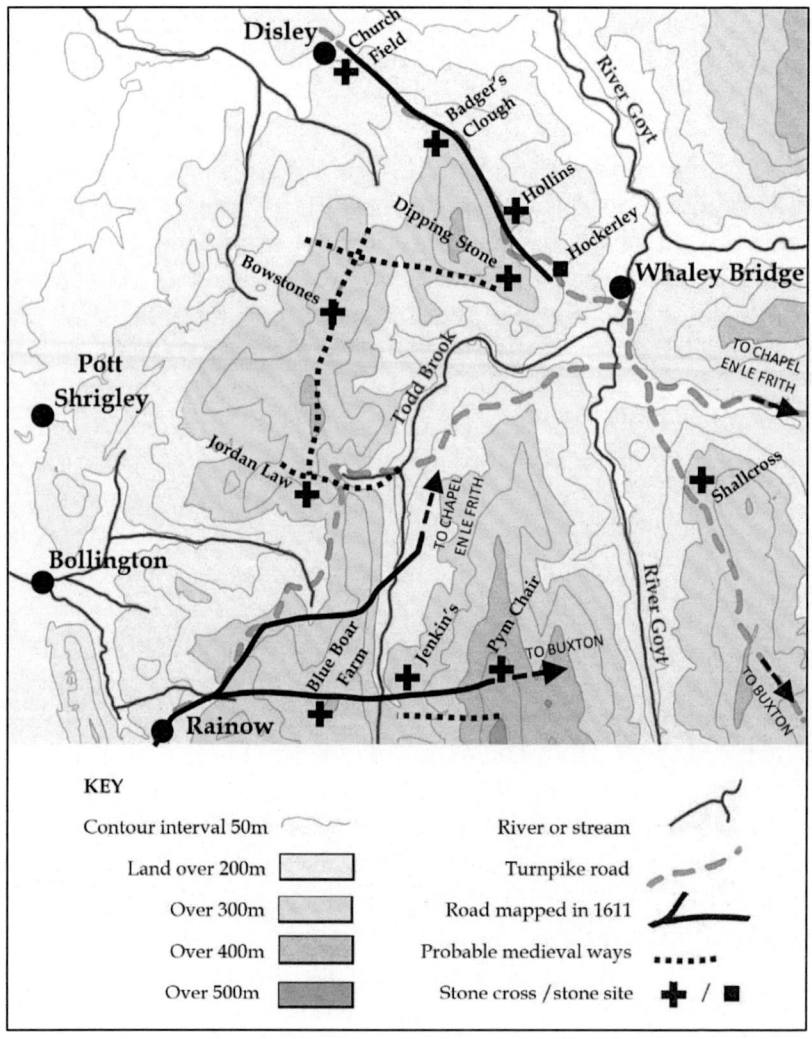

Figure 3: Cross and stone sites in the northern part of the Forest of Macclesfield.

Ways and Meres in the East Cheshire Peak District

Surveyors on Kerridge Hill

Immediately prior to survey work for the first edition 6 inches to 1 mile OS maps, boundaries in the Macclesfield Hundred were walked by a surveyor together with a meresman from the township on each side of the boundary. Robert Hidey of the Ordnance Survey recorded in his notebook that on 4 February 1869 he walked the townships boundary along Kerridge Hill with John Rowson of Rainow and Samuel Knight of Bollington.[14] Hidey drew neatly across the pages of his book a continuous strip map based upon the tithe maps of the 1840s, marking along the strip the form of boundary, wall or hedge, or 'not defined' if no physical barrier was present. Hidey showed a physical barrier as a continuous solid line, indicating the boundary on one side with a dashed line and the abbreviation FW for face of wall or RH for root of hedge (Figure 4). The distance from root of hedge was the space allowed by custom beyond the middle of a hedge for maintenance, a distance confirmed for each township by a note from the meresman at the back of the surveyor's notebook. Any uncertain or disputed section of boundary was noted and it might surprise some present-day Bollingtonians that there appeared to be no dissent to Hidey indicating the summerhouse building Northern Nancy at the north end of Kerridge Hill to be entirely within the township of Rainow. This monument is now called White Nancy and is one of the best known landmarks in the whole of east Cheshire (Plate 4).

    The Bollington and Rainow meresmen each signed their name but not all township meresmen were literate, as Hidey's companions on other boundary walks confirmed their presence by making their mark in the surveyor's book. The details of any markers along the boundary were noted with care, some like 'birch tree' being more temporary than others. In 1869 Hidey recorded a dressed merestone inscribed with the letters K, B

Landscapes Past and Present

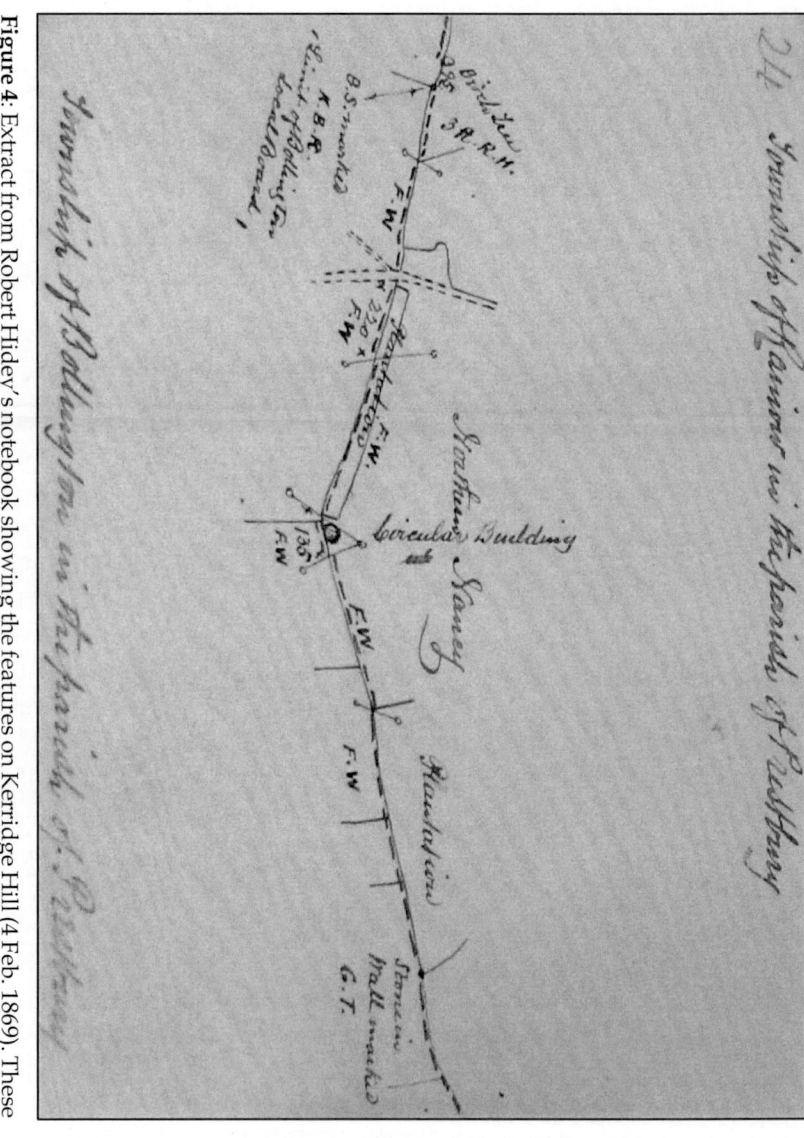

Figure 4: Extract from Robert Hidey's notebook showing the features on Kerridge Hill (4 Feb. 1869). These include a boundary stone marked K-B-R, Northern Nancy and a stone marked G-T. (The National Archives UK, ref. OS 26/1063, reproduced by permission.)

and R on three faces. In 2012 this merestone was found buried in the base of the hedge and it has now been restored by volunteers to an upright position at the meeting place of the boundaries of Kerridge, Bollington and Rainow (Figure 5). Robert Hidey is not one of the nine members of Ordnance Survey staff whose names are recorded in print on the 6 inches to 1 mile map showing the Kerridge Hill boundary; for his walking of the boundaries and his meticulous attention to detail, he deserves a mention too. The present Kerridge Hill boundary wall is built partly of a softish, blocky gritstone that occurs at the top of the hill, higher in the coal measures geological strata than the Milnrow sandstone still quarried along the western side of the hill. A very large rectangular block of shaped stone in the base of this wall was recorded by Hidey

Figure 5: Nineteenth-century boundary stone on Kerridge Hill. This undated stone bears the letters K, B and R and is now restored to an upright position.

in 1869 as bearing the letters G and T. On one face, now partly below ground, is the date 1839, an inscription not noted by Hidey. The position of this marker stone coincides with the place at which the township boundary wall is joined by a tumbledown plantation wall and, given the present-day maturity of the oldest of the plantation trees, it is tempting to take the stone as evidence for the date of the plantation enclosure. We cannot take the merestone date as the date for the whole of the boundary wall, as in 1809 William Marriott saw a 'stone fence' running south to north along Kerridge Hill and then onward down the hill towards Bollington. At the top of the hill, presumably where White Nancy now stands, was 'a small rotunda of brick, bearing the same construction of a sea mark with that at Alderley'.[15] The first detailed map of the area is undated but on examination it is beyond any reasonable doubt the companion to another map dated 1611, plotted and surveyed by Edward Maunsell.[16] This early seventeenth-century map shows a change in direction of the Kerridge Hill boundary very close to White Nancy but gives no clue about the physical form of the boundary or of any marker there. A primary aim of Maunsell's survey would have been to define the boundaries of commons and wastes so that their area and hence value could be calculated, so survey and recording of linear and point features would tend to be limited to what was needed to achieve this.

Highways to London
In the absence of a road atlas, the seventeenth-century traveller who did not know the way would ideally have the help of someone who did, either to travel with, or to provide directions. A carrier acted as guide for young teenager Edward Barlow's walk of about 183 miles from Manchester to London in 1657.[17] Barlow's journey entered Cheshire across the River

Ways and Meres in the East Cheshire Peak District

Mersey at Stockport and left Cheshire for Derbyshire by crossing the River Goyt at Whaley Bridge, ending over a week later at the Axe in Aldermanbury. Together with the Beare in Bassingshaw and the Two-Neck'd Swan in Lad Lane, the Axe was a preferred London lodging for 'The Carriers of Manchester'.[18] After a dozen years or so away from home, Barlow hired a horse for the return journey from London to Prestwich to carry him and his possessions, choosing the company of the slow-moving carrier over travelling alone.

Maintenance of the bridge at Whaley would usually have been the responsibility of the counties that it linked, but the old manorial system seems to have endured here as in 1650 the lord of the manor of High Peak still claimed a toll for 'packs and carryages passing at Hayfield and Walley Bridge'.[19] In 1606 Edmund Jodrell had been granted, by a warrant of James I, 4 acres of waste and common land in recompense for giving up freehold land 'for the erection of a new bridge at Waylie within the Forrest of Macclesfield and for a waye leading to the said bridge'.[20] The taking of land for the bridge approaches may have provided for gentler gradients local to the river crossing to suit occasional wheeled traffic in addition to livestock, packhorses, pedestrians and equestrians, but seventeenth-century travellers could not always expect a bridge to take them over a watercourse, even on a major highway. Floods in summer 1718 had scoured the channel of the River Lathkill at Alport and made the ford probably used by Edward Barlow impassable for over a week. It was argued at the court of Quarter Sessions that a horse bridge was needed as the crossing was used by 'great gangs of London Carriers Horses as well as great drifts of Malt Horses as well as other carryers and passengers'.[21] The first road atlas was supplied in 1675 in the form of John Ogilby's *Britannia*. The 1 inch to the mile strip map for the Manchester to Derby road shows landmarks along the journey, including the 'stone bridg' at Whaley and, at 18¼ miles from Manchester, beyond Shawcross and just east of the road, a cross (Figure 6).[22]

Gordon Dickinson checked the accuracy of Ogilby's maps and found 'it is safest to assume that no scale can be applied to off-set distances', so the distance of the cross from the road is uncertain.[23] Early in the twentieth century W.J. Andrew found part of a round-shaft stone cross re-used as a sundial shaft in the garden of Fernilee Hall.[24] The owner made enquiries and found that 'the stone is said by tradition to have been brought down from the old road above the hall' so Andrew concluded that it must have stood at an old crossroads at Elnor Lane Head. Ogilby's map shows the cross on a hill top some 1½ to 3 furlongs south of a crossroads, with the Manchester to Derby road cutting across the flank of that hill. This pictorial evidence points to the hill partly within Black Edge Plantation and south of the crossroads as a possible alternative original cross site. The 'Shallcross' was removed from the garden at Fernilee Hall and is preserved today at the junction of Elnor Lane and Old Road. Neville Sharpe identified three cross sites further into Derbyshire along the way to Buxton; one at Wainstones, where he saw a cross base, and two sites based on documentary evidence, the first near White Hall called The Woman's Cross, Weeping or Lady's Cross and a second just over half a mile to the south-east called Rough Lowe Cross.[25]

There is evidence that a number of stones or crosses were visible to the medieval traveller on the highway from Disley to Whaley Bridge (Figure 3). In 1957 a large stone base with sockets for a pair of circular shafts was found near a spring in 'Church Field', Disley. No cross is marked here on Edward Maunsell's 1611 'Plott of the Prince his Highnes Comons in the Mannor and Forrest of Macclesfield' but the large area of unenclosed waste to the immediate south-west is named on the

Ways and Meres in the East Cheshire Peak District

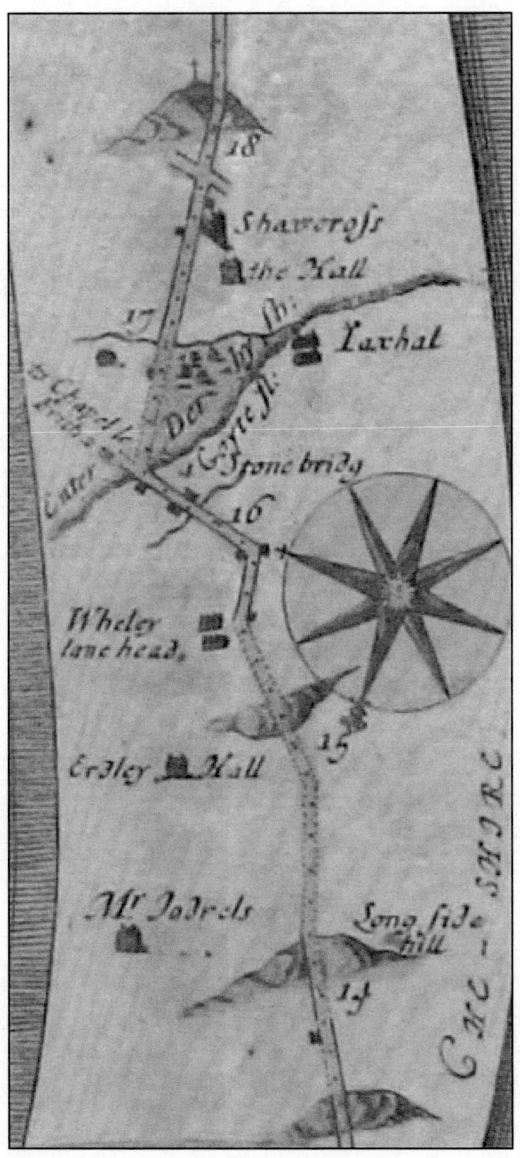

Figure 6: Extract from Ogilby's Strip Map (see endnote 22), showing a cross on a hill near Shallcross.

map as Crosleighe.[26] In 1611 Maunsell named Hollins Cross near the junction of present-day Diglee Road and Buxton Old Road and Hockerlye Stone about a kilometre further southwest along the main road. No remains of stone monuments have been found at either place but the hamlet Stoneheads may have been named after Hockerley Stone. The regular occurrence of hollin (hollin = the tree, holly) as a place-name element in the Forest of Macclesfield has been discussed in an earlier paper.[27]

Ornamented cross fragments were often treated by nineteenth-century gentry as portable antiquities which could be removed and re-used as garden ornaments. Isaac Watt Boulton (Figure 7) viewed two incomplete stone crosses in the gardens to the south of Lyme Hall and was informed that the fragments had been found at Badger Clough, about 100 yards north of Red Moor Lane end and 20 yards west of the road, by Thomas Armfield whilst clearing gorse for Peter Swindells of Black Farm, Whaley Moor.[28] No evidence of a base was found in the ground. A badger was 'one who buys corn and other commodities and carries them elsewhere to sell', therefore the place-name, Badger Clough, is most likely associated with a packhorse route crossing or joining with the main highway.[29] The crosses seen by Boulton are believed to be the upper sections of a particular type of round-shaft cross, of which the Shallcross shaft in Derbyshire is an example, although the geographical distribution of the type is very much centred in east Cheshire. The oldest marker associated with this highway is also a round gritstone shaft, a Roman milestone of about 0.33 metres diameter and 0.61 metres high, found in 1862 and now in Buxton Museum.[30] The translation of the incomplete Latin inscription on the milestone includes '... from Navio 11 miles', it being about 11 Roman miles from Buxton to the Roman fort of Navio at Brough. From near where the milestone was found,

Ways and Meres in the East Cheshire Peak District

Figure 7: Amateur antiquarian Isaac Watt Boulton with cross fragments at Lyme Park. 'IWB' carved his initials on a number of landmark stones beyond Cheshire and into the hills of Derbyshire and south-west Yorkshire. (Image reproduced by permission of New Mills Local History Society.)

a northbound traveller would leave the Derby to Buxton road, Margary's Roman road number 71a, to travel east along Batham Gate, road number 710a, for Navio.[31]

In 1618, on his 'Pennyles Pilgrimage', John Taylor (*alias* 'The King's Water Poet') travelled north by a more westerly route, avoiding the Peak District moors crossed about 40 years later by Edward Barlow.[32] The water-poet lamented the state of the way between Talke o'th Hill in Staffordshire and his comfortable lodgings as a guest in east Cheshire:

> And kindly every step entreats me stay,
> The clammy clay sometimes my heels would trip,
> One foot went forward, the other back would slip,
> This weary day, when I had almost past,
> I came unto Sir Urian Leigh's at last,
> At Adlington, near Macclesfield he doth dwell,
> Belov'd, respected, and reputed well.

It is quite likely that Taylor went via Congleton to Gawsworth, then via the old way that formed the western boundary of the Forest of Macclesfield, to Broken Cross, Prestbury and then Adlington. Taylor may have seen the cross that gave Broken Cross its place-name, a broken round-shaft cross at Upton near Prestbury and at least one broken round-shaft cross near Adlington. Two round-shafts are now ornaments at Adlington and the field-name 'Cross Leech' on a map for a diversion of the turnpike road in 1810 suggests that one at least stood close to the road past Adlington Hall.[33]

Macclesfield Roads and Tracks

The old way north-east out of Macclesfield runs across both of the 1611 maps of the Forest of Macclesfield. The way crossed Hurdsfield common to join the present-day line of Cliff Lane for the steep climb up 'Millstone Cliff' and then followed Calrofold Lane to Rainow. This challenging section was bypassed entirely, possibly when the road was turnpiked in 1770.[34] Through Rainow, the way divided in two near Gin Clough (Figure 3), one branch continuing across the 'Harrop Pastures' towards Chapel-en-le-Frith via Kettleshulme. Some sections of this early seventeenth-century Chapel-en-le-Frith way would be impassable by wheeled traffic which may explain the absence of eroded hollow ways where otherwise they might be expected, given the steepness of the terrain. A still older footway to Chapel-en-le-Frith, instead of going by Kettleshulme, probably took a direct route into Taxal via a notch or nick point in the ridge called Wynd Yatts on the 1611 map (yatt = gate or way). The other branch of the way from Rainow takes a very direct route east towards 'Buckstons' (Buxton) across the 'Cheaswayes', entering the 'Salters Ford Pastures' via a gate at 'Buckstor Stoops', then continuing on to 'Pims Chayre' (Figure 8). Bank Lane, a later less direct alignment on this old way to Buxton, now known locally as 'the Corkscrew', provided gradients to suit wheeled traffic, but is manageable now only by motor sports enthusiasts and its present condition shows what happens to a steep road with inadequate surfacing and drainage (Figure 9).

In order to make a durable road on a steep hill, a hard surface must be laid down and then maintained to prevent rutting by wheels, or erosion by the hooves of draught animals or laden pack horses, as ruts or channels once formed will become channels for rainwater and surface run-off which in turn will cause further erosion. Secondly, drainage must be provided and maintained to divert water away from the road into a natural watercourse otherwise the road itself will become an open drain, prone to erosion during heavy rain. Eroded hill roads or tracks, when abandoned completely, like the old way up from Saltersford Hall to Oldgate Nick, become marshy

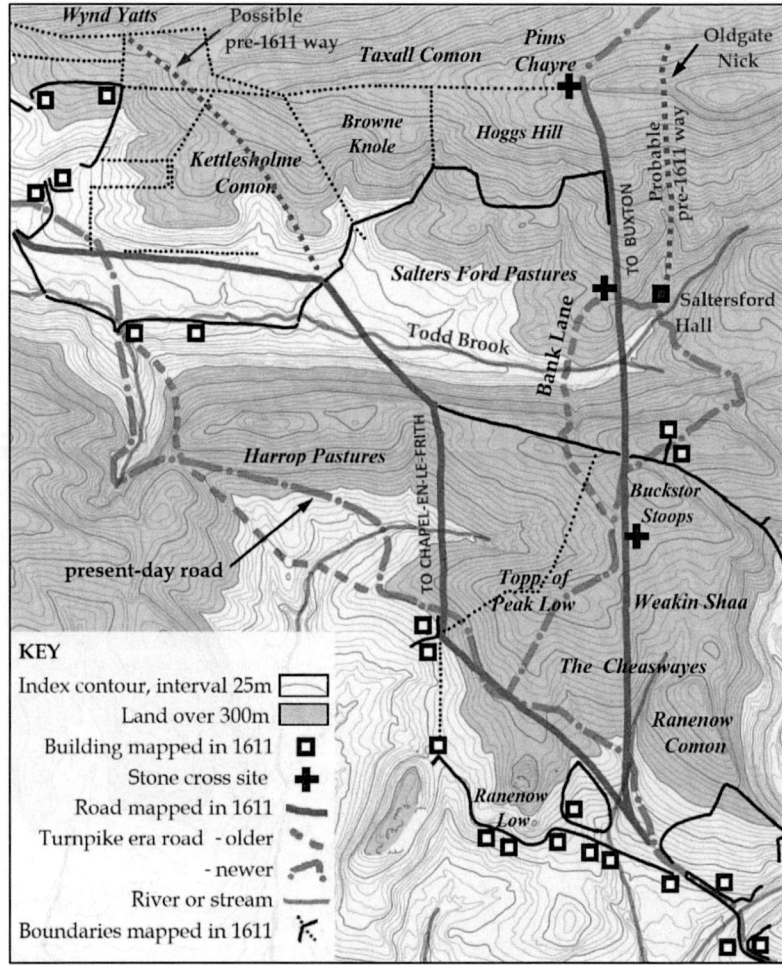

Figure 8: Roads and tracks via Rainow from Macclesfield to Buxton and Chapel-en-le-Frith. The names in italics are from Edward Maunsell's maps of 1611 (original spellings retained).

hollow ways easily mistaken in field survey work for natural gullies and indistinguishable from them on even the earliest OS map.

Ways and Meres in the East Cheshire Peak District

Figure 9: Bank Lane, Rainow. Volunteers clearing a drainage ditch to divert water away from the badly eroded surface of the former turnpike era road now used mainly by walkers (Photograph: Bob Langstaff).

The place-names of 1611 are clues to the early seventeenth-century traffic on this old way to Buxton where the highway to London might be joined. Cheshire cheese was famous as one of the port of Chester's principal exports to London in the second half of the seventeenth century, but earlier overland regional trade via routes that must have included 'the Cheaswayes' are not well documented.[35] Salt from the 'Cheshire wiches' was probably taken by packhorse train to the Roman centres of Brough via Chapel-en-le-Frith and Buxton via Oldgate Nick, crossing the River Goyt by salters' fords at Taxal and Errwood respectively (Figure 8).[36]

Marking the way towards Buxton in 1611 was Jenkin Cross, which according to Ormerod was close to where Jenkin Chapel (Saltersford) was built in the 1730s (Figure 3).[37] A cross probably once stood just south of Blue Boar Farm as a piece of sculpted stone was found there early in the twentieth century, almost certainly part of the upper section of a round-shaft cross, but when the cross was broken or removed is unknown.[38] There is no sign today at Pym Chair of the stone cross base with circular socket that was seen early in the twentieth century.[39] Stone guide stoops were erected in the Peak District at the beginning of the eighteenth century on the order of the justices of the peace to mark ways across the moors.[40] This appears to be the most likely purpose of three standing stones without inscriptions found and recorded in east Cheshire by William Marriott in 1809 (Figure 10). Marriott described the way to the first stone from a prominent hill that he called 'Round Hoo', identifiable now as standing in a field named in the 1849 tithe apportionment as 'Round Oven', near the hamlet of Bottom-of-the-Oven.[41] Marriott followed what he called Hoo Lane to the first stone, near where the OS map marks 'Cross, site of'. From this stone he noticed a track southward along the edge of the peat moor to another similar stone east of Shuttlings Low (now called Shutlingsloe). Based on Marriott's descriptions and on some evidence on the ground of old trackways, the likely position of this stone and also of a second Shutlingsloe stone can be estimated; the two stones together give the traveller the line down to a likely fording point for the stream in Wildboarclough and then on towards a meeting place of packhorse trails at Panniers Pool.

Looking for a possible packhorse trail from Panniers Pool to Macclesfield involves considering a near-direct route. This is necessarily an imagined walk into the past using maps and aerial photographs on paper and computer screen, as a modern right of way exists only intermittently. Walking north-west from the second Shutlingsloe stone, we cross the flank of the hill and in doing so enter territory covered by the 1611 map of

Ways and Meres in the East Cheshire Peak District

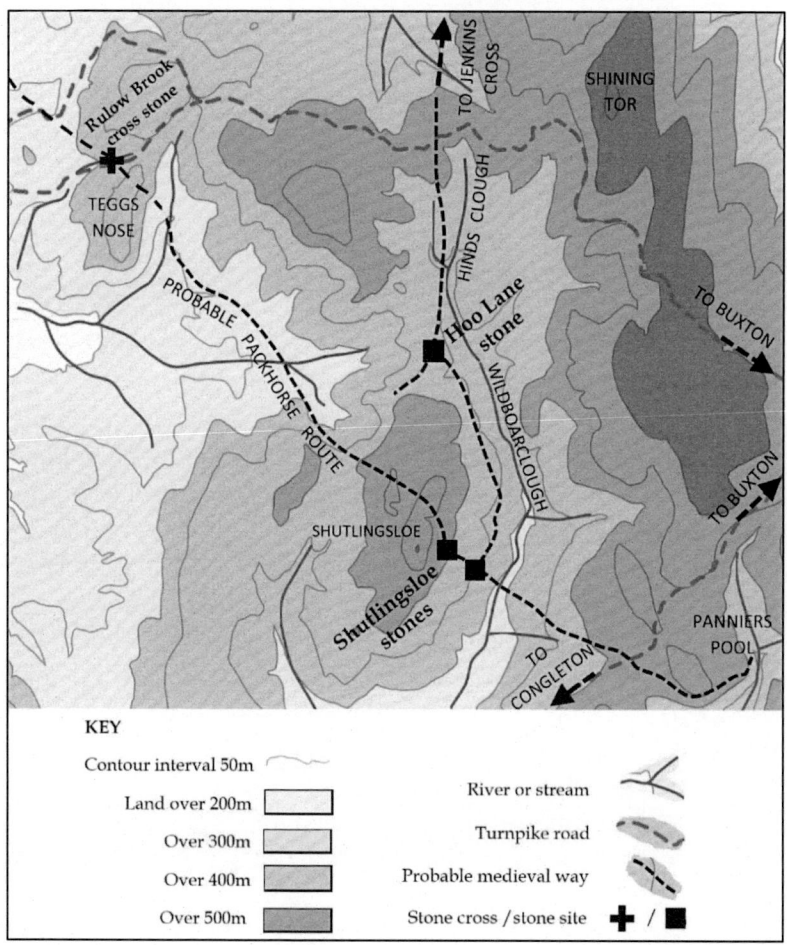

Figure 10: Location map showing Rulow Brook, Hoo Lane and Shutlingsloe stones.

the southern part of the Forest of Macclesfield. No way is marked here on the map, but following a boundary line that is marked on the map takes us to the flank of Tegg's Nose which we climb at a steady gradient, then continue down the other side. The descent from Tegg's Nose follows a hollow way, crosses over Buxton Old Road, then takes an old track down to Rulow Brook. Just before the brook a large cube of gritstone stands to the south side of the track; Edward Maunsell helpfully marked this distinctive stone on his map of 1611 as 'cross stone'. The descent continues, the steeper sections in a prominent hollow way, before re-entering the present day on New Buxton Road, just above the town of Macclesfield (Figures 11 and 12). Jane Laughton has provided us with the names of some of the probably medieval users of the old hollow way.[42]

Whilst the way from Macclesfield towards Buxton is marked explicitly on the Forest of Macclesfield maps of 1611, the map evidence for an old way between Leek and Macclesfield is indirect. Arthur and Molly Dodd identified what they believed to be an old way across the River Dane into Cheshire by a ford that they used themselves, presumably as an experiment, about half a mile down river from the present bridge at Danebridge.[43] The Dodds' way ran half a mile east of Wincle Grange (a grange of Combermere Abbey), past Bennettshill Farm to a crossroads below Cleulow Cross. The evidence for the exact line of this old way from field survey and examination of aerial photography is uncertain, but there is no doubt that the siting of Cleulow Cross, shown in Figure 13, made it a significant and highly visible landmark along an old south to north route. The 1611 map for the southern Forest of Macclesfield marks Clulow Cross but also, a little to the south, Blayklow Cross and, just over two kilometres to the west, Cross in Mind (mind = minn, a long hill) (Figure 14). The Cross in Mind was near the head of a stream that now feeds Bosley Reservoir and on a likely pre-turnpike way from Congleton to Buxton. There is no sign of Cross in Mind or Blaylow Cross now, but perhaps their shafts are amongst the three relocated to a park in Macclesfield. A stone close to the road north of Cleulow Cross and on the boundary between Wincle and

Ways and Meres in the East Cheshire Peak District

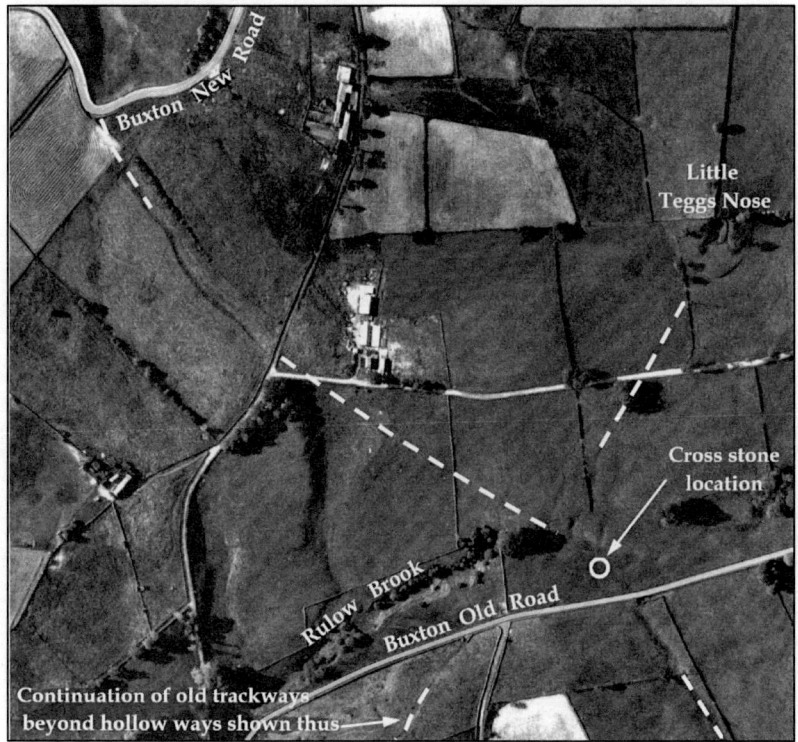

Figure 11: Aerial photograph showing the context of the Rulow Brook Cross Stone. (The aerial photograph is from the 1971-73 Aerial Survey of Cheshire. Copyright 2006 Cheshire West & Chester Council & Cheshire East Council © All rights reserved. Flown and captured by Hunting Surveys Ltd 1971-73. Digitally converted by Genesys International Ltd & The Aerial Surveyor Ltd 2005/6.)

Sutton is marked on Bryant's 1831 map of Cheshire as 'Old Cross'.[44] This stone appears to be the very bottom part of a large diameter round shaft to a cross of about the same size as Cleulow Cross, but if there is a socketed base stone here, it is under the turf. Is the shaft of this cross the third of the group in the park in Macclesfield? On the boundary between Wincle and Bosley in 1611 were two named stones. Golding Slate may have

Figure 12: Rulow Brook Cross Stone.

Figure 13: Cleulow Cross, Wincle.

Ways and Meres in the East Cheshire Peak District

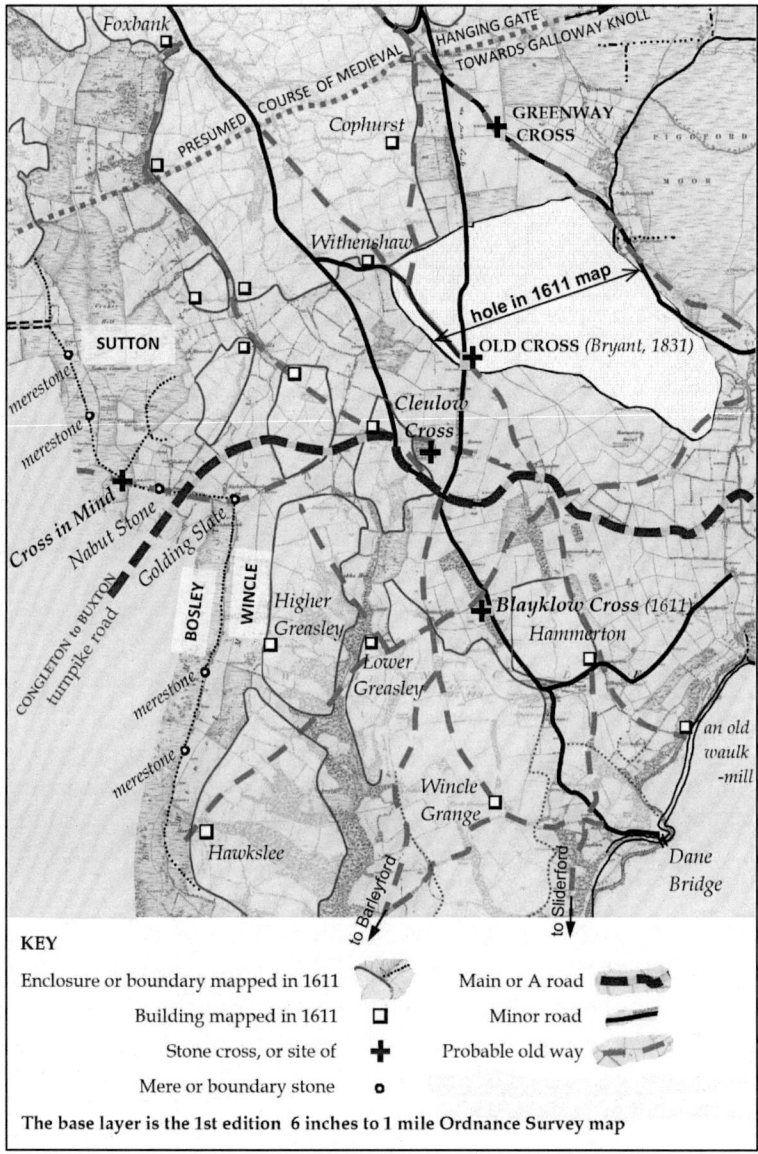

Figure 14: Cross and stone sites in the southern part of the Forest of Macclesfield.

been a slate or flagstone standing or lying in a damp place amongst marsh marigolds, or a name misheard, as the present-day name of the place is Golden Slack (slack = the slope below the top of a hill). Certainly a mishearing may explain the name of the next stone along the boundary; was Edward Maunsell informed by his local guide that the evocatively named Nabut Stone was na[ught]but stone, i.e. simply a stone with no name?

Understanding the Stones
The present paper has sought to provide more complete evidence for the original locations of stones and crosses in the landscape. Map analysis and fieldwork has enabled the surviving remains of two stone crosses to be found *in situ*, one near Rulow Brook in Macclesfield and the other on the boundary between Wincle and Sutton. The former locations of three further named crosses (Hollins Cross, Blaylow Cross and Cross in Mind) and three named stones (Hockerlye Stone, Golding Slate and Nabut Stone) have been established using two early seventeenth-century maps. An alternative former location for the cross at Shallcross alongside the principal old way out of east Cheshire has been proposed, based on pictorial evidence from a late seventeenth-century strip map and on a nineteenth-century report of the relocation of the cross shaft. Interpretation of historical accounts, supported by the use of modern maps, fieldwork and aerial photograph analysis, has enabled approximate former locations to be given for stone crosses at Badger Clough and Jordanlaw and for two standing stones on the eastern flank of Shutlingsloe. An early nineteenth-century name, 'Hoo Lane Stone', has been re-attached to the 'Cross, site of' on the south-east side of the present-day Macclesfield Forest. Field-name evidence has been found that appears to confirm the approximate location of crosses at Adlington and south-west of Disley Church.

Ways and Meres in the East Cheshire Peak District

Visibility is considered a key to understanding the early movement of people through the landscape, particularly 'across the grain' of a ridge and vale upland landscape like the east Cheshire Peak District. For example, the old ways heading east from Rainow cross the ridges bordering the Todd Brook and River Goyt valleys at rounded saddle or angular nick points, natural features visible from a distance. Before the ways were diverted to reduce gradients to suit wheeled traffic or 'confused' by enclosures, they were straight and the traveller moved 'as the crow flies' between landmarks. The original setting for the stone crosses or stones referred to in this paper, with one or two exceptions, was close to a way, in some cases an important highway, in other cases a moorland track walked by packmen and their packhorses. Neville Sharpe's conclusion that the crosses of the Derbyshire Peak District first marked ways and that some later became boundary markers is believed to hold true for east Cheshire too.[45] At many of the known or probable cross sites the visitor is struck on a clear day by the views. At a simple level, stone crosses and standing stones served a practical purpose as way finders. Where ridges limit the east to west viewshed of a stone cross site in a valley, then companion stone crosses occur alongside the way to the east or west and on or just beyond the ridges. Where views from and of a cross in the middle of a moorland stretch of way are blocked by the edges of the moorland plateau, a cross or stone on the slope up to the moor provides a viewshed across the plain below.

The immediate setting of some of the stone crosses is associated with a natural landscape feature that may have had past social or religious significance. Cleulow Cross, for example, stands on a large natural mound that might have been a gathering place and a destination in itself, relatively close to the prehistoric Bullstones monument.[46] Places of pagan worship at springs, stones and trees were not razed with the introduction of Christianity but by deliberate policy of the Church were re-consecrated, so some crosses may have been placed near more ephemeral sacred landscape features.[47] The wider significance of stones and crosses in the landscape beyond their way-marking function is outside the scope of the present paper. However, it is hoped that the more complete pattern presented here of the crosses and stones that once stood in the east Cheshire Peak District will enable better informed speculation about them.

Endnotes
1. J.C. Cox, 'Early Crosses in the High Peak', *The Athenaeum* (1904), 56–58.
2. J.C. Cox, 'Plans of the Peak Forest', in J.C. Cox, ed., *Memorials of Old Derbyshire* (London, 1907), 281–306.
3. Map of Mellor Moor and Common, Derbyshire, c.1640: TNA, MPC1/20. The map is not dated, but the catalogue suggests '? Chas I'.
4. J.C. Cox, *The Royal Forests of England* (London, 1905), 178–80.
5. D. Hey, *A History of the Peak District Moors* (Barnsley, 2014), 92–93.
6. Cross base, Primrose Lane (NE side), Mellor Moor: NGR: SJ 99249 87479: Grade II, Historic England List description, entry number 1260017.
7. Wayside boundary cross known as 'Robin Hood's Picking Rods' (Chisworth Parish, High Peak, Derbyshire): NGR: SK 00612 90938: Scheduled Ancient Monument, Historic England List description, entry number 1008595.
8. C. Kerry, 'A History of Peak Forest', *Journal of the Derbyshire Archaeological and Natural History Society*, XV (1893), 73–77.
9. R.N. Bailey, *Corpus of Anglo-Saxon Stone Sculpture, IX: Cheshire and Lancashire* (Oxford, 2010), 33–38.

10. W. Marriott, *The Antiquities of Lyme and its Vicinity* (Stockport, 1810), 1–7.
11. *The Legh of Lyme Survey*, J. and B. Fothergill et al., eds (Ranulf Higden Society, 2011) CD-ROM edition.
12. F. Renaud, *Contributions towards the History of the Ancient Parish of Prestbury* (Manchester, 1876), 72.
13. L.V. Grinsell, *The Ancient Burial Mounds of England* (2nd edn, London, 1953).
14. Ordnance Survey Boundary Remark Book of Robert Hidey for Bollington township, Prestbury, 4 Feb. 1869: TNA, OS 26/1063.
15. Marriott, *Antiquities of Lyme*, 207–8.
16. Map of Bollington, Bosley, Gawsworth, Macclesfield and Rainow, c.1611: TNA, MR1/354.
17. B. Lubbock, ed., *Barlow's Journal of his Life at Sea in King's Ships, East and West Indiamen and other Merchantmen from 1659 to 1703*, I (London, 1934), 21–22, 175.
18. J. Taylor, *The Carriers Cosmographie or a Brief Relation, of the Innes, Ordinaries, Hosteries and other Lodgings in, and near London, where the Carriers, Waggons, Foote posts and Higglers, doe usually come*, etc. (London, 1637); B. Capp, 'Taylor, John (1578–1653)', *Oxford Dictionary of National Biography* (Oxford, 2004). Available online: <<http://www.oxforddnb.com/view/article/27044>>, accessed 9 Nov. 2015.
19. D. Hey, *Packmen, Carriers and Packhorse Roads: Trade and Communications in North Derbyshire and South Yorkshire* (2nd edn, Ashbourne, 2004), 19.
20. Records of a Court of Survey, Manor and Forest of Macclesfield, 3 to 27 Sep. 1611: TNA, LR 2/200, original manuscript page numbers 269–70.
21. J.C. Cox, *Three Centuries of Derbyshire Annals*, II (London, 1890), 223.
22. J. Ogilby, *Britannia*, I (London, 1675), plate 90.
23. G.C. Dickinson, 'Britain's First Road Maps: The Strip-Maps of John Ogilby's Britannia, 1675', *Landscapes*, I (2003), 93.

24. W.J. Andrew, 'The Shall-Cross: A Pre-Norman Cross, now at Fernilee Hall', *Journal of the Derbyshire Archæological and Natural History Society*, XXVII (1905), 201–14 and plate.
25. N.T. Sharpe, *Crosses of the Peak District* (Ashbourne, 2002), 51, 95–97.
26. E. Maunsell, 'A Plott of the Prince his Highnes Comons in the Mannor and Forrest of Macclesfield ... taken by Edward Maunsell Anno Dom 1611 ...': TNA, MPEE1/110.
27. T. Swailes, 'Fields in the Forest of Macclesfield', in V. Greatorex and M. Headon, eds, *Field-names in Cheshire, Shropshire and North-East Wales* (Chester, 2014), 116.
28. I.W. Boulton, 'Ancient Crosses at Lyme', Garside scrapbook, n.d. (newspaper cutting, possibly *Manchester City News*): New Mills Local History Society Archive, D983/11, 76 (cutting), 77 (image).
29. W.T. Little, C.T. Onions, et al., *Shorter Oxford English Dictionary*, I (3rd edn, Oxford, 1973), 146.
30. R.G. Collingwood and R.P. Wright, *Roman Inscriptions of Britain: Inscriptions on Stone*, I (Oxford, 1965), RIB 2243 fragmentary milestone. Available online: <<http://romaninscriptionsof britain.org/inscriptions/2243>>, accessed 21 Feb. 2016.
31. I.D. Margary, *Roman Roads in Britain* (3rd edn, London, 1973), 359–61.
32. J. Taylor, *The Pennyless Pilgrimage ... of John Taylor, Alias the Kings Majesties Water-poet. How he travailed on foot from London to Edenborough ...* (London, 1618).
33. Plan of the proposed diversion of the Turnpike Road leading from London to Manchester, May 1810: Adlington Hall Archives, DLA 38/8.
34. A.G. Crosby, 'New Roads for Old: Cheshire Turnpikes in the Landscape, 1700–1850', in *LHDNW*, 190–227, at 208–9.
35. C.F. Foster, *Cheshire Cheese and Farming in the North West in the 17th and 18th Centuries* (Northwich, 1998), 3–6.
36. A.E. Dodd and E.M. Dodd, *Peakland Roads and Trackways* (3rd edn, Ashbourne, 2000), 123–28.
37. Ormerod (1819), 377.
38. Bailey, *Anglo-Saxon Stone Sculpture*, 98–99.

39. Andrew, 'The Shall-Cross', 203.
40. Hey, *Packmen, Carriers and Packhorse Roads*, 23–35.
41. Marriott, *Antiquities of Lyme*, 150–56.
42. J. Laughton, 'Life in a Medieval Forest', in Rainow History Group, *Patchwork*, I (2014), 17–18.
43. Dodd, *Peakland Roads and Trackways*, 53.
44. A. Bryant, *Map of the County Palatine of Chester* (London, 1831).
45. Sharpe, *Crosses of the Peak District*, 115.
46. J. Kirton, 'Locating the Cleulow Cross: Materiality, Place and Landscape', in H. Williams, J. Kirton and M. Gondek, eds, *Early Medieval Stone Monuments* (Woodbridge, 2015), 52–53.
47. A. Walsham, *The Reformation of the Landscape: Religion, Identity and Memory in Early Modern Britain and Ireland* (Oxford, 2011), 18–48.

4

KEYS TO THE PAST: UNLOCKING THE SECRETS OF THE LANDSCAPE OF PEEL

Sharon M. Varey

Introduction

Eight miles to the east of Chester, to the north of the A54, between Tarvin and Kelsall, lies the civil parish of Horton cum Peel. Originally part of the large parish of Tarvin, Peel is located to the north-west of Ashton with commanding views over the Cheshire and Welsh countryside. From the public footpaths close to the Hall, it is possible to look beyond Tarvin Church to Beeston and Peckforton Castles to the south and also westwards into Wales.

Walking the landscape today, one cannot help but be intrigued by the enigmatic building sitting amidst lumps, bumps, dips and hollows in the surrounding fields. This article therefore aims to reveal some of the secrets of the landscape surrounding Peel Hall. It will show how an analysis of: old maps, surveys, estate and probate records, diaries, various contemporary accounts and secondary sources, alongside the landscape itself, can reveal much about the history of a small part of the Cheshire countryside. As Muir reflected back in 1981: 'the evidence is locked in the details of scenery, in old maps and documents, air photographs and earthworks. It lies all around you. ... [These are] our keys to the past.'[1]

To the landscape historian there is indeed much to 'unlock'.

It would seem logical to use the landscape today as our starting point – what we have inherited from past generations, who adapted and moulded the environment to suit their

Unlocking the Secrets of the Landscape of Peel

present-day needs. To Hoskins, the landscape itself was 'the richest historical record'.[2] Written over sixty years ago, his statement is still true today.

Discussion will begin with the fields that surround Peel Hall, before considering the building and associated features which make up this complex landscape.

The Fieldscape

Today the farm at Peel Hall comprises 250 acres. With the exception of 'The Ashton Field' which has been added to the estate since 1962, the fields are bounded to the north by Ashton Brook and to the south by Pentre Brook. Figure 1 shows their relationship to each other and the field-names in use today.[3] Comparison with the Tithe Map and Apportionment of c.1850 (Figure 2) reveals considerable continuity in the names of fields, although a number of the field boundaries have become more rectilinear in outline since 1870.[4] The most westerly fields belonging to Peel cross the township boundary and are partly in Barrow.

An early eighteenth-century estate map reveals that the fieldscape depicted in 1717 had changed little by the mid-nineteenth century (Plate 5). Although sadly the accompanying book of survey is missing, the 1717 map contains a wealth of detail pertaining to the landscape of Peel. Meadows (coloured green), marl pits, pools (shaded), woods, coppice (shown as trees), rough or gorse (speckled), hedges, ditches and streams are all shown; fields are named and entry gates drawn.[5]

One noticeable feature to the north of the map is a pool marked 'Decoy' indicating that there may have been a shooting pond or trap. Wildfowl were an important source of food in the eighteenth century, and as such, the shooting or trapping of ducks and geese played a significant part in the rural economy. The idea of a permanent structure for entrapment originated in

Landscapes Past and Present

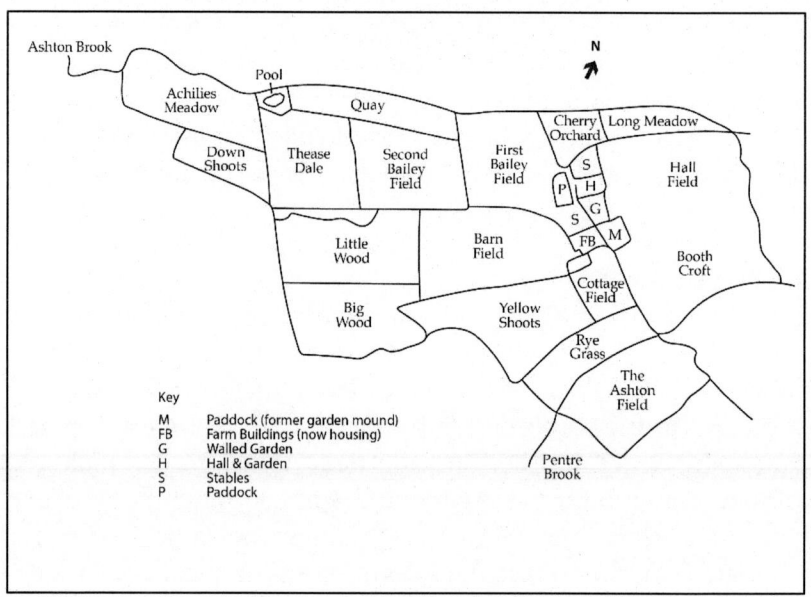

Figure 1: Field-names on the Peel Hall estate, 2015.

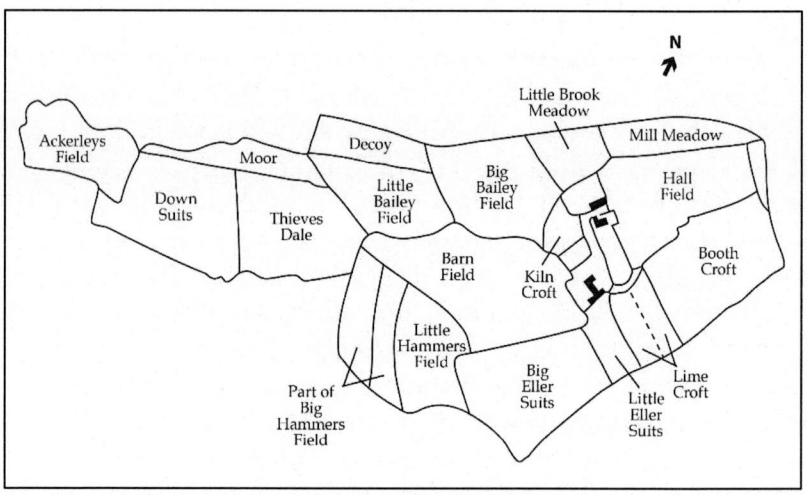

Figure 2: Field-names on the Peel Hall estate, *c*.1850.

Unlocking the Secrets of the Landscape of Peel

Holland in the sixteenth century. These traps were known as 'eendekooi' meaning 'duck cage'. Heaton suggests that the earliest English examples probably date to the 1620s although their heyday did not occur until the following century. One imagines that the idea became increasingly popular following the construction of a decoy in St James's Park for Charles II in 1665.[6]

A decoy consisted of a central pond, from which a number of arms or pipes radiated outwards and this was surrounded by trees. The arms, which typically numbered between three and eight, gradually tapered as they radiated outwards, ending in a net or cage which trapped the bird. They were most common in eastern counties and Somerset; Cheshire had few recorded duck decoys. The best surviving Cheshire example is that at Hale (with five arms), which has been reconstructed in recent years. Other, incomplete, remains can be found near Decoy Farm on the Lache Eyes on the outskirts of Chester.[7]

Perhaps the safest interpretation of the feature shown on the 1717 map would be as a shooting pond for there is no contemporary documentary evidence to suggest this area of wetland had additional radiating arms. Nevertheless, this feature was already part of the landscape in the 1680s for Colonel Roger Whitley, landowner of the estate during the last quarter of the seventeenth century, refers to the shooting of wildfowl and the 'decoy' in his diary. The earliest reference occurs in June 1684, a second in July 1686 when 'Mr Farrington came from Chester to go a duck hunting'. In September 1686, Colonel Whitley mentions that he 'went to Wrench and the other workmen at the decoy'. One cannot help but wonder what the workmen were doing and wishes he had said more! In January 1688, visitors were taken after dinner 'to see the gardens, decoy etc'. However, perhaps the most tantalising snippet is the reference to a 'coyman' in March 1692. This may have been the decoyman, an individual responsible for the entrapment of wildfowl, who would have lived in a cottage nearby. It is interesting to note that the 1717 estate map does in fact show a dwelling next to the gate that leads into the wooded enclosure and the decoy. A final reference in the diary to stolen ducks in December 1696 reminds us of the economic value of wildfowl to the local inhabitants of Ashton and Mouldsworth.[8]

Considering this feature in its wider context, it must be noted that Colonel Whitley spent a significant proportion of his life in London as a Member of Parliament for Flintshire. It is therefore not unreasonable to suggest that he would have been familiar with the decoy in St James's Park. Less known perhaps is the fact that he owned land in Marlston-cum-Lache.[9] A decoy was constructed here in 1634 by Sir William Brereton.[10] By 1709, the 'old' decoy on the Lache Eyes had been superseded by a

Figure 3: Wetland habitat in the vicinity of the former 'Decoy', 2015.

Unlocking the Secrets of the Landscape of Peel

'new' one.[11] Although it is not known whether Whitley was familiar with the 'new' decoy and whether it was constructed during the Colonel's lifetime, for he died in 1697, one can assume that he would have been aware of a decoy on the Lache Eyes. Given these links, it is indeed possible that the feature indicated on the 1717 map was a decoy.

Drainage work to Ashton Brook most likely resulted in the loss of the original pool although the field-name was still in use in 1870. Today this area is known as 'Quay' and the owner of the estate is allowing the area to be reclaimed by nature. Smaller ponds have developed ensuring that the area is once again inhabited by wildfowl and becoming a haven for wildlife (Figure 3).

On the outer edge of the estate lies a field which is known as 'Achilies Meadow'. Recorded as 'Ackerley's Field' in the Tithe Award, and 'Acrely's Field' in 1717, this field was named

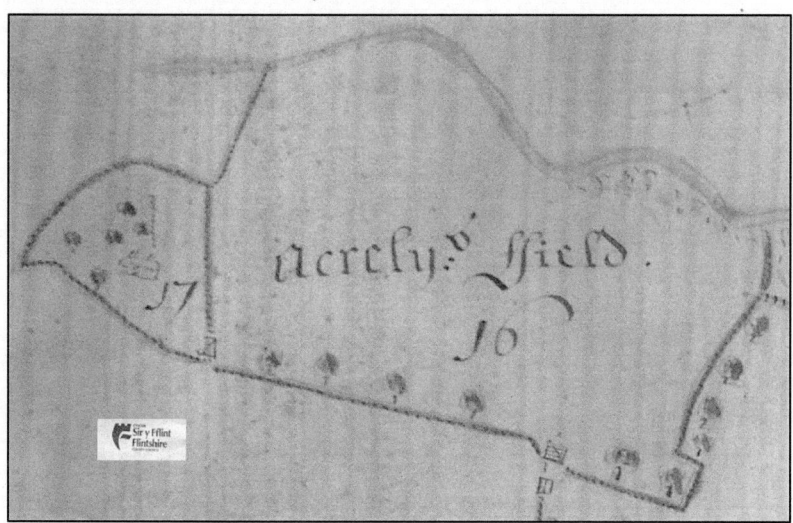

Figure 4: Acrely's Field and croft (enlarged), taken from an estate survey commissioned by the earl of Plymouth, 1717 (reproduced by permission of Flintshire Record Office).

after a former tenant of Colonel Whitley. Living in a one-hearth dwelling and described as a yeoman, Oliver Ackerley lived and farmed on the estate for over 30 years. Whitley's diary records a visit to his 'new house' in 1694. This is probably the cottage depicted in the adjoining croft on the 1717 map (Figure 4). By July 1696 Ackerley had died but his widow remained in the house until the following year for the diary records that it was suggested to Whitley that 'she should quit my house before May and leave it to the justices to provide another for her in Barrow or Mouldsworth'.[12]

The above example demonstrates the enduring nature of the field-names in this locality. This is borne out by a rental nearly 100 years earlier which refers to: 'Boothes Croftes', 'Hall Feilde', the 'Great' and 'Little Bealyfeilde', 'Little Barnefeildes', 'Theevesdale', 'Dounshuttes', 'Great' and 'Little Hammons feilde' and the 'Great' and 'Little Elershawe'.[13] Given the continuity in names, one could suggest that the field boundaries were probably broadly similar to those of the eighteenth century.

Field-names often reveal clues about individuals, structures, the topography and previous farming systems. However, they need to be used cautiously in conjunction with additional evidence as in the example of 'Acrely's Field' above. One might have assumed that the name referred to land assigned to the manorial ploughman from the OE *acer-man*.[14] Similarly, initial consideration of the field-name 'Booth Croft' could easily lead one to assume the name was connected with the nineteenth-century landowner Booth Grey. However, the 1610 rental clearly reveals this was not the case.

A further consideration is the need to discover the earliest derivation of a name for field-names are prone to transcription errors. They were often passed on by word of mouth leading to

Unlocking the Secrets of the Landscape of Peel

the 'Chinese Whisper' effect. The field-names shown in Table 1. reveal how names can change subtly through time.[15]

2015	1870/1850	1815	1765	1717	1610
Yellow Shoots	Eller Suits	Hilly Shoots	Alley Shoots	Elasheth	Elershawe
Down Shoots	Down Suits	Down Shoots	Down Shoots	Down Shoots	Doun Shuttes
-	Hammers Field	Hanmors Field	Amous Field	Hammons Field	Hammons Field

Table 1: Field-names through time.

'Elershawe' refers to a copse or wood of alder trees whereas the modern derivation might lead the unwary to think that the name could have derived from a piece of productive land or a field where rape seed was grown. 'Dounshuttes' probably derives from the OE 'sceat' meaning a long strip of arable land, the basic unit of cultivation in an open field system. 'Hammon's Field' may derive from a personal name or individual. On initial reading 'Theevesdale' may conjure visions of thieves stealing produce. However this could be a derogatory name for a piece of unproductive or unattractive land. The 'dale' element may relate to a hollow or valley, or, could possibly derive from a 'dole' – a strip in a common field.[16]

With its wealth of detail, the 1717 map does help to explain some of the anomalous lumps and bumps in the landscape of Peel such as the elongated tear-shaped mill pond located on the far side of the brook. Although there are no remains of the old mill house or workings, it is still possible to make out the line of the leat beyond the brook and the former mill pond survives as a grass depression (Figure 5). Documentary references to the mill are sparse; however, eighteenth-century rentals reveal that the mill underwent considerable repairs *c.*1739 to 1744 which included two new millstones and work on the mill dams.[17]

Figure 5: Former mill pond. Note the depression visible behind the horse's head.

The lumps, bumps, dips and hollows in the 'Cottage Field' are perhaps more difficult to explain. Turner has suggested they could be the remains of ridge and furrow. However, this is difficult to substantiate with any certainty.[18] Within both the 'Cottage Field' and 'Booth Croft' it is possible to make out a slight ridge. This would appear to mark the boundaries of the former 'Lime Croft' (Figures 2 and 13).

Unlocking the Secrets of the Landscape of Peel

Buildings and Gardens: Past and Present

In order to understand the changing landscape of Peel, a brief overview of the ownership of the estate is helpful.

Although the estate has changed hands a number of times since the mid-sixteenth century, there have been long periods of stability. Peel was acquired by the Hardware family c.1560 upon the marriage of Henry Hardware to Ann Gee, daughter of Henry Gee, one-time Mayor of Chester. By 1683, Peel had been purchased by Colonel Roger Whitley and it was subsequently inherited, after the latter's death, through marriage by the earl of Plymouth. The estate belonged to the absentee earls of Plymouth until the early nineteenth century when it was purchased by William Booth Grey. In 1819, Booth Grey exchanged Peel with Samuel Aldersey, for the manor and lordship of Ashton. Peel was subsequently purchased c.1870 by William Atkinson, who had already purchased the Ashton Hayes estate and lands in Mouldsworth from Booth Grey. The entire estate was ultimately sold at auction in 1923. Owned by the Bridge family from the 1920s and subsequently Kilverts Farm Products, Peel was purchased by the Kinseys in November 1961.[19]

Plate 6 shows the south front of Peel Hall. Built of Manley sandstone in 1637 for Henry Hardware IV, the building is a dominant feature in the present landscape. However, this imposing southerly aspect hides an enigmatic past. L-shaped in plan, the west front suggests that all is not quite as it seems. Figure 6 reveals a wing reduced in height and a blocked arched doorway. Irregular stonework above the nineteenth-century porch suggests windows have been removed. It is however the view from the north-east which is most revealing (Figure 7). The presence of a semi-circular headed door case with an

Figure 6: Peel Hall: west wing. Note the former doorway to the left of the porch.

ornate date plaque, a 'hanging' capital and an elliptical medallion, flanked on either side by two Renaissance pilasters at first floor height, indicates that these must have been internal walls; a view which is reinforced by the 'suspended' moulded fireplace at ground floor level. These features are sadly all that remain of a 'sumptuous' Great Hall.[20] At the northern end of the west wing, there are two blocked doorways, one above the other. Undecorated, the lower doorway probably led into the service rooms and was part of a screens passage (Figures 7–8). The upper doorway may have led onto a gallery overlooking the hall.[21] Taken together, the evidence suggests that the present-day hall is indeed but 'a tantalising fragment',[22] a mere 'shadow of its former self'.[23]

Unlocking the Secrets of the Landscape of Peel

Figure 7: Peel Hall: back view of the west wing.

Figure 8: Ornate doorway at first floor level, leading from the Great Hall into the south wing, with date plaque above.

Unlocking the Secrets of the Landscape of Peel

In 1810 Lysons described Peel Hall as 'a respectable old mansion'. At this date the Great Hall and north wing may have still been in existence. By 1819 these structures had certainly gone. Ormerod, was not impressed with Peel, stating:

> ... if an opinion could be formed from the wing which remained until its demolition by the present proprietor, it did but ill deserve the eulogiums which have been bestowed upon it, being but an indifferent specimen of the taste which prevailed on the restoration of Italian architecture in this country. The whole as a mass, might have an effect which the relics were incapable of giving.[24]

Since the nineteenth century, the building has attracted much speculation. Writers and local people alike have conjectured as to the presence of a chapel, secret attic rooms, passages, tunnels and even a dungeon! Doubt has also been expressed as to whether the northern wing of the house was ever realised.[25] Some myths can easily be dispelled, others hold a grain of truth. However, other than the fabric of the present building there appears to be very little documentary evidence about the structure itself.

The Hearth Tax returns of 1664 and 1674 both record eleven hearths which in itself suggests that the northern wing of the Hall was a reality. Interestingly, the returns of 1665 state that there were fourteen hearths but that two were discharged (not in use). Colonel Whitley's diary sadly tells us very little about the fabric of the Hall. He occasionally refers to rooms where he has entertained or met with visitors: the hall, parlour, buttery and his own chamber. Unfortunately, the 1717 estate map does not shed any light on the matter for it depicts the outer garden wall and gateways but the inner area is blank. One imagines that the house itself was of little interest to the absentee landowner, the earl of Plymouth, and so it was not drawn. An undated print of Peel Hall by J. Musgrave, originally bound by Broster in 1817, would suggest that the north wing had disappeared by this time.[26]

Regarding the presence of a chapel,[27] this seems unlikely. The grand interior archway, which has been interpreted as part of a chapel, would have led directly into and from the Great Hall at its upper end. The writer feels that had the Hall possessed a chapel, Colonel Whitley would have used it and mentioned it in his diary. He makes regular references to his attendance at church on a Sunday. His non-attendance is similarly stated – as on Sunday 29 January 1688 when he writes: 'the ways were so bad, I could not goe to church'.[28]

A number of the comments which have been made about the Hall appear to stem from a short piece written by Cash in 1897. She refers to two underground passages, later interpreted as tunnels, which 'unite into one', extending out beyond the Hall, which 'are said to appear on the surface again about a mile distant at a place called Swinford Mills'. Cash interprets the passages as places of refuge. However, her comments would suggest that she is not really familiar with the local area, although she did visit and sketch the Hall.[29] Her comments also reveal that the 'myth' surrounding the length of the tunnel was already in existence by the late nineteenth century. In more recent times, the tunnel has been said to extend to Barrow Church, Hockenhall and Horton Hall![30]

Two brick lined culverts undoubtedly exist. One of these was discovered to the north-west of the main house during 2012. Measuring 0.4 metres x 0.6 metres, a section of approximately 3 metres in length was exposed. The bricks were contemporary to others found in the garden walls and have been dated to the late sixteenth/early seventeenth centuries. Pottery dating to the late seventeenth/early eighteenth centuries was found in the backfill. This feature may have been a drain which served the house. Interestingly, estate rentals for

Unlocking the Secrets of the Landscape of Peel

1728 record a payment to Mr Sayer, plumber, for £32 8s. 5d. One wonders if this substantial payment included work on the drains/culvert. A similar length of tunnel to the one discovered in 2012 has also been exposed in a field running towards the brook.[31]

Two large barrel vaulted, brick lined cellars can be accessed from the present kitchen. These extend beyond the footprint of the house, beneath the garden to the west. At the end of the furthermost cellar there is a door, now sealed, which separates the cellar from a tunnel, the exact extent of which is largely unknown and has given rise to local tales.[32] Given the date when the Hall was constructed, it is indeed possible that a tunnel was constructed as a means of escape from the house. However, in the absence of further exploration, 'the jury remains out' on the exact length of the passage.

Extensive amounts of brick walling survive in close proximity to the Hall. Today these enclose a stable area to the north-east of the house, the outer edge of a garden to the east,

Figure 9: Former gateway. This is one of two which are in direct alignment on either side of the present stable yard.

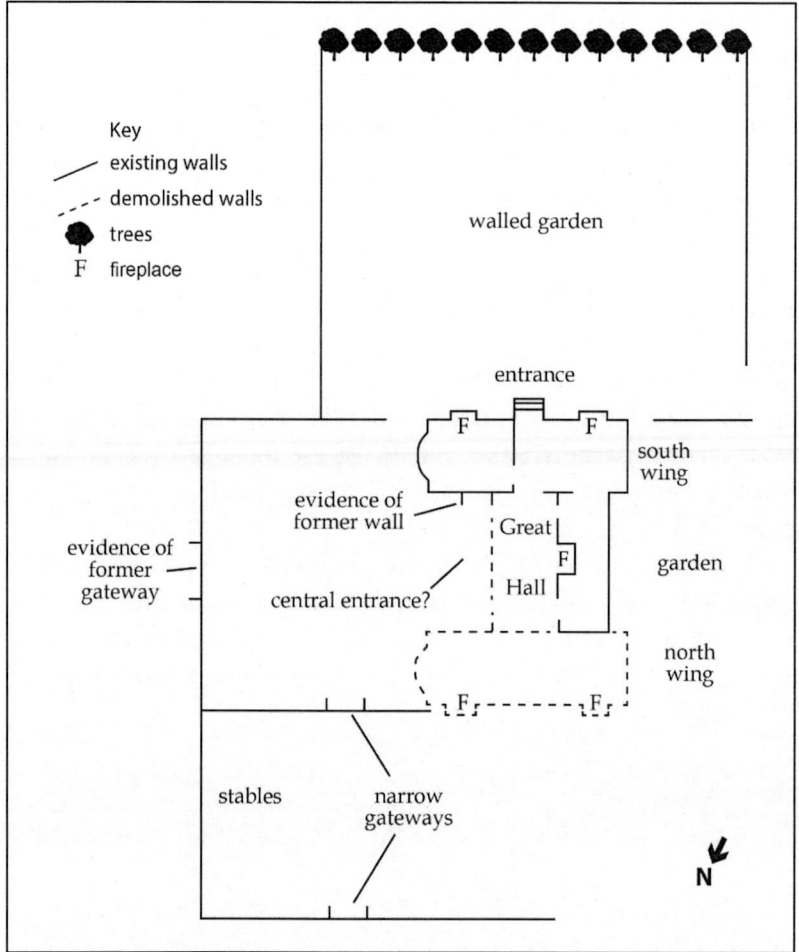

Figure 10: Simplified plan of Peel Hall and gardens.

a smaller garden to the west and a former walled garden to the south. It would seem likely that the brickwork is contemporary with the house. The present stable area to the north-east was probably a former walled courtyard or garden. Figure 9 shows

Figure 11: The partial remains of a decorative escallop on the west side of the garden wall.

the remains of one of two former gateways, which are in direct alignment and form part of the walling in this area (see also Figure 10). The footings of a larger gateway, beneath the east garden wall, were discovered by the owner during 2015. This is centrally located along the east wall of the former garden/ courtyard area directly in front of the house and aligned with a central main entrance (Plate 5). An ornate gateway on this aspect would have allowed visitors to view the front of the house as they approached. However, the topography and a lack of evidence to suggest there was a carriage driveway leading to the house from the east might indicate that the gateway was a visual attraction rather than a functional accessway. Evidence from the 1717 estate map (Plate 5) would suggest this was the case.

Figure 10, based on the work of Turner and the writer's own observations, is a simplified plan of Peel Hall with its walled courtyard and gardens. The slightly different alignment of the walled garden to the south of the house suggests that this was possibly a later feature than the courtyard/garden areas to the east and north-east.[33]

Decorative escallops used to form a part of the brickwork to the former walled garden to the south. The partial remains of one of these is shown in Figure 11. Writing in 1819, Ormerod commented that: 'The gardens were large, and the old brick wall which surrounded them fancifully arranged in escallops and semi-circles.' Additional evidence for this feature is provided by the Tithe Map which, when enlarged, shows four escallops, grouped together on both the west and east sections of the wall. In 1897, Cash also refers to 'six or eight semi-circular loops' in the high wall.[34] These decorative features were still in evidence in the twentieth century for Jackson, writing in 1960, states: 'Now very much dilapidated, the brick garden wall, with its scalloped ornamentation, was until twenty years or so,

Unlocking the Secrets of the Landscape of Peel

Figure 12: The remains of the garden mound and moat to the south of the walled garden. Note the depression and uneven ground surface highlighted in white.

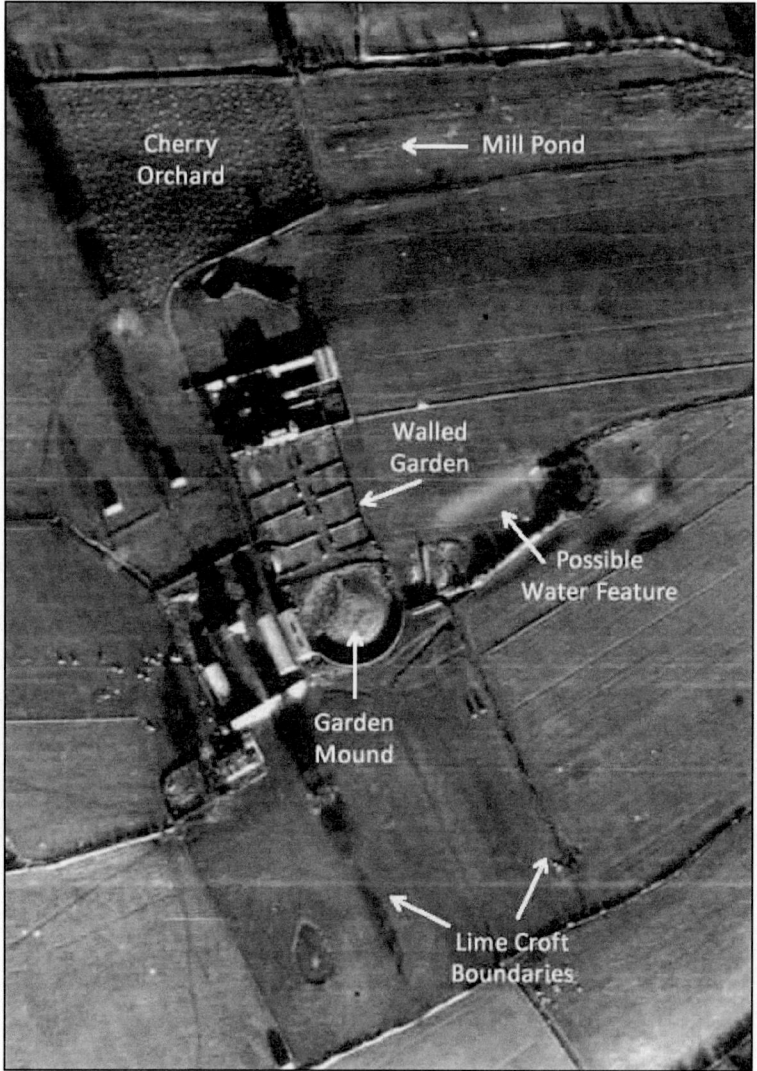

Figure 13: RAF aerial photograph of the landscape of Peel (17 Jan. 1947), showing the garden mound and causeway. (CALS, CPE_UK_1935_3038: reproduced by permission of Cheshire Archives and Local Studies and the owner/depositor to whom copyright is reserved.)

standing in good repair.'[35] One suspects that the walled garden became a victim of more intense farming during the war years.

Just beyond the remains of the walled garden in existence today, a paddock contains a circular depression. This is the bulldozed remains of the garden mound, a feature which was demolished in 1948 (Figure 12). The RAF aerial photograph, taken in January 1947, (Figure 13) and a description written shortly before it was bulldozed give a good impression of this feature:

> Both motte and moat are still plainly to be seen within the enclosure – once no doubt carefully cultivated – which was originally the chief garden or orchard of the hall. At the present time this causeway is covered with a mass of bushes and weeds.[36]

Cash sketched the bridge over the moat in 1897. At that time it was 'in a good state of preservation'.[37] The aerial photograph clearly shows the moated area, causeway and the garden wall just beyond the mound to the south. Enhanced magnification of the wall would also suggest the survival of the scalloped wall decoration to the east. The bridge, wall and a ruined building on top of the mound, were all lost in 1948.[38] The garden mound or mount would have been intended as a focal point at the most southerly extent of the garden. Any structure on top of the mount would have afforded good views of the surrounding countryside: Tarvin Church, Beeston Crag and the Welsh hills. The presence of a building on top of the mound is revealed in Whitley's diary. An entry from June 1686 records: 'Hussey went with Houseman to the top of the garden house to take the plan of the ways from Ashton, Tarvin etc.'[39]

Close to the site of the garden mound, the adjoining 'Hall Field' contains numerous dips and hollows. The largest area is roughly rectangular in shape and gives the impression it could have been a former pool, marl or possibly clay pit used for making bricks. This feature is depicted on most of the historic maps and is clearly visible on the 1940s aerial photograph. It would not be unreasonable to suggest that the pool may have been incorporated as an additional garden feature to be viewed from the top of the mount.

Colonel Whitley's diary records a vineyard. In May 1691, Whitley met with a craftsman about making seats for the vineyard and arbour. The following spring, stones were needed for the arbour. There are also references, such as those in July and August 1691, to people from Chester visiting the house and gardens, suggesting that, on a local scale, both house and gardens were noteworthy.[40]

Whether the vineyard shown on the 1717 map (Plate 5) is the one referred to in the diary is impossible to say. However, the map additionally shows a hop yard, what appears to be a small orchard within the walled area, an 'old orchard', beyond the walled area, close to the site of the garden mound, and what may be orchard trees to the front of the house. There is one reference to an orchard in the eighteenth-century estate accounts, relating to 1744, when Ralph Tinney, gardener, was paid £2 14s. 8d. for 'cutting superfluous branches off the orchard trees'. Such a significant sum would suggest a large orchard or one that had suffered considerable neglect.[41]

The aerial photograph clearly reveals the presence of an orchard to the north of the house and garden. Today this field is known as the 'cherry orchard'. Jacob's article suggests this had disappeared by 1962.[42]

Brief consideration should be given to the brick farm buildings on the site. A dairy herd was kept at Peel until the latter years of the twentieth century. A subsequent change in direction to a livery stables led to many of the farm buildings going out of use. These were converted to housing c.2006–7. An archaeological survey of the barns, carried out prior to building

Unlocking the Secrets of the Landscape of Peel

work, suggests these were built in the first half of the eighteenth century. The tallest, northern wing is the earliest structure, dating to the early eighteenth century. The long range and south wing was probably added soon after: it is of similar handmade brick but is not keyed into the earlier structure. This would suggest the barn complex was constructed whilst Peel Hall was owned by the earls of Plymouth. Although the eighteenth-century rentals do not state when the barns were constructed, the accounts for the years 1728 and 1736 to 1744 include substantial sums of money spent on slates and carpentry work. Even taking into account the fact that Peel Hall may have needed re-roofing, one imagines that at least some of these monetary figures can be attributed to the construction of part of the barn complex. It is interesting to note that in 1740 the list of disbursements includes a sum of £2 16s. 10d. to Edward Briscoe for flagging a barn floor – the only direct reference to the structures.[43]

House and Gardens: In Context

To Turner, Peel is 'an imposing Artisan Mannerist gentry house'.[44] This was a style of English architecture which prevailed from c.1615–75, created by masons rather than qualified architects.

An engraving of Crewe Hall, which was built between 1615 and 1636 by Sir Randle Crewe, reveals some similarities to the existing structure of Peel Hall. Built on a much larger scale than Peel (it had 42 hearths in 1674), the illustration shows a symmetrically designed E plan house. A small arched gateway is visible to the front of the house. There are formal gardens with high walls close to the house, and a rectangular ornamental pond.[45]

Influenced by years spent in London, Fuller eloquently suggests that Sir Randle Crewe 'first brought the model of excellent building into these remoter parts, yea, brought London into Cheshire, in the loftiness, sightlines and pleasantness of their structures'.[46]

Turner describes Crewe Hall as a 'model building'. Another contemporary building, Dorfold Hall (built in 1616 by Sir Ralph Wilbraham) has a centrally placed hall built between two cross-wings as at Peel. This plan form is also visible at Nerquis Hall in North Wales which was built c.1635–40. This leads Turner to conclude that:

> For the period 1615–1640, a group of wealthy Cheshire merchants and professional men, many with London connections, were inspired to build country houses in the style of their contemporaries and social equals in the capital. This interest was fostered by Sir Randolph Crewe and Crewe Hall but developed and continued to incorporate new trends up to the Civil War. Of the later houses Peel Hall, Ashton would seem to have been the most ambitious.[47]

It is worth noting, in this context, that the Wilbraham family of Dorfold were related by marriage with the Hardwares of Peel. Both Ralph and his son, Roger Wilbraham, were mentioned in the will of Henry Hardware III of March 1612/13 suggesting close contact between the families.

A Previous House

Evidence regarding an earlier house at Peel is fragmentary and one is reliant on wills and inventories. William Webb, in his description of Cheshire written in 1623, refers to 'the goodly ancient house' at Peel.[48] It has been assumed that this was a timber-framed structure although there is no direct evidence to suggest that this was the case.[49]

Colonel Whitley's diary has one reference to the previous house. In July 1686 he wrote: 'An old woman came to see me,

Unlocking the Secrets of the Landscape of Peel

sayd she had bin borne in the old house of Peele, was 74 yeares old.'[50]

This suggests she was born c.1612 when the house was in the ownership of Henry Hardware III. His probate inventory of 1613 suggests that the house was substantial. The document lists 27 rooms and the contents therein. The house undoubtedly had two floors; numerous chambers with a great many beds, including one in the dining room and a large number of service rooms. There were rooms over the parlour and hall, but nothing is specified over the dining room. Careful consideration of the route the appraisers took through the house would suggest there was a staircase in close proximity to the hall and parlour. One would imagine that the service wing, especially the kitchen and milk house faced north. In addition to the usual service rooms recorded in a large house, there were numerous closets, store rooms, an additional kitchen and a clock house! Furniture, rather than possessions, made up the vast majority of the items listed.[51]

A near contemporary rental of 1610 gives a tantalising glimpse of the landscape beyond the dwelling house for it mentions two gardens, two orchards, a dove house, hop yard, pools, hemp yard, rabbit warrens and a croft.[52]

An earlier mention of the house can be found in the will of Henry Hardware I, 1582, which refers to the glass and wainscot in his 'now dwelling house called the Peel'. It would not be unreasonable to speculate that Henry built the house, or greatly extended any existing house at Peel, for this was land he acquired through his marriage with Ann Gee c.1560.[53]

The place-name Peel has been spelt variously over the centuries: Peel, Peele, Pile and Pyle. Christopher Saxton's map of Cheshire, 1577, shows 'The pyle' in relation to the villages of Ashton and Mouldsworth. Its inclusion would suggest it must have been a noteworthy structure topographically.[54] Dodgson suggests that the name derives from *pēl* meaning a stockade or fortification.[55] Peel or Pele Towers were often small fortified keeps or tower houses built along the English and Scottish borders. Intended as watch towers, beacon fires could be lit to warn of approaching danger. However, such structures were not exclusively confined to the north of England.

It is unclear whether Saxton's depiction shows Henry Hardware's house or an earlier defensive feature. Writing in c.1819, Ormerod, makes reference to an earlier building:

> Peel Hall was preceded by a mansion, which as its name imports, was, most probably, either formed out of the remains of a building erected for defence against the ravages of the Welsh, or occupied its site. This earlier building is supposed to have stood within a circular moat in the garden, and to have furnished at its demolition the materials for the barns and outbuildings of the fabric which succeeded to it and which is now destroyed.[56]

Many earlier writers refer to the garden mount in terms suggestive of a motte: Jackson (1960), Glasgow (1948), Aldcroft (1908) and Cash (1897). Aldcroft says of the mound at Peel:

> There occur here and there perfectly circular moats, wet or dry and of great strength, which may have been the exterior defences of small castles analogous to Pele towers. In a case like that of Peel Hall Moat, between Ashton and Mouldsworth in Cheshire, there can be little doubt that there once stood a pele tower for the protection of the Welsh Marches, the more so as the island, 80 feet across and considerably raised above the natural level, bears a strong likeness to a somewhat truncated mount of the normal kind. The moat here has a width of about 60 feet.

Writing a few years earlier, Cash entitled her article 'Peele Castle and Hall' and interpreted the garden wall escallops mentioned earlier as part of the defensive features.[57]

Unlocking the Secrets of the Landscape of Peel

Interpretations change; clearly the mound at Peel was used in the seventeenth century to form part of the formal gardens. However, it may have had earlier origins and there may have originally been a pele tower situated at Peel. Topographical evidence would suggest the site could have previously been used in this way with extensive views in all directions. A beacon lit at Peel would be visible for miles around. Analysis of the location of the fortified sites in west Cheshire when plotted on a map, would appear to reveal a double series of medieval defences similar to the pattern along the Welsh border in Shropshire identified by Eyton. Figure 14 reveals that the location of Peel fits neatly within an inner chain.[58]

Field-name evidence from the 1610 rental is also suggestive. The presence of a 'Great' and 'Little Bealyfeilde' is indicative of a previous structure. Turner believes the name to be a corruption of bailiff, which is of course a possibility, but the fields are located on low-lying land close to the brook and may indeed form part of a bailey to an earlier defensive feature. Further supporting evidence comes from the 1765 valuation of the Peel estate which lists 'Sheriffs Dale' (the earliest mention of the name), in addition to the two 'Bailey Fields'. This suggests that the former is a corruption of 'Thieves Dale' which was used previously, adopted again in the nineteenth century, and has continued in use to the present day (2015).[59]

Concluding Comments

This article has considered the landscape of Peel, and tried to explain how and why the landscape looks the way that it does today – its evolution through time. Although it has been possible to pinpoint numerous changes and when they occurred, the writer feels that this continues to be a work in progress for there are still questions to answer. Although change has taken place, there is considerable continuity in the

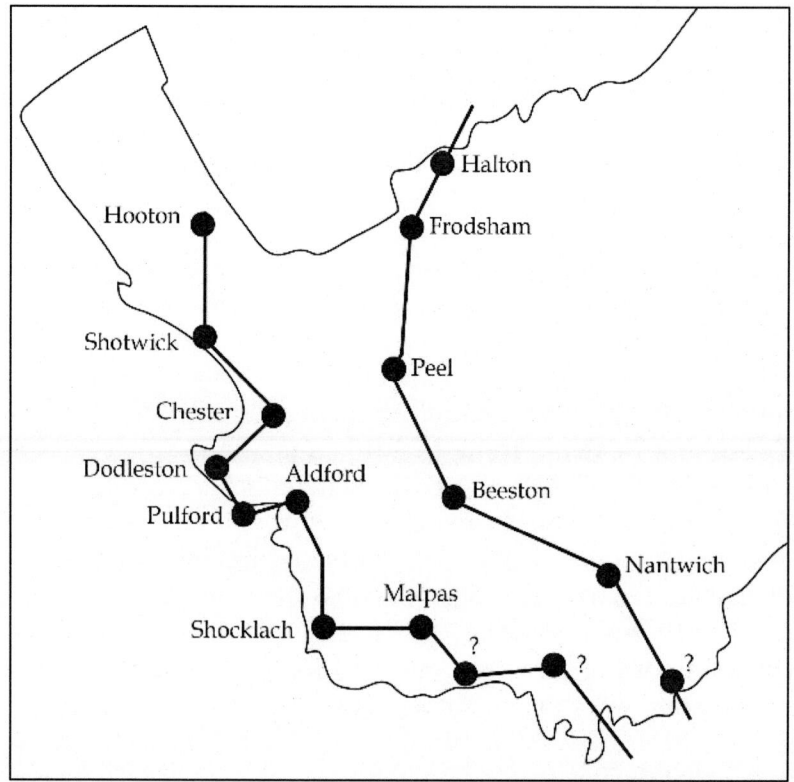

Figure 14: Location of known and possible medieval fortified sites in west Cheshire.

landscape: the location of fields, their field-names, the house – albeit much reduced in size – and the walled garden. In an era when places change beyond recognition, there are still a number of recognisable features of the seventeenth-century landscape of Peel.

There could, however, easily have been a different end to this story if it had not been for the Kinseys of Peel. By the end of 1961 the south wing of the Hall was uninhabitable: the roof was leaking and in need of repair and many of the floorboards were rotten. Years of neglect, combined with having been used internally as a poultry farm for a number of years, resulted in the County Council having no objection to the demolition of the south wing. Had it not been for the current owner's family, grant aid and Tarvin Rural Council,[60] the later twentieth-century and early twenty-first landscape history of Peel might have been very different!

Acknowledgement
Richard and Julie Kinsey of Peel Hall have shown great interest in this project. I would like to thank them for kindly allowing me to photograph the house and grounds, and for their numerous cups of coffee!

Endnotes
1. R. Muir, *Shell Guide to Reading the Landscape* (London, 1981), 16, 17.
2. W.G. Hoskins, *The Making of the English Landscape* quoted in M. Aston, *Interpreting the Landscape: Landscape Archaeology in Local Studies* (London, 1985), 12.
3. R. Kinsey, Oral Communication, 19 Mar. 2014.
4. Tithe Map of Horton cum Peel, 1850: CALS, EDT 209/2. Available online: <<http://maps.cheshire.gov.uk/tithemaps/TwinMaps.aspx?township=EDT_209-2>>. Plan of Peel Hall Estate, 1870: CALS, DDW 3765/172/2.
5. Plymouth Estate Map, 1717: FRO, D-DM 540/7.
6. A. Heaton, *Duck Decoys* (Princes Risborough, 2001), 5–6.
7. Hale Duck Decoy, <<http://www.thefriendsofpickeringspasture.org.uk/hale-duck-decoy.html>>; D. Nuttall, 'Cheshire Duck Decoys', *Cheshire History*, XXXVIII (1998-99), 35–39. One of the former decoys on the Lache Eyes is clearly visible during the winter months and can be seen from the A55 in close proximity to the Chester to Wrexham railway line.
8. Diary of Colonel Roger Whitley, 1684–97 <<http://www.british-history.ac.uk/no-series/roger-whitley-diary/1684-97>>,

accessed 13–20 Oct. 2015. Entries for: Jun. 1684, Jul. 1686, Sept. 1686, Jan. 1688, Mar. 1692 and Dec. 1696.

9. D. Lysons, *Magna Britannia; Being a Concise Topographical Account of the Several Counties of Great Britain*, II (London, 1810), 629.

10. Nuttall, 'Cheshire Duck Decoys', 35.

11. Abstract of title to an estate in Marlston-cum-Lache, 1711–18: CALS, DBC 1102/11/1.

12. Cheshire Hearth Tax Returns: CALS, Mf 13 located within E179/86/244/34 (1663), E179/86/145 (1664), E179/86/244/37 (1665), E179/86/155 (1674); Plymouth Estate Records Lease 8–9 March 1676/7: National Library of Wales (hereafter NLW), Plymouth MSS 1080; Col. Roger Whitley's Diary: Nov. 1694, Jul. 1696, Oct. 1696 and Mar. 1697.

13. Rental of lands belonging to Henry Hardware, 1610: CALS, DF 148.

14. J. Field, *English Field Names: A Dictionary* (Gloucester, 1989), 2.

15. Peel Hall Estate, 1870: CALS, DDW 3765 172/2; Tithe Map, c.1850: CALS, EDT 209/2; Valuation of Several Farms in Cheshire, 1765: Glamorgan Archives (hereafter GA) DPL 888/2; Estate Map, 1717: FRO, D-DM 540/7; Rental, 1610: CALS, DF 148.

16. Field, *English Field Names* and H.D.G. Foxall, *Shropshire Field-Names* (Shrewsbury, 1980).

17. Estate rentals and accounts, 1737–44: GA, DPL 944/3.

18. CHER: RN 1902, 'Peel Hall', RCHME (1986), 3.

19. Will of Henry Gee, 1545: CALS, Mf 164/1; Abstract of Title to lands in Cheshire, 1669–1773: NLW, Plymouth MSS 1072-1074, 1078-1080, 1897; Deeds of Peel Hall Estate, 1800–70: CALS, DDW 3765/165/2, DDW 3765/172/2; Sale Particulars Ashton Hayes Estate, 1923: CALS, D 4336/2; R. Kinsey, Oral Communication, 19 Mar. 2014.

20. CHER: Listed building details for Peel Hall.

21. CHER: Listed building details for Peel Hall.

22. P. de Figueiredo, *Cheshire County Houses* (Chichester, 1988), 6.

23. S. Jackson, 'Historic Buildings: Peel Hall, Ashton Hayes,' *The Cheshire Historian*, X (1960), 37.

24. Lysons, *Magna Britannia*, 797; Ormerod (1819), 180. Available online: <<https://archive.org/stream/historyofcountyp02orme #page/180/mode/2up/search/Peel>>.
25. S. Cash, 'Peel Castle and Hall', *Cheshire Notes and Queries*, II (1897), 190-91; D. Jacob, 'Peel House, Ashton', *Cheshire Life*, XXVIII (1962); 'Peel Hall', *Cheshire Observer*, 3 Mar. 1962; C. Hartwell, M. Hyde, E. Hubbard and N. Pevsner, *The Buildings of England: Cheshire* (London, 2011), 109.
26. Cheshire Hearth Tax Returns: CALS, Mf 13. Undated print of Peel Hall by J. Musgrave, available to view online, <<http://cheshireimagebank.org.uk>>.
27. The earliest reference to a chapel would appear to be in Jacob, 'Peel House', 31.
28. Col. Roger Whitley's Diary: Jan. 1688.
29. Cash, 'Peel Castle and Hall', 191. Sarah Cash wrote a number of short pieces, illustrated with her own sketches, about various aspects of Cheshire's history, namely families, their residences and churches, which can be found in *Cheshire Notes and Queries*, c.1896-1900.
30. Jacob, 'Peel House', 31; R. Ellington, 'Down on the Farm: Peel, Ashton Hayes', *Cheshire Life*, XXXVIII (1972), 59; oral communication with various local inhabitants of Ashton and Peel.
31. CHER, event ID ECH5515; Rental of lands in Cheshire and Flintshire, 1728: GA, DPL 968/4.
32. Site visit by author 5 Oct. 2015.
33. R.C. Turner, 'Peel Hall, an Artisan Mannerist Puzzle in Cheshire', *THSLC* CXXXVI (1986), 30-31.
34. Ormerod (1819), 180; CALS, EDT 209/2; Cash, 'Peel Castle and Hall', 190.
35. Jackson, 'Peel Hall', 38. A reliable source, Jackson was Headmaster of the local school who lived and worked in Ashton from 1927.
36. R. Glasgow, *The Hardwares of Cheshire* (London, 1948), 31.
37. Cash, 'Peel Castle and Hall', 190-91.

38. CHER card: oral communication, Mr W. Horsburgh, Manager, Peel Hall Farm, 16 Jul. 1959.
39. Col. Roger Whitley's Diary: Jun. 1686.
40. Col. Roger Whitley's Diary: May, Jul., Aug. 1691.
41. GA, DPL 944/3.
42. Jacob, 'Peel House', 31.
43. P. Frost, 'Peel Hall Barns, Ashton Hayes, Cheshire: Archaeological Building Assessment', Castlering Archaeology, Report CLV (2003); GA, DPL 968/4; DPL 944/3.
44. Turner, 'Peel Hall, an Artisan Mannerist Puzzle', 29–30.
45. D. King, *A Description of the County Palatine of Chester* (1656), 75; R. Gladden, (ed. J. Park), *The Crewes of Crewe Hall: A Family and a Home* (Nantwich, 2011), 12–13.
46. T. Fuller, *The History of the Worthies of England* (1662), 178.
47. Turner, 'Peel Hall', 34–36.
48. King, *Description of the County Palatine of Chester*, 101.
49. Glasgow, *Hardwares of Cheshire*, 31; S. Jackson, *Ashton Hayes: Glimpses into the Story of a Cheshire Village* (Chester, 1994), 47.
50. Col. Roger Whitley's Diary: 9 Jul. 1686.
51. Inventory of Henry Hardware, 1612/13: CALS, EDA 2/2 1613.
52. Rental, 1610: CALS, DF 148.
53. Will of Henry Hardware, 1583: CALS, WS 1583.
54. Christopher Saxton's map of Cheshire, 1577. Available online: <<http://www.cheshirehistory.org.uk/archive/large.php?id=12>>, accessed 19 Nov. 2015.
55. J. McN. Dodgson, *The Place-Names of Cheshire*, III, XLVI (Cambridge, 1971), 276.
56. Ormerod (1819), 180.
57. Jackson, 'Historic Buildings: Peel Hall', 37; Glasgow, *Hardwares of Cheshire*, 31; Cash, 'Peel Castle and Hall', 190–91; A. Hadrian Aldcroft, *Earthworks of England* (London, 1908), 443.
58. Figure 15 includes the possible fortified sites at: Coddington, Newhall (outer chain) and Manley, Alvanley and Doddington (inner chain); M. Salter, *The Castles and Tower Houses of Lancashire and Cheshire* (Malvern, 2001), 9–21; Medieval fortified sites in Cheshire, <<http://www.gatehouse-gazetteer.info/Indexs/

EngCounty/Cheshire.html>>, accessed 19 Nov. 2015; S.M. Varey, 'Little Ness in the Second Millennium' (Chester College, MA thesis, 2000), 12, Figure 2.3; Rev. R.W. Eyton, 'The Castles of Shropshire and its Borders', *Transactions of the Shropshire Archaeological Society*, X (1887), 15.
59. Turner, 'Peel Hall', 1; GA, DPL 888/2.
60. *Cheshire Observer*, 3 Mar. 1962, reproduced in Jackson, *Ashton Hayes*, 185-87; *Chester Chronicle*, 20 Apr. 1963: CALS, Mf 204/144.

5

TRACING THE EIGHTEENTH-CENTURY LANDSCAPE OF THELWALL IN CHESHIRE

Mike Taylor

Purpose of This Study
Surviving records give a wealth of detail about the lifestyle of the inhabitants of the small township of Thelwall during the eighteenth century.[1] From a study of this archive, it is apparent that most residents never strayed more than about eight kilometres from the village but naturally developed an acute knowledge of their local landscape since it was their workplace as well as their home. Whilst researching the local history of this area, it is highly instructive and entertaining to 'walk the job' to see just how much of the eighteenth-century landscape survives. With regard to the survival of land boundaries within the township, an estate map for the Manor of Thelwall dated 1743 provides an excellent basis for this work.[2] The project is unfinished but this paper defines its scope and offers a progress report.

Introduction: The Township of Thelwall
Of the townships and chapelries in eighteenth-century north Cheshire, Thelwall was one of the smallest with a population of about 280 people. Today, it is the smallest ecclesiastical parish in the deanery of Great Budworth and it no longer has an individual civil parish council, having been merged with that of Grappenhall about 80 years ago. The area belonging to Thelwall township has shrunk over the past 130 years and the principal cause was the digging of the Manchester Ship Canal around 1890. This divided the township, leaving about a third of all its farmland isolated on the north side of the canal with

The Eighteenth-Century Landscape of Thelwall

the rest, including most of the houses and farmsteads, remaining on the south. The land thus isolated on the north side was later transferred to other parishes that had easier access to it. However, in 1884, even before the Canal was dug, two detached areas of Thelwall land that were partially enclosed by bends in the river (known as 'The Warps' and 'West Eye') were transferred to Latchford: so Thelwall was already shrinking.

Before these changes, Thelwall was a township of roughly 1,500 acres (about 600 hectares) containing about 65 houses and 334 inhabitants in 1850.[3] During the eighteenth and nineteenth centuries, its population had grown only slowly. For instance, there were 309 inhabitants in 1801 and surviving records suggest about 60 houses and 250–280 inhabitants in the mid-1700s.[4] Throughout this period, Thelwall was a reasonably prosperous, agriculture-based community deriving its income from a mix of fishing (that ended around 1800 when the river became too polluted) plus beef and dairy farming on the flood-prone Eyes and more mixed farming on the better-drained rising ground south of the river. The community was largely self-sufficient, possessing a blacksmith, a wheelwright or millwright and, by the 1740s, a shoemaker. Flax was grown, linen thread and wool were spun and cloth was woven. Willow was woven into fish traps or baskets to carry goods such as coal. Sometime between the late 1600s and the 1730s, potato-growing became popular in Thelwall and 'delving' became a widespread if onerous activity with many villagers renting small strips in a larger field to grow this staple crop. Individual patches were measured after the diggers had exhausted either themselves or their stock of seed potatoes and a rent was then calculated.

The townships adjacent to Thelwall were Latchford, Grappenhall and Lymm plus hamlets at Statham and Appleton (Figure 1). Naturally, there was a cross-flow of people working

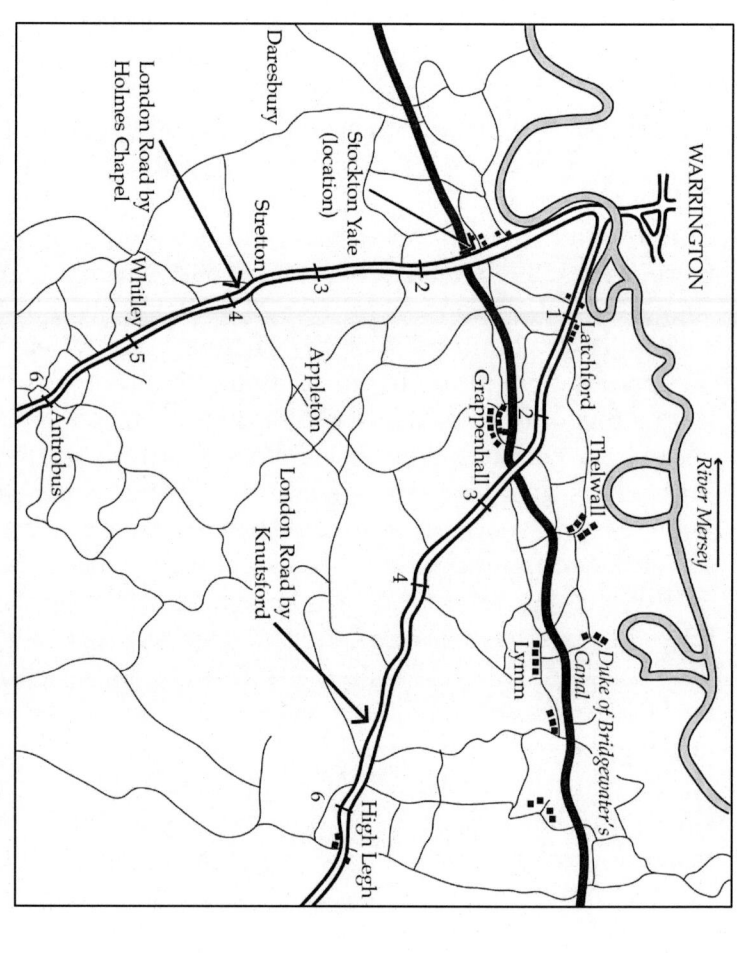

Figure 1: Thelwall and the surrounding area in the mid-1700s (based upon Burdett's Survey – see note 12). The Bridgewater Canal was not constructed at Thelwall until 1761. The figures alongside the London roads are miles from Warrington. Although Stockton does not appear on Burdett's map it has been included for locational purposes.

The Eighteenth-Century Landscape of Thelwall

the land and family links across township borders were the norm. However, in the eighteenth century, most residents of Thelwall seem never to have travelled outside this area except for visits across the county boundary to Warrington where there were markets, merchants, bankers, a post office and horse fairs and an occasional chase on a horse. In addition, local records contain many mentions of the Heath at Stockton so this too must be included in the orbits of Thelwall people.

Only the wealthy travelled further and there were few such people in the village. However, in the 1740s, one man from Thelwall went to Norfolk, a considerable journey. He went for pleasure and was gone three months.[5] No-one else in Thelwall could have afforded such a journey or could have spared the time. Thirty years earlier, the Lord of the Manor used to travel on the stagecoach from Warrington to London because he was a lawyer at Gray's Inn. Now retired and hard up, he never went far and an invitation to dine at, for instance, Dunham Massey Hall was a rare treat! Thus, in their lives, most villagers never strayed far from their homes. They could earn a penny for walking to Warrington to post a letter for someone (although few in Thelwall could write one) but the urge to enjoy the sights of places further afield seems to have been eclipsed by the need to work. Much of peoples' lives was spent outdoors so they developed a far better knowledge of the local countryside than most of us today.

Available Records
In 1920, the last Lord of the Manor of Thelwall, Admiral Jones Parry, died. He had married twice and his second, much younger, wife, who preferred to live at Bournemouth, emptied the Hall and took the manorial records back to her home. On her death in 1955, these records were dispersed by her executors and most are now in private collections in the USA.

Landscapes Past and Present

Thus, this corpus of manorial records relating to Thelwall and dating from the fourteenth century onwards is unavailable to us. Fortunately we know some of what has been lost because, in the 1840s, an earlier Lord of the Manor, James Nicholson, published a digest of records that were then held at the Hall. His long paper was published in two parts and gives extracts from many of the manorial records and discusses them in detail.[6] This tells us about some of what was in that archive but we cannot judge his accuracy nor do we know what he omitted.

Happily, many other records of the township survive. For instance, there are the Overseers, Constables and Surveyor of the Highways accounts and the minutes of township meetings plus rating and rental lists. There is a good collection of Wills and Inventories and two late-seventeenth or eighteenth-century diaries that contain much local detail. There are estate valuations and maps and a large collection of legal documents and letters relating to activities at the Hall that survived because they were probably lawyers' copies.

Many local names crept into surviving written records, field-names being just one example; some lanes were also named. Whilst studying these records, especially the detailed ones from the eighteenth century, one frequently reads place-names that are unfamiliar today and which beg the question 'Where was that?' Happily, much of the landscape around Thelwall village remains undeveloped having escaped the insensitive mass development that has blighted neighbouring townships such as Lymm and Appleton. As a result, therefore, there is still time to read the records and then look at the landscape and search for traces which would still be familiar to inhabitants of Thelwall from 300 years ago.

The Eighteenth-Century Landscape of Thelwall

Figure 2: Neglected frontage of the old Red Lion coaching inn at Warrington.

The Built Landscape Surrounding the Township of Thelwall

Warrington

Much of the old busy, cramped centre of the town has been destroyed since the 1960s. However, there are still a few buildings that would have been familiar to eighteenth-century travellers from Thelwall who would have crossed the river into Bridge Street, a street that, by the 1700s, was lined with inns. Stagecoaches started from here and others passed through – at least 60 a day by the mid-1700s. Warrington had a stagecoach service to London by 1704 when Matthew Henry noted seeing the Warrington Stage stuck in mud.[7] In 1757, one of the first fast stagecoach services, the Warrington Flying Stage, began a twice-weekly service to London from the Red Lion Inn. Travellers from Liverpool joined here and the journey to London took three days (summer only) and seats cost two guineas.[8] It was in the Red Lion that the incoming Lord of the Manor of Thelwall finally confronted creditors who had forced the jailing of both his father and grandfather for debt. In a stormy meeting in 1752, all debts were settled but at a discount of about 70%.[9] The Red Lion survives, albeit carrying a Victorian face-lift and suffering serious neglect (Figure 2). However, the coach passage into the yard and stables at the rear are reminders of a building that was once a hub of cutting-edge transport in the area.

Latchford
The lane from Thelwall to Warrington joined the old London Road[10] at Latchford which, until its development in the early 1800s, was a small agricultural community with much of its land remaining unenclosed and often referred to as heath. It was on Latchford Heath in the eighteenth century that famous early race meetings were held with a grandstand being erected and entry tokens sold. These tokens are collectors' items today. Latchford's rural landscape has completely gone. In the early 1800s, a silk mill was established there and the heath began to fill with workers' houses, not only to provide labour for local employment, but also because it was within easy walking distance of Warrington. It is difficult to recognise remains of the earlier landscape but alongside the old road from Thelwall is the Cheshire Cheese Inn (Figure 3). This was a well-known eighteenth-century landmark visited by Thelwall residents. Thomas Percival referred to 'catching a fox in the Cheshire Cheese' meaning he had drunk too much.[11] Money was lent at

The Eighteenth-Century Landscape of Thelwall

Figure 3: The Cheshire Cheese – an amenity for ale, conversation and banking in the eighteenth century.

the door of the Cheshire Cheese, a reminder of how an essential service was delivered before modern banking. The building is sometimes described as an 'old coaching inn' but, being just 1 mile from the Warrington terminus, this it is hard to understand; it may have served as a pick-up point but no sign of a yard or coach entrance survives.

Stockton Heath

The sparsely populated open heathland extended westwards from Latchford across to Stockton. As late as the 1770s, any settlement there was insignificant – it was heath. Stockton was not even named on the Burdett Map of Cheshire (1777)[12] and was regarded as part of the township of Appleton, itself only a chapelry under Runcorn. Two important roads crossed the heath, one running north–south, the other east–west and these were heavily used by coaches and pack horses even though the going was described as 'heavy'. Throughout the 1700s, there was a well-visited rendezvous at Stockton Yate where contracts

Landscapes Past and Present

Figure 4: Part of the wharf on the Bridgewater Canal at London Bridge, Stockton Heath.

were signed, debts settled or incurred and hunts organised. The Yate was a formal entrance onto the heath and it is logical to expect that it was located at the cross-roads since there was no other significant landmark.

Change came with the cutting of the Bridgewater Canal in 1772 when a wharf was built at the intersection of the canal with the London Road,[13] close to the Yate. The wharf was called Stockton Quay. At the same time, possibly attracted by this, Robert Hamblett, a blacksmith from Stretton, built his Spade Works on open ground close to the road intersection on the heath (i.e. the Yate) and this business developed into Stockton Forge.[14] Housing and other workshops followed and Stockton Heath was quickly transformed into a village, becoming an ecclesiastical parish in 1838.

The Eighteenth-Century Landscape of Thelwall

Today, the Heath has gone, as has the Forge, although it continued to manufacture hand tools until the 1990s. Of all the settlements around Thelwall, Stockton has changed most. Our eighteenth-century predecessors would be lost in the modern village although they might draw comfort from the wharf, warehouse and canal bridge that survive even though goods traffic along the canal has been replaced by leisure cruising (Figure 4).

The Rural Landscape Surrounding Thelwall Township

Most of the landscape surrounding Thelwall in the eighteenth century was open country. If Thelwall was typical of this part of north Cheshire, then common land was still only partially enclosed giving easy access across it. This view seems reasonable and is supported by a recent review[15] of Sylvester's earlier work on settlement in Cheshire and helps explain why, in the mid-eighteenth century, huntsmen could race across surrounding parishes and townships without any apparent impediment. For instance, a diary kept by Thomas Percival (a local farmer who acted as steward to the Lord of the Manor at Thelwall) records 'I started a doe in Thelwall and chased and killed it in Whitley' – a chase of at least ten kilometres.[16] Obviously, some land was enclosed and regarded as private and so too were some roads, hence statements such as: 'Dined at Dunham Hall and returned home [to Thelwall] by the Bent Lane at Warburton by the permission of Mr Arnold Drinkwater'.[17] Use of such roads or private land was often negotiated if they offered a short cut when carting heavy loads such as clay, marl or bricks. For instance: 'Mr. Thomas Worsley spoke to me in Warrington about carting through Leigh's Horse Croft'.

Naturally, villagers on foot had near-total access – after all, this was their world. However, some outings caused more interest than others.

In March 1749, Percival wrote: 'John Rigby and Nurse Coumbs were seen to walk together from Grappenhall into the fields towards Grimsditches or Witherwing and were suspected to be too kind together for which they were posted'. Rigby and Miss Coumbs (also spelled 'Coombs') lived in Thelwall and it is obvious that this was no innocent outing but we may ask why Percival was so inflamed that he felt it right to advertise their tryst by posting information in a public place? Grimsditch (after a local family name) was a wood situated at the edge of the mosses in Appleton (OS SJ 653837). Witherwing was also in Appleton township and its name earns a substantial but unsatisfying entry in the English Place-Name Society's volume for this area.[18] The name 'Witherwins' *[sic]* survives as a farm and road name. What is important is that these two places lie well away from Thelwall in a sparsely populated landscape. So, John Rigby and Nurse Coombs chose to walk over 2 miles (about 4 kilometres) from Thelwall across Grappenhall parish to reach quieter ground. Theirs was a vain hope because the people of both communities would be in the fields and they were bound to be noticed.

Their affair raises an interesting aspect of local social behaviour. Diaries about the village did not often remark on extra-marital activities even though the Overseer of the Poor's accounts show that several illegitimate children were being looked after in Thelwall and were named after their natural fathers. However, the Coombs family was on the breadline, looking for any casual or occasional work to make a living. Nurse Coombs was probably an elder daughter working as a nursemaid and her income would be seen as vital in maintaining the family without recourse to the Poor Rates.

The Eighteenth-Century Landscape of Thelwall

Percival, who chose to inform (or 'post') the village of the affair and thereby use public pressure to suppress it, often wrote up the accounts of the Overseer of the Poor in Thelwall. As such, he recognised that if Nurse Coombs became pregnant, there would be an extra mouth to feed in the Coombs family and a wage lost, possibly leaving the entire Coombs family rather than just the child needing assistance. Thus, rather than making any moral judgement, it seems he was prompting the community to react to the relationship in order to contain the township's Social Security payments.

Despite the passage of some 270 years, we can find that the landscape of Witherwings survives with small, well-hedged fields that would be as attractive to Rigby and Miss Coombs today as they were in 1749. In fact, they are probably quieter nowadays than in the 1740s.

The Landscape Within the Township

The land within Thelwall township divided naturally into three areas. In the south, there was the Waste. In the centre but high enough to avoid flooding was the rich land around the village. Further north and close to the River Mersey were the rich but flood-prone grasslands known as the Eyes.

The Waste of Thelwall

The Waste is usually understood to have been most of the triangle of rising ground on the south side of the Mersey valley and delimited by Weaste Lane that runs east–west across the township.

The Waste still is the most difficult land to work in Thelwall because of the presence of boulder clay in the soil. A Roman road ran along the ridge above the Waste (known as the Ridgeway and excavated at High Legh and Tatton Park) possibly following an even earlier roadway. Two tracks run down from this ridge across the Waste towards the river (where there were fords across the Mersey). One of these tracks, now known as Cinder Lane, has been described by Crosby as an 'ancient trackway'[19] and during the eighteenth century served as an access route for enclosure of the Waste.

When the estate was mapped in 1743, the Waste was in the process of being enclosed (but no enclosure award is known). The map is entitled 'Lands belonging to John Pickering Esq.' (Plate 7). He was Lord of the Manor and many of the fields are edged in green, others are not. It is assumed that Pickering's lands were those with green boundaries so it seems likely that he was driving through the enclosure of the Waste. Since he was bankrupt, we may suspect that he was doing this either to sell land or to increase the rent yield.

It is interesting to note how the process of enclosure was being achieved. From the map, we can see that a strip of land with uniform width had been marked out to the west of the track. This strip was then divided up into fields of varying lengths. Beyond this, another strip of identical width had been measured and the process repeated. The width of these strips, as scaled off the map, was about 130 yards. The surveyor at this time, Thomas Percival, normally used a 32-yard chain[20] (called the 'customary' or 'Cheshire' measure rather than the 'standard' measure chain of 22 yards), hence the width of each strip was 4 chains. The 2 strips enclosed to the east of the track were also four chains wide. Thus we see that the enclosure was being planned as a unified development by taking regular strips, each 4 chains wide out of the Waste, using the track as the baseline.

So, what remains of that earlier landscape? On comparing the eighteenth-century estate plan with later maps such as that for the Tithe Award of c.1845, it is apparent that extensive adjustments were soon made to the enclosure boundaries with

The Eighteenth-Century Landscape of Thelwall

some fields being merged and boundaries moved or destroyed (Figure 5). This raises the question of the age of today's hedges. Those on either side of Cinder Lane stand well back from the roadway leaving wide verges typical of many enclosure roads. Alongside the track, the hedges on this lane are always 32 feet apart (centre-to-centre, i.e. a third of a chain apart). Thus, while the trackway might be ancient, the laying out of the boundaries on which hedges presently sit was probably part of the enclosure of the 1740s when the limits of the fields were defined. For fans of Hooper's hedgerow hypothesis,[21] the hedges are a disappointment and suggest a more recent date than 1743 because they consist almost entirely of hawthorn with only an occasional second species. Hedgerow trees and also those trees left marooned in fields as remnants of grubbed-out hedges are all mature oak. In a landscape like the Waste, it is hard to see how these oaks could all have appeared without being deliberately planted. The only variation in tree species comes around isolated water-logged marl pits (where we find mainly alder) and on the banks of the Massey Brook whose deep valley marks the boundary of the township. Apart from the coppiced hazel and willow around this brook, there is no evidence for management of trees on the Waste and the hedges have never been layered and so were never intended to be stock-proof. All this points to an enclosure of the Waste to give arable fields or hay meadows with boundaries being marked by trees, posts or stones and with hedges being planted much later. More recently still, probably well into the twentieth century, more of the hedges were grubbed out to enlarge fields and accommodate more mechanised farming (Plate 8).

However, returning to the 1743 plan, an important exception is found at the southern end of the Waste where the landscape points to some earlier enclosure on this, the highest point in Thelwall. Here, on the plan, there are strips labelled 'shoots' (from OE *sceat* meaning strip or furlong)[22] and the modern farm occupying this ground is called 'Howshoots' (OE *hoh* 'land on spur of a hill')[23] (see Figure 5 and Plate 7). The name 'Howshoots' appears several times on the 1743 plan so the name was established by then. Thus, the enclosure of this farm and its strips may well pre-date the more radical enclosure of the Waste that was in progress. The area in question is triangular in shape so its shoots were of varying lengths up to about 290 yards and more typically 240 yards long (265 and 219 metres). The shoots, which were straight rather than having a 'reverse-S' shape, were on either side of Cinder Lane but their

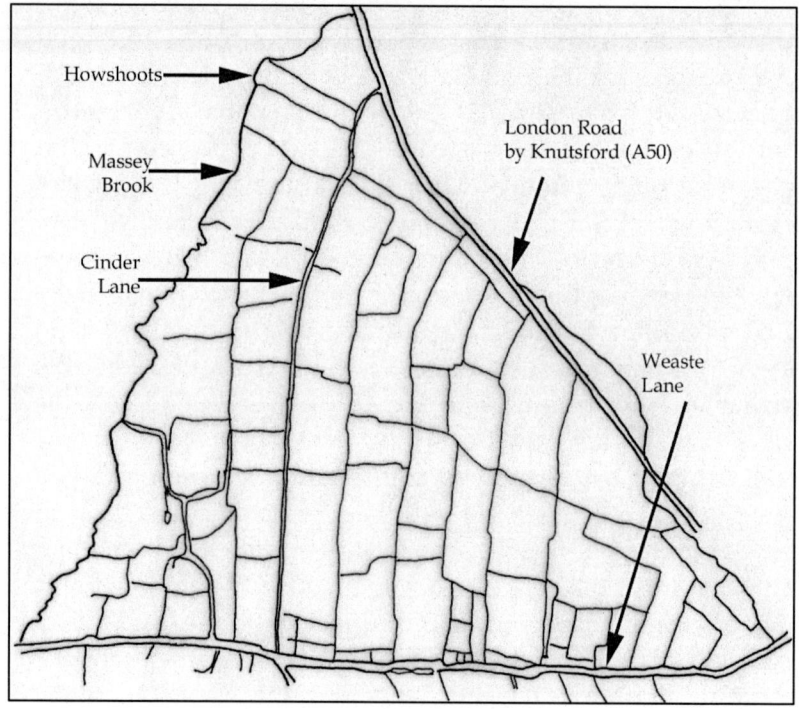

Figure 5: The Waste in 1845; by this date it was fully enclosed (drawn from Tithe Map of *c*.1845).

The Eighteenth-Century Landscape of Thelwall

boundaries were not in register with each other across the track so the track is presumed to pre-date the strips. These remain to be studied.

Thus, the 1743 estate map gives a snapshot of the landscape during a planned and systematic scheme to divide up and enclose a large part of the Waste whilst respecting one corner that had already been enclosed. By the time of the Tithe Award (1845), all the Waste had been enclosed and some consolidation of fields had already occurred.

The Central Part of the Township
Although they are difficult to identify in surviving maps, the great open fields of Thelwall were probably close to the principal group of farms and dwellings that is situated around a bend in the River Mersey where there were two minor fords. The likely names of the fields were Ascroft, Marstow(e) and, possibly, Town Field.

The 1743 map has a surprise because it shows strips (called 'Loonts' – a dialect name for strips) surviving in two of these fields. For example, in Figure 6, we can see that the field closest to the village was divided in this way. Someone (judging by the handwriting, it was Thomas Percival) helpfully added the names of the occupiers of each strip, for instance 'Ellin Rowson's Loont', plus a measure of the area of that strip. These names include most of the farming families in Thelwall at that time. As drawn, the loonts are short and straight and their presence is challenging. It is doubtful that these strips were the product of traditional open field farming where ploughing year after year would be expected to produce 'reverse-S' strips. However, in the 1700s, a major change was happening in Thelwall and by 1743 many villagers had started growing potatoes in small patches dug out of larger fields such as this one. One task for the future will be to see whether any of the

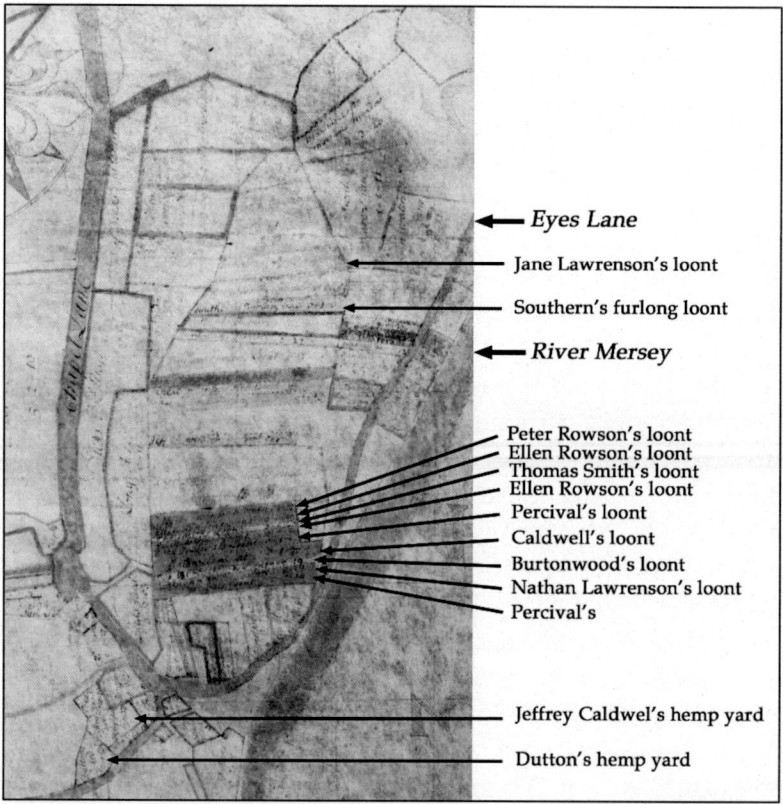

Figure 6: Part of the 1743 Estate map showing a large field, thought to have been an open field, at the centre of the village. It is divided into strips called 'loonts', labelled with the name of the occupier (examples are arrowed). (CALS, DWW 430: reproduced by permission of Cheshire Archives and Local Studies and the owner/depositor to whom copyright is reserved.)

areas shown on this plan correspond with the sizes of potato patches that were measured so that rents could be calculated; these measurements survive. Alas, one field now lies under housing but part of a second, Ascroft, is also shown as strips on the estate map and some of this survives although no signs of the strips are presently visible. They may therefore have been a

The Eighteenth-Century Landscape of Thelwall

short-term feature of the rush to grow potatoes rather than more established plough strips.

The Eyes of Thelwall

Because of their susceptibility to flooding, the Eyes or meadows close to the Mersey have remained undeveloped and retain many characteristics of the eighteenth-century landscape. For instance, the network of ditches and streams flowing towards the Mersey not only survives but still serves its old purpose. Maintenance of these drains used to be a responsibility of the Surveyor of the Highways since, whilst these waterways did not prevent flooding, they speeded up the recovery of the land once water levels receded. In the tracks leading onto the Eyes, we can find small stone bridges, probably built at the township's expense in the eighteenth century. There is a record of one such bridge collapsing into a stream. Local labourers were paid by the Surveyor to recover the stones from the stream and a skilled mason was recruited to rebuild the bridge.

Whilst the Eyes were of great agricultural value, much of the land was lost by a decision to dump spoil on the remoter parts of this riverside land. Part of that area is, today, the Woolston Nature Reserve. However, those fields south of the Canal and closer to the village survive and their boundaries and hedges are still as shown in the 1845 Enclosure Award. They have not changed in 170 years although they have been undergrazed since the BSE epidemic of the 1990s and are tumbling back to scrub. This is the only part of the old Eyes that can now be explored.

The 1743 estate map is of little use here since most of this land some distance from the village was not mapped – presumably because the Lord of the Manor had no financial interest in it or did not intend to enclose it. Fortunately for us, he did keep a close watch on the fishing rights that he owned along with land on the north side of the river, known as Wilgreaves. The Wilgreaves was surveyed for the 1743 plan and, importantly, the map locates the two minor fords in Thelwall, referred to in other records of the 1700s as the 'upper' and 'lower' fords. These allowed farm workers to cross the river. It is said that people, animals and carts were all rafted across the Mersey from one side to the other, a practice which was continued (and photographed) well into the twentieth century for crossing the Ship Canal until a calamitous capsize ended the practice.

From Percival's diary entries, we know that, in the 1740s, one field on Wilgreaves was called 'Ports', another was called 'Barn Field' and a third was 'Port Common'. All of these features are identified on the 1743 map along with some of the strips in Town Field on the south side of the river (Plate 9). The use of the word 'Port' in field-names on the Wilgreaves is puzzling because none of the common meanings of this word (such as 'market') seem to fit here. It occurs elsewhere (for instance, 'Port Meadow' in Oxford) on similar riverside land. It is suggested that for Thelwall, it may derive from 'portage' where cargoes might have been carried across the neck of land for onward shipment to ease navigation over the shallows (including two fords) and a difficult bend in the river.[24] A little nearer to Warrington, another bend in the Mersey was known by sailors as 'Hellhole' and that at Thelwall was equally daunting.

Conclusions
This has been a progress report on a project to compare the present landscape around Thelwall with maps and records of the eighteenth century. In the intervening 300 years, the population of Thelwall has risen from about 300 to at least ten times that today.[25] Much of the manorial park has now been

The Eighteenth-Century Landscape of Thelwall

built on with ribbon development along all the roads and lanes. There is much pressure to build more but there is still time to examine the landscape and identify features that have survived over this period.

So, what has survived? In the surrounding built environment, there is very little. Some remarkable buildings have gone in the last 60 years (for instance, the shameful destruction of Thelwall's Dovecot and its timber-framed Garland Hall (Figures 7, 8)) and the few old buildings that remain are under persistent threat. For instance, the 1770s warehouse at Stockton Quay, contemporary with the building of the Bridgewater Canal, survives only because of public action. The other major change to Thelwall's landscape dates to the closing decades of the nineteenth century when the Manchester Ship Canal was cut through the Eyes, severing several hundred acres from the rest of Thelwall and destroying most of it.

However, much of the remaining landscape in Thelwall and Grappenhall is still agricultural and it is here that we can look for signs of centuries of farming. The eighteenth century saw the enclosure of the Waste in Thelwall. Despite some consolidation of fields, traces of those efforts can still be seen.

Figure 7: Sketch of Columbarium before demolition. The dovecot was a relic of the old hall at Thelwall which was replaced in 1755. The Columbarium survived until the mid-1950s.

Figure 8: Garland Hall in Weaste Lane, Thelwall.

The Eighteenth-Century Landscape of Thelwall

Further down the slope, much of the best agricultural land in the township has been built on so there is now little evidence of the large fields that must at one time have constituted an enviable and productive mixed arable and pasture environment. Out on the surviving areas of grazing land on the Eyes, the landscape appears unaltered since the 1845 Tithe Award; fields and hedges seem the same. There is no reason why these features should not date back much further than 1845 but the evidence is absent because they were not surveyed for the earlier map.

There is plenty of walking and photography still needed to record the landscape of Thelwall. Some of the surviving part of the Eyes has not yet been explored. A photographic record is also needed of the historic built landscape; an intact eighteenth-century farmhouse in Thelwall with its set of barns is presently being 'developed'. An application to list this group of buildings was rejected because 'they are not rare in Cheshire'. Maybe not but it was the last in Thelwall. So, there is plenty of scope for further research.

References and notes
1. The most important records are the EGT/4 series (about 84 papers) of the Egerton of Tatton Muniments held at John Rylands Library, Manchester. The Town Book for Thelwall (Mf. ENGL18010/41/6/170120 MF49) and the Pocket Books of Thomas Percival of Thelwall (3 vols), reference MS1648, are both held in the Local History Section at Warrington Library. The Estate Maps (1743) of John Pickering, reference DWW 1/429-31, are held at CALS, Chester (see note 2).
2. Estate Map of Lands Belonging to John Pickering Esq, 1743; Extracts reproduced with the permission of Cheshire Archives and Local Studies: CALS, DWW 1/429-31 (3 sheets).
3. *Bagshaw's Directory*, 1850, reproduced in CALS township pack 88 'Thelwall' (1999).

4. The Town Book (see note 1) for the 1740s records 62 rateable properties, a few of which were not houses but only land. However, cottages accommodating people on the Overseer of the Poor's lists were not subject to Town Rate so it is suggested that the best estimate of houses is about 60.
5. Journey mentioned in the Pocket Books of Thomas Percival (see note 1).
6. J. Nicholson, 'Chronicles of Thelwall, Co. Chester', *The Topographer and Genealogist*, I (1846), 379–94 and 431–68.
7. A.H. Judson, A.J. Linnard, M. Henry, *Christian Biography: Lives of William Cowper* (Religious Tract Society, London, 1 Jan. 1799).
8. See 'Lancashire Online', <<http://lan-opc.org.uk/warrington/>>, accessed 4 Apr. 2015.
9. The chaotic financial affairs of the Pickerings of Thelwall are described in M.F. Taylor, *Debtors' Retreat* (Thelwall, 2013).
10. Known as 'London Road by Knutsford' to distinguish it from the 'London Road by Holmes Chapel' road that ran through Stockton Heath.
11. M.F. Taylor, *Thomas Percival's Pocket Books: The Pocket Books of an 18th Century Resident of Thelwall in Cheshire, 1741 to 1755* (Thelwall, 2014).
12. P.P. Burdett, *A Survey of the County Palatine of Cheshire of 1777*, eds J.B. Harley and P. Laxton (Hist. Soc. of Lancs. and Ches., occasional ser., I, 1974).
13. The present London Road (A49).
14. J. Dolan, *From Barn to Chapel, The Story of Stockton Heath Independent Methodist Church* (Cheshire, 1989).
15. B.K. Roberts and S. Wrathmell, *Region & Place: A Study of English Settlement* (Swindon, 2002), 97.
16. Taylor, *Pocket Books*, 3 Jan. 1750.
17. Taylor, *Pocket Books*, 25 Jan. 1743.
18. J. McN. Dodgson, *The Place-Names of Cheshire*, II (Cambridge, 1970), 97.
19. A. Crosby and J. Haynes, *Warrington for Ever* (Barnsley, 2006), 135.
20. Taylor, *Pocket Books*, 8.

21. E. Pollard, M.D. Hooper and N.W. Moore, *Hedges* (London, 1974), 79–85.
22. Dodgson, *Place-Names of Cheshire*, II, 140.
23. H.D.G. Foxall, *Shropshire Field Names* (Shrewsbury, 1980), 15.
24. Oral communication with M. Handley, following a talk given by the author to Merseyside Archaeological Society, 21 Jan. 2016.
25. All modern population estimates are for the combined Civil Parish of Grappenhall and Thelwall and there is no separate figure for Thelwall. A reasonable guess would be between 3,000 and 4,000.

6

WHEN WAS COLWYN BAY?

Mike Headon

Colwyn Bay is a town and formerly prosperous holiday resort in North Wales. Old Colwyn, still identifiable as a distinct settlement, lies 2 kilometres east of Colwyn Bay's parish church of St Paul, built in 1887–95.

This paper looks at when and how Colwyn Bay acquired its name, and how Old Colwyn became 'Old'. It also looks at a number of other names that were used for the emergent settlement, and tries to identify the geographical, social, commercial and political factors that led to their use (Figure 1).

Geographical and Administrative Background

The resort town of Colwyn Bay was created within the parish of Llandrillo-yn-Rhos in the extreme north-western corner of historical Denbighshire,[1] and extended from what is now Rhos-

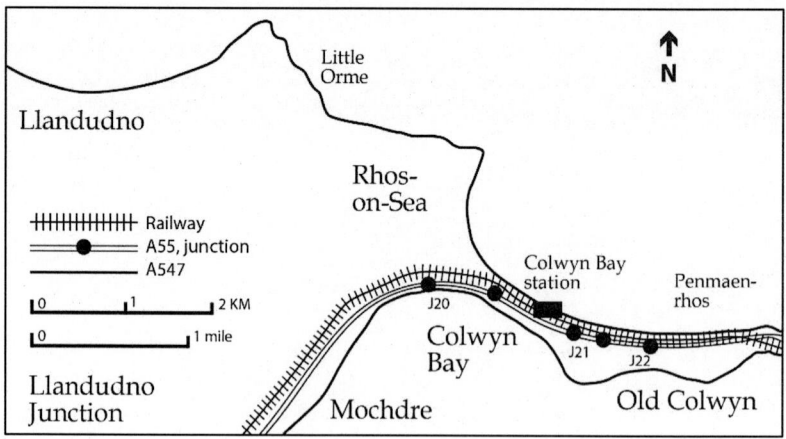

Figure 1: Location of Colwyn Bay today.

188

When was Colwyn Bay?

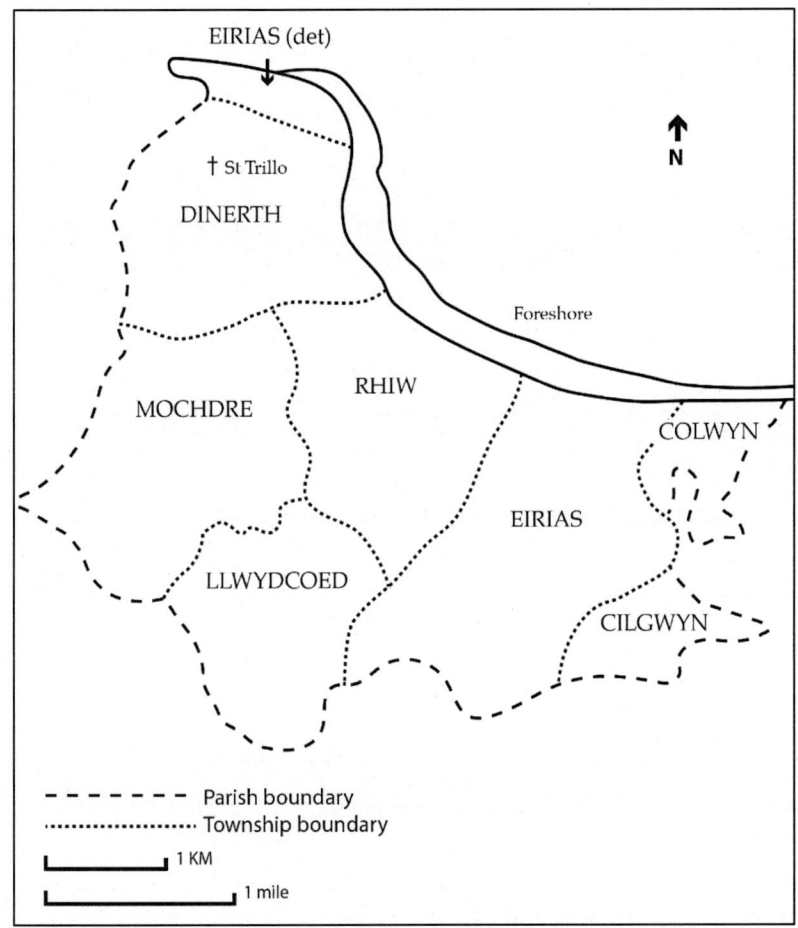

Figure 2: Townships within the parish of Llandrillo-yn-Rhos, 1847.

on-Sea in the west to the headland of Penmaenrhos in the east, and southwards nearly as far as the Holland Arms on the B5113 to Llanrwst.

At the time of the Tithe Award in 1847, the parish contained the townships of Cilgwyn, Colwyn, Dinerth, Eirias, Llwydcoed,

Mochdre and Rhiw, and was 2,128.6 hectares (5,260 acres) in extent, including the 392.6 hectares (970 acres) in Eirias township, a detached part of Caernarvonshire (Figure 2).

At the beginning of the nineteenth century, there were two small nucleated settlements in the parish: Mochdre ('pig farm') in the west, overlooked by Bryn Euryn, and Colwyn in the east, straddling the Afon Colwyn which separated Colwyn and Eirias townships. *Colwyn* is an obsolete Welsh word for a puppy or small animal, applied to frisky streams that tumble over rocks; the township name is recorded as *Coloyne, Coleyne* in 1334.[2] There were also a few small hamlets, generally with one or two farms and their cottages; the largest was Groes, at what is now the entrance to Eirias Park. Plate 10 shows a view across the fields of Colwyn to the sea in 1845; Rhiw township is on the extreme left.

Tenurial Background

The Tithe Award of 1847 shows the parish in multiple ownership – indeed, a list of the owners of the land crossed by the Chester to Holyhead Railway (C&HR), whose building coincided with the tithe survey, reads to some extent like a *Who's Who* of the landowning gentry of North Wales: from east to west, John Hughes, solicitor; Edward Lloyd of Cefn; John Lloyd Wynne of Coed Coch; Catherine Clough of Min-y-don, a member of the Denbighshire Clough family; Henry Hesketh of Glan-y-don, a member of the Hesketh family of Chester and Gwrych; Lady Erskine of Pwllycrochan; Whitehall Dod, a member of the family of Llannerch Park; John Foulkes, a local freeholder; Thomas Peers Williams of Craig-y-don near Beaumaris; Robert Jones of Bryn-ffanugl; and Edward Mostyn Lloyd Mostyn of Mostyn Hall, a member of the Mostyn dynasty.[3]

When was Colwyn Bay?

One section of the parish did, however, form a compact block in single ownership. The whole township of Rhiw, 287 hectares (708 titheable acres), along with 243 hectares (600 acres) of the adjacent township of Llwydcoed, formed the Pwllycrochan (or Pwllycrochon) estate. The estate belonged to the dowager Lady Erskine of Pwllycrochan. She had inherited the estate as Jane Silence Davies in 1809, and had married Sir David Erskine of Cambo in Fife, who died in 1841. It was the decision of their son Thomas to sell the estate in 1865 that is usually seen as the beginning of the development of the resort of Colwyn Bay. The house Pwllycrochan (Welsh *pwll*, pool, pit, hollow, *y*, definite article, *crochan*, cauldron, probably referring to the stream serving the house) stood near the top of what is now Pwllycrochan Avenue. The present building (rebuilt in 1821; remodelled in 1841; Figure 3)[4] is now part of Rydal Penrhos School.

Figure 3: Pwllycrochan, *c.*1905. By permission of Conwy Archive Service.

Landscapes Past and Present

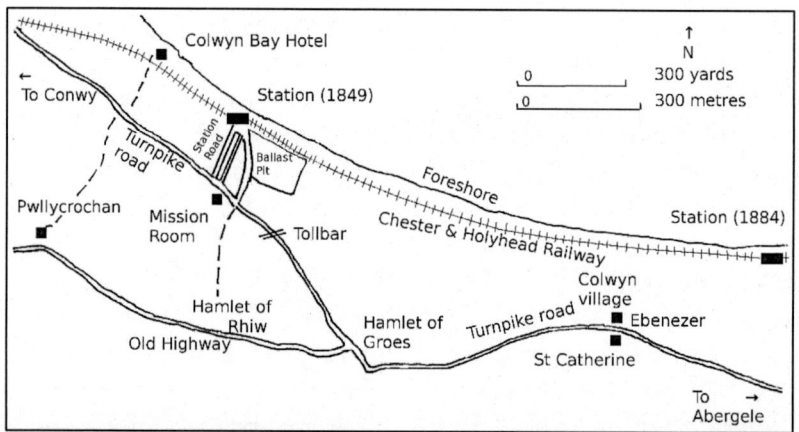

Figure 4: Places mentioned in the text.

Rhiw township (Welsh *rhiw*, a hill) lay on the north coast of the parish, between Eirias and Dinerth townships (Figures 2 and 4). A narrow flattish coastal strip, no more than 260 metres wide, lay to the north of the modern A547, and then the land rose steeply to the south. No nucleated settlement existed in Rhiw at the start of the nineteenth century; a small hamlet called Rhiw, made up of two or three farms and their cottages, clustered around the junction of Rhiw Road and the Old Highway. The Old Highway was the original west–east highway, running across the hillside to avoid the more difficult ground down by the sea. Otherwise, settlement consisted of dispersed farms. The census returns show that there were about twenty named places in 1821 – a number which does not vary by more than one or two between 1841 and 1861.[5]

The Name of the Bay
The northern boundary of the parish is formed by the sea bay that lies between Rhos Point and Penmaenrhos (Figure 1). The most prominent landmark between these points is St Trillo's,

When was Colwyn Bay?

the parish church of Llandrillo-yn-Rhos, standing on the top of its hill, traditionally whitewashed. Its tower is said to have been built in 1552.[6] A turret was added to the south-west corner of the tower, *c*.1600, to act as a beacon or lookout, making the profile of the church unmistakable. It was said to be called 'the Rector's Chair'. It was and still is possible to beach small boats in the bay. The tithe map of 1847 shows a coal yard situated at the mouth of the Afon Colwyn, but later in the nineteenth century cargo boats would have regularly moored at the small industrial settlement that stood where Rhos-on-Sea now stands. Their cargo was limestone, brought down to the quay from the quarry on Bryn Euryn by a tramway running parallel to Rhos Road; remnants of its course were still visible in the 1970s. This hamlet was known as Glan-y-mor or Rhos-fynach; the name Rhos-on-Sea did not become current until the area was developed for tourism at the turn of the twentieth century.

Before the development of the resort town, the bay was known by several names, all taken from the parish name or elements within it: 'Llandrillo-yn-Rhos Bay', 'Llandrillo Bay', 'Rhos Bay'. For example, in 1797 the Revd Edward Edwards, rector of Llanrwst, wrote to the government expressing his concerns about the possibility of an enemy landing at 'Llandidno, *Llandrillo Bay*, or both'.[7] In 1840, on the first Ordnance Survey 1-inch to the mile map of the area (sheet 79, Denbigh; NW quarter), the bay is marked as *RHÔS BAY*, as it is on the first edition of the OS 6-inch map (Denbighshire sheet 3), published in 1879.[8] The shipping news published regularly in the *Liverpool Mercury* generally referred to 'Rhos Bay', as on 30 September 1853: 'The flat *Rhydland Trader*, bound for Llandudno, was driven on shore in *Rhos Bay* on Monday morning. The crew were saved',[9] while in 1895, the Board of Trade Harbour Department gave its assent to the construction of an outfall sewer in *Llandrillo Bay*.[10]

It is clear that the new settlement did not take its name directly from the bay. Even so, we shall see that the name 'Colwyn Bay' was occasionally applied to the sea bay in the nineteenth century.

Early Days
The old village of Colwyn, straddling the townships of Colwyn and Eirias, was the most densely populated part of Llandrillo-yn-Rhos parish but the furthest from the parish church. Nonconformist causes grew rapidly from the late eighteenth century, and in 1815 Ebenezer Independent chapel was founded in the village.[11] To combat the growth of Nonconformism, St Catherine's church was built opposite it in 1837 as a chapel of ease (Figure 4), and in 1844 the townships of Colwyn and Eirias were detached to create the new ecclesiastical parish of Colwyn, with St Catherine's as the parish church.[12]

It is also in 1844 that we find the first recorded use of the name 'Colwyn Bay', though not yet with reference to any settlement. Figure 5 shows an advertisement for a property sale that appeared in the *Chester Chronicle*, the *North Wales Chronicle* and the *Liverpool Mail* in November 1844 and again in August 1845.[13]

The house referred to as 'Cefn Elian' is the one more usually known as 'Cefn-y-ffynnon' (Welsh *cefn*, ridge, back, *ffynnon*, well), whose grounds contain the notorious cursing well of St Elian – a sort of negative holy well. It stands above Colwyn village in Groes Road on the parish boundary, less than a kilometre from St Elian's church in Llanelian-yn-Rhos. It was 'Cefn-y-ffynnon' (various spellings) in 1817 (Llandrillo-yn-Rhos parish registers),[14] 1840 and 1879 (OS maps), 1847 (Tithe Award), and the 1851 and 1861 censuses, so calling it 'Cefn Elian' was presumably a marketing ploy to emphasise the

When was Colwyn Bay?

> IN NORTH WALES.
> PEREMPTORY SALE OF SINGULARLY INTERESTING FREEHOLD PROPERTY, ADMIRABLY ADAPTED FOR THE ERECTION OF A MARINE RESIDENCE, AND A MOST ADVANTAGEOUS INVESTMENT.
> On TUESDAY, the 19th instant, at Three o'clock in the Afternoon, at the Bee Hotel, Abergele, in the county of Denbigh—subject to conditions then to be produced,
> ALL that MESSUAGE or DWELLING-HOUSE, with the Outbuildings, Farm, and LANDS thereunto belonging, called "Cefn Elian," containing by a recent survey 66A. 1R. 27P. or thereabouts, situate in the parish of Llandrillo, in the county of Carnarvon, now in the occupation of William Williams.
> This Estate is most delightfully situated on an eminence midway between Abergele and Conway, overlooking the beautiful Bay of Colwyn, and commanding a most extensive view of the Irish Sea and the magnificent promontories of the Great Ormshead and Penmaenmawr, and within One Mile of the Chester and Holyhead Road, along which her Majesty's mails pass and repass four times a day. The new line of Railway from Chester will traverse the coast of Colwyn Bay. The farfamed Well of St. Elian, better known as "Ffynon Elian" on this Property, forms a feature of interest to the curious, by the many traditions and reputed mysteries connected with it.
> The Land is in a good state of cultivation and very productive.
> For further particulars apply to Messrs. WILLIAMS and BARKER, Solicitors, Portmadoc, from whom a plan of the Estate may be obtained; to T. LL. ROYLE, Esq., Llanfyllin; or C. B. TEECE, Esq., Shrewsbury.

Figure 5: *Liverpool Mail*, 16 Aug. 1845. By permission of the British Newspaper Archive.

connection with the well. The seller, presumably Edward Lloyd, owner of the Cefn estate, was clearly expecting the area to be developed with the coming of the railway, and to present the well as a tourist attraction. The 'recent survey' will have been the survey for the Tithe Award (not confirmed till 1847), which gives this exact figure for the total area. The house was bought by Lloyd Hesketh Bamford Hesketh of Gwrych Castle; William Williams remained as the tenant.

We may note that the author of the advertisement uses 'Bay of Colwyn' for the bay itself and 'Colwyn Bay' to mean 'the recreational area along the coastal strip, associated with Colwyn village'. These names were by no means established usage. Seven years later, the *Liverpool Mercury* carried an advertisement on 18 July 1851 for the sale of the house called 'Tŷ-newydd' in Eirias township. The advertisement is headed LANDRILLO IN RHOS BAY and subheaded 'Delightfully adapted for bathing', indicating that the area was regarded as a bathing venue well before the resort town was constructed.[15] The advertiser has created a new place-name by adding 'the marketable *Bay*'[16] to the anglicised parish name to give 'Llandrillo in Rhos Bay'. Commercial considerations were already in play in the naming of places.

As far as mail was concerned, the address for those houses that might receive mail was simply 'near Conway': a notice in the *Carnarvon and Denbigh Herald* of 24 August 1850, reporting that Lady Erskine entertains local schoolchildren to tea and buns, was headed PWLLYCROCHON, CONWAY;[17] a lease dated 24 December 1853 refers to *Whitehall Dod of Bryn Dinarth near Conway*.[18]

The Railway Station
The Chester and Holyhead Railway began operations on 1 May 1848. Stations were opened at the towns of Abergele to the east and Conwy to the west. The opening of a station at Colwyn had been discussed, but for cash flow reasons it was opened in the second batch of stations the following year; it appears in the January 1850 edition of Bradshaw's monthly timetable as *Colwyn*.[19] In Norman Tucker's *Colwyn Bay: its origin and growth*, the standard history of Colwyn Bay, published in 1953 and on which all subsequent historians have drawn, it is stated that there was an earlier stop to the west called *Pwllycrochan Halt*, said to be for the convenience of Lady Erskine:

When was Colwyn Bay?

> It was stated that Lady Erskine imposed a condition that the Company should provide a 'halt' for her convenience. This was apparently first made at a spot west of Marine Road bridge ... Old residents say that "Pwllycrochan Halt" was the name applied to the first stopping place arranged for Lady Erskine.[20]

Unsupported statements such as 'It was stated that ...', 'Old residents say ...', are untypical of Tucker, a conscientious historian who usually credited specific sources and named his informants. His friend Ivor Wynne Jones describes how Tucker became frustrated with '[t]he strange contract between the old Colwyn Bay Borough Council and [himself]'. The council had required the book to be printed (but not published) in instalments, and 'refused to allow him to make amendments to any of the sheets printed'.[21] In truth, no documentary evidence has been found to date to confirm that there was ever a stopping-place west of the present site of Colwyn Bay station, or with the name 'Pwllycrochan Halt'.

The railway runs westwards along an embankment from the western portal of Penmaenrhos tunnel, continues elevated to cross the Afon Colwyn and other streams, and first drops to the natural ground level at the present (2015) site of Colwyn Bay station (Figure 4). Adjacent to the station was the *Ballast Pit*, from which ballast was obtained for building the railway and which was later used for railway sidings; the site is now occupied by the Bay View Shopping Centre and the modern A55. Station Road forms the main axis of the resort town. It is a short road that links the station to the point near St Paul's church where the main road (now A547) from Abergele to Conwy changes its name from Abergele Road to Conway Road.

The station opened in 1849 and was constructed on the site where the modern station stands (as shown by the mileages given in the January 1850 *Bradshaw*), an easy half an hour's walk westwards from the centre of the village of Colwyn, on land acquired from the Pwllycrochan estate and perfectly convenient for a carriage descending from Pwllycrochan Hall. The *Weekly News* of 8 December 1899 carried an obituary for John Porter, whose importance to the development of Colwyn Bay will be described below. The author of the obituary was in no doubt:

> ... the station on the Chester and Holyhead Railway for the village of Colwyn was where Colwyn Bay station now stands ... No doubt the station was placed at this point, a mile and a half from the village, through the influence of Lady Erskine and as part of the consideration for the purchase of the land.[22]

The story of 'Pwllycrochan Halt' may be a rationalisation of this local railway history, or it is also possible, of course, that 'Pwllycrochan Halt' was an unofficial local name for Colwyn station – the inhabitants of Colwyn would have observed that the station was much nearer to Pwllycrochan Hall than to their own homes. In addition, Colwyn was a low status, 'second class' station with few facilities and so may have been seen as a 'halt'. While the 1851 census records stationmasters at Abergele and Conwy, there was not one at Colwyn. The census records the only resident as eighteen-year-old William Fox, Assistant Clerk in Railway Station Office, with his address given simply as *Station*.

The First Sale of the Pwllycrochan Estate
The first of the two sales of the Pwllycrochan estate that define the development of the resort town took place on 12–15 September 1865.[23] The bulk of Pwllycrochan estate was bought by John (later Sir John) Pender, a submarine cable magnate of Scottish origin. Pender had local connections; his wife's mother, Mrs Denison, lived at Conwy.[24] Pender appointed his former

When was Colwyn Bay?

butler, John Porter, as his land agent. Porter leased Pwllycrochan and opened it as a hotel in 1866. Although Pender is credited with beginning the development of the new resort town, it was Porter and his descendants who were to become important figures in the development of the resort.

Newspaper advertisements for the sale refer to the estate as 'Pwllycrochon ... in the parish of Llandrillo ... close to *the Colwyn Station*'.[25] The sale plan, reproduced by Tucker,[26] is labelled PWLLCROCHON ESTATE IN THE PARISH OF LLANDRILLO YN RHOS. It labels RAILWAY STATION and BALLAST PIT, and, most significantly, it labels the sea bay as COLWYN BAY. The plan shows the estate divided into lots, with access roads laid out in a pattern that can be traced in the present roads of Colwyn Bay, but with no buildings other than Pwllycrochan itself and the existing farms.

The Colwyn Bay Hotel, the Tollbars, and the Vicar's Road

The early 1870s saw the flowering of the resort town. At first, the settlement was defined in terms of its proximity to the railway station. Tucker says that 'an official Calvinistic Methodist record gives this entry: "November 19th, 1871. Report of *Colwyn station* school – average attendance 29". In 1872 the report appears under the heading "*Colwyn Bay*"'.[27] It has not yet been possible to trace this record, but the name 'Colwyn Station' is clearly seen as defining the settlement in 1871.

The most significant development, though, was the opening of the Colwyn Bay Hotel the following year, 1872 (Figure 4). Although the Pwllycrochan Hotel, in the old Erskine mansion, was the first hotel in Colwyn Bay, the first purpose-built structure was the Colwyn Bay Hotel. It stood at the

Figure 6: The Colwyn Bay Hotel, c.1900. By permission of Conwy Archive Service.

junction of what is now Marine Road with the Promenade. The earliest reference to the enterprise is in the name of the development company, which was incorporated in 1871. The *Morning Post* of 30 January 1871 reports 'The following joint-stock companies were registered during the past week ... Colwyn Bay Hotel – capital £20,000, in £10 shares' and Board of Trade records have *Colwyn Bay Hotel Company Ltd* 1871.[28]

As for the physical structure itself (Figure 6), the *North Wales Chronicle* of 1 June 1872 has 'COLWYN BAY HOTEL. – This magnificent building, which stands so prominent upon the brink of the *Colwyn bay*, is fast approaching completion ...'. The issue of 6 July 1872 reads,

> COLWYN BAY HOTEL
> This large and commodious Family Hotel, beautifully situated on the *Bay of Colwyn*, and within a few minutes' walk of the *Colwyn Railway Station*, on the Chester and Holyhead Railway, will be opened for Tourists and Visitors, on Monday, the 15th inst. A limited number of Visitors can be accommodated a few days previous to the above date. –

When was Colwyn Bay?

> Apply for particulars to Miss Liddell, Manager of *Colwyn Bay Hotel, Colwyn, North Wales*;

and on 3 August 1872, the *North Wales Chronicle* reported:

> COMPLETION OF THE *COLWYN BAY HOTEL*
> The delightful neighbourhood of *Colwyn* is becoming more popular as a summer resort for visitors every year. ... a few weeks since the above hotel ... was completed.

[followed by a report of a dinner for the construction workers on Friday 26 July 1872]; while the *Cheshire Observer* of 20 July 1872 has

> THE *COLWYN BAY HOTEL*. – This beautifully-situated hotel, overlooking the magnificent *Colwyn Bay*, was formally opened on Monday last.

As a hotel, its name was fixed from the start, but these extracts provide useful information about the other Colwyn names. The sea overlooked by the hotel is *the Colwyn bay* (= 'the bay by Colwyn') or *Colwyn Bay* (the curve of the sea called Colwyn Bay). The address is given as *Colwyn, North Wales*, with no need for reference to nearby post-towns such as Conwy or Abergele.

The hotel name was devised by adding 'the marketable *Bay*' to the name of the original settlement, 'Colwyn'. A newly built road, 450 metres long (later lost to development), linked the hotel to the railway station, emphasising the fact that these were the two most significant structures in the new development. It was the hotel that had the edge, though, and the change from 'Colwyn Station' to 'Colwyn Bay' in the Calvinistic Methodist record mentioned above illustrates this.

Nevertheless, other names were also used, even in a semi-official context. The *North Wales Chronicle* of Saturday 11 May 1872 reports and comments on a dispute over turnpike tolls. There was a turnpike gate on the road from Abergele to Conwy (later the A55, now the A547) at the junction of Abergele Road and Station Road. With the construction of new roads in the resort, it became possible to bypass the tollgate. The trustees responded by erecting another gate at the junction of Abergele Road and what is now Greenfield Road, to intercept traffic from (Old) Colwyn. Both gates were therefore in what is now Colwyn Bay; the newspaper comments:

> THE *COLWYN* TOLLGATE
> The iniquitous ... action in erecting a tollbar opposite a public refreshment rooms ... the inhabitants of *Colwyn* were justified in testing the legality of such an obstruction. If trustees are empowered to erect two gates, as they have done at *Colwyn*, within three hundred and sixty yards of each other ...

Following litigation, the original tollgate was demolished, leaving only the new gate (or its replacement) standing at the junction with Greenfield Road, and with a name on it. The same newspaper reports on 1 June 1872, 'The late litigation has, let us hope, ended the strife between the road trustees and the inhabitants of *New Colwyn* ... The Trustees have the name of the gate up – "*New Colwyn*"'. This gate is shown on the first edition of the OS 6-inch map as *Colwyn New T.P.* (Figure 4). We might note that the relationship between railway stations and place-naming practices has frequently been examined, but that with tollgate names less so.

There is further contemporary evidence for the use of the name 'New Colwyn'. Earlier in 1872, the *North Wales Chronicle* of 23 March carried the following as the first of two significant reports:

> COLWYN
> PROPOSED NEW ROAD. – It is with the greatest pleasure that we hear that a scheme has been set on foot to make a new road from the magnificent new hotel at *New Colwyn*, to join the road from Llandudno, near the Little Ormeshead.

When was Colwyn Bay?

> Should this be carried out, the distance to Llandudno would be shortened by about 3½ to 4 miles. The boon to the visitors to Llandudno would be greater even than to the visitors of *Colwyn Bay*, …

The road was indeed built. It was known originally as 'the Vicar's Road', and is now (in 2015) part of the B5115 from Colwyn Bay to Llandudno. The Revd W. Venables Williams, vicar of Llandrillo-yn-Rhos, paid for its construction and charged a toll where the road now enters Penrhyn Bay; this area is still known locally as 'The Tollbar' (Figure 7).

The newspaper report is followed immediately by an extended account of John Pender's ceremonial visit to his new development. Pender had recently been elected MP for Wick Burghs, and 'Upon its becoming known that Mr Pender intended visiting his estate, it was resolved … to give him a hearty welcome after his success'. The report locates the Pwllycrochan estate in 'the neighbourhood of *Colwyn*'; the Pwllycrochan Hotel is so busy that it had been found necessary

Figure 7: The B5115 that replaced the Vicar's Road, looking east from The Tollbar; the tower of St Trillo's church is visible top centre.

to build a new hotel (the Colwyn Bay Hotel) 'located in the very centre of *Colwyn bay*' (here the coastal strip is meant), and 'it may reasonably be hoped that *Colwyn* will be in a few years one of the most populous watering-places on the Welsh coast'. As Pender and his party arrived at *Colwyn Station*, the town was decorated, the militia band played, cannons were fired, a local holiday was declared, and the Revd W. Venables Williams read an address from the parishioners of Llandrillo-yn-Rhos, signed by himself and the two churchwardens. It is interesting to note that the Vicar uses only the old parish name, with no reference to 'Colwyn'. Pender's party included his wife, his land agent Charles Ewing of Golden Grove, Chester, and his architect John Douglas of Chester.

Venables Williams was a figure of equal stature with Porter in the development of the new resort, though for different reasons. He was an enthusiastic writer of letters to the local press, and much can be learned about the early history of the resort from the entertainingly vituperative correspondence that he generated, often concerning financial matters. One group of his enemies were the local Nonconformist farmers, who staunchly refused to pay tithes to the established church.[29] Venables Williams's argument with the Nonconformists seems to have been fiscal rather than doctrinal – he invited Porter, a Scots Presbyterian, to become a churchwarden at St Trillo's.[30]

On Saturday 17 August 1872, the *North Wales Chronicle* published a letter from Venables Williams that, by implication only, illustrates another of his concerns:

> Sir.-
> Last year in consequence of the fast increasing population at *Rhos Bay*, near the Colwyn station, it occurred to me that it was necessary to have a Sunday service there, accordingly in the second week in June I commenced an afternoon service in a long open shed used for a sawing machine,

When was Colwyn Bay?

> kindly lent me for the purpose by Mr Abel Roberts. ... However, in the spring of this year ... I determined upon building a *mission chapel* on a piece of land given by Sir Thomas Erskine, Bart. The first sod was cut on Tuesday, May 21st. The building, which is a very neat one, was opened June 18th.

There are two points of interest here. The first is the reference to the 'mission chapel'. This building can be seen marked on the first edition of the OS 6-inch map (1879) as *Mission Room*. The original structure was burnt down in 1886 following threats from tithe agitators. Significantly, this structure stood in the exact spot where St Paul's church would be erected from 1887 onwards (Figure 4).

The second point is Venables Williams's use of the name 'Rhos Bay'. By using the traditional name of the sea bay for the new resort, he may have been consciously or unconsciously attempting to ensure that the new development should have a name that associated it with the parish name of Llandrillo-yn-Rhos rather than with the village name 'Colwyn'. Venables Williams, who had held the incumbency since 1869, would have been aware that the most densely populated part of Llandrillo-yn-Rhos parish, the village of (Old) Colwyn, had been detached to create the new ecclesiastical parish of 'Colwyn' in 1844. Now a new densely populated nucleated settlement was growing up, its nucleus being the area around the railway station and the new mission room. The census reveals that the population of Rhiw township increased from 175 in 1871 to 1,050 in 1881.[31]

He would have had the foresight to realise that this new concentration of population might also be lost to the mother parish, and this did indeed happen during his incumbency, in 1893, when the new ecclesiastical parish of Colwyn Bay was created out of the townships of Rhiw and Llwydcoed, leaving only the townships of Dinerth and Mochdre in the mother parish.

The following year, the *Cheshire Observer* of 2 August 1873 reports on a choir outing:

> This year they avoided Snowdon, and proceeded to *Colwyn*, where they enjoyed a day of pleasure not soon to be forgotten by those who shared in it. The day was fair and beautiful, and the *Bay of Colwyn* lay like a huge crystal set in an emerald frame of wooded hills. What the Bay of Naples is to Italy, truly is *Colwyn Bay* to Wales. ... Having explored the neighbourhood, they returned to *Colwyn Bay Hotel*, where a sumptuous tea was provided ....

Here, 'Colwyn' is the old village, 'Bay of Colwyn' is the sea, 'Colwyn Bay' is the recreational coastal strip, and 'Colwyn Bay Hotel' is used as a place-name – note the absence of the definite article.

The hotel was demolished in 1974–75, a sad loss to the architecture of the town, which had grown up in the area defined by the railway station and the hotel. Its importance to place-name studies is, as suggested by Owen and Morgan,[32] that the name of the hotel was a strong influence on the naming of the settlement.

The Second Sale of the Pwllycrochan Estate

Suffering cash flow problems following the breaking of one of his submarine cables, Pender put the estate up for sale again. This second sale took place on 12 October 1875. Porter bought the freehold of the Pwllycrochan Hotel, while the bulk of the estate was bought by the *Colwyn Bay and Pwllycrochan Estate Company*, a Manchester syndicate. Like Porter, the Estate Company (Figures 8a, 8b) was to play an important part in the development of the resort.

When was Colwyn Bay?

Figures 8a and 8b: The Estate Office of the Colwyn Bay and Pwllycrochan Estate Company, in Conway Road as it appears today – note engraved sign (Figure 8b) which is top left in Figure 8a.

To some extent the name chosen for the development company appears tautologous; it suggests uncertainty about what is exactly defined by the name 'Colwyn Bay'. Possibly it was simply a recognition of the commercial difference between the resort development on the shore ('Colwyn Bay') and the estate farms on the hillsides ('Pwllycrochan Estate').

A report headed COLWYN BAY, by a correspondent of the *Christian World*, was published in the *North Wales Chronicle* (4 September 1875) and several other newspapers. It said 'I ... fled the following week to the peaceful tranquillity of *Colwyn Bay*. A more striking disparity between the stillness of last Sabbath at *Colwyn Bay* and the bustle of the previous one at Blackpool would be difficult to find.' Subsequent mentions of 'Colwyn Bay' show clearly that the town itself is meant, and the fact that this report was syndicated widely in newspapers throughout England and Wales demonstrates that the name for the town was now instantly recognisable.

The railway station had been raised to first-class status in 1873 following the opening of the Colwyn Bay Hotel, as reported in the *Llangollen Advertiser* of 16 May 1873: 'In consequence of the increasing traffic at *Colwyn*, it will be raised to the position of a first-class railway station ...'. Now, in 1876, when the name of the new resort had settled, the station was renamed 'Colwyn Bay' – Bradshaw's timetable guide for December 1875 has *Colwyn*, that for January 1876 *Colwyn Bay*.[33] One may speculate that the impetus for the change came at least partly from the development company, the Colwyn Bay and Pwllycrochan Estate Company, keen to market its new product. It is from this date, January 1876, that we can say that the resort town was unambiguously known as 'Colwyn Bay'.

When was Colwyn Bay?

Getting Old

Like many smaller railway companies, the Chester and Holyhead Railway Company was soon swallowed by one of the giants: the line was worked by the London & North Western Railway from 1856 and vested in the LNWR in 1859.[34] In April 1884, perhaps in an attempt to capitalise on increased local traffic caused by the growth of the resort, they opened another station in what is now Old Colwyn. This was called 'Colwyn'. Figure 9, taken from the *Llangollen Advertiser* of 25 April 1884, reveals that this caused some confusion for holidaymakers. A year later the *North Wales Express* reported that 'the London and North Western Railway Company have decided that the name of *"Colwyn"* Station will be altered to *"Old Colwyn"*'. An advertisement for the Pwllycrochon (*sic*) Hotel in the July 1888 edition of Bradshaw warns 'Please note the Station – *Colwyn Bay* – not *Colwyn*'.[35]

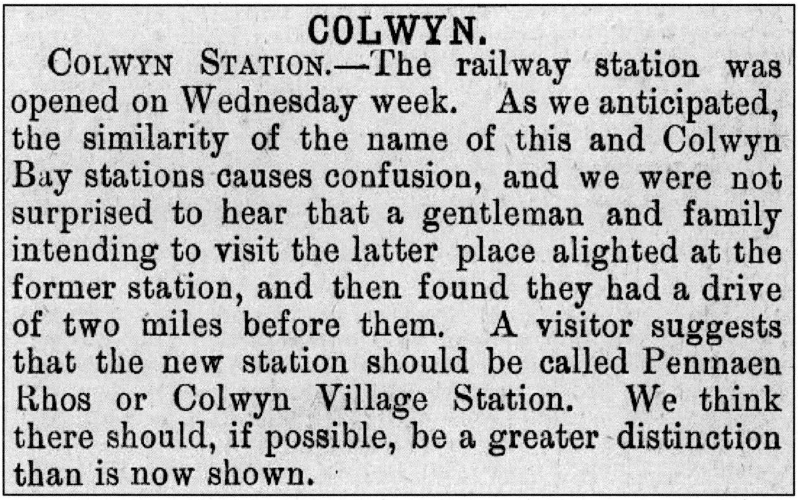

> **COLWYN.**
> COLWYN STATION.—The railway station was opened on Wednesday week. As we anticipated, the similarity of the name of this and Colwyn Bay stations causes confusion, and we were not surprised to hear that a gentleman and family intending to visit the latter place alighted at the former station, and then found they had a drive of two miles before them. A visitor suggests that the new station should be called Penmaen Rhos or Colwyn Village Station. We think there should, if possible, be a greater distinction than is now shown.

Figure 9: *Llangollen Advertiser*, 25 Apr. 1884. By permission of Llyfrgell Genedlaethol Cymru/The National Library of Wales.

The name 'Old Colwyn' had been in use for several years by then: on 8 June 1878, the *Wrexham Guardian* reported on a case of drunken assault on a policeman by the farmer of *Tŷ-newydd, Old Colwyn*, and on 31 August 1878, the *North Wales Chronicle* reports on a dishonest cabman whose passenger had wanted to go from Llandudno to *Colwyn Bay* and then decided to go on to *Old Colwyn*.

As with Colwyn Bay, we may say that the village of Old Colwyn became unambiguously known by its affix 'Old' following the renaming of the new station. This was not the case with officialdom, however, which recognised the distinction between the two settlements but ignored the affix: the local government reforms of the 1880s and 1890s saw the creation of the *Colwyn Bay and Colwyn Urban Sanitary District* and subsequently the *Colwyn Bay and Colwyn Urban District Council*.[36]

Later Developments

The name *New Colwyn* was revived in the next generation, when its former use had presumably been forgotten: on 2 November 1900, the *Welsh Coast Pioneer* has a report headed 'The Development of *New Colwyn*'. This refers to the development of Rhos-on-Sea, a separate resort settlement from Colwyn Bay, by the landowner Sir Everard Cayley; here, *New Colwyn* is new not by comparison with Old Colwyn but by comparison with Colwyn Bay itself. The name *Rhos-on-Sea* itself is not recorded before 1898 (*Llandriloo yn Rhos (Rhos-on-Sea)*).[37]

Conclusion

At the end of the nineteenth century, the writer of John Porter's obituary claimed that it was Porter who coined the name 'Colwyn Bay': 'Someone wanted to call it *Pendertown*, but Mr Porter suggested the adoption of the name of the bay on which

When was Colwyn Bay?

it stood.'[38] 'Pendertown' was surely a joke; the second claim sounds feasible, but it is a foundation myth. As we have seen, the process by which places acquire names is liable to be far more complex.

The name 'Colwyn Bay' is interesting for a number of reasons. The township name 'Rhiw' was also the name of an existing hamlet, and so it was never in question as the name of a new settlement. The traditional names of the sea bay, based on the parish name, did not influence the naming of land settlements; rather the other way round. The original names of the railway stations opened in 1849 and 1884 were changed to reflect the newly developed names of the localities they served, the reverse of what often happened elsewhere. The forms 'New Colwyn' and 'Old Colwyn' were not in use contemporaneously – 'New Colwyn' had dropped out of use well before 'Old Colwyn' was adopted. Forms derived from the parish name, like 'Rhos Bay', yielded to forms derived from the name of the nearby ancient village of Colwyn. When 'Colwyn' was used in the name of the Colwyn Bay Hotel, the success of the name 'Colwyn Bay' was assured.

Endnotes
1. Denbighshire pre 1974.
2. *Survey of the Honour of Denbigh 1334*, eds P. Vinogradoff and F. Morgan (British Academy Records of the Social and Economic History of England and Wales, I, London, 1914), 308, 312. Following usual onomastic practice, illustrative instances of place-names are italicised in this study, although they will not have been in the source.
3. Tithe Award for parish of Llandrillo-yn-Rhos: TNA, IR 29/49/57, IR 30/49/57.
4. E. Hubbard, *The Buildings of Wales: Clwyd (Denbighshire and Flintshire)* (Harmondsworth and Cardiff, 1986), 140.

5. Llandrillo-yn-Rhos Vestry Books, 1821: Denbighshire Record Office, PD/46/3/3; Census enumerators' returns: TNA, HO107/1403/11 fos 4–7 (1841); HO107/2519 fos 211–214 (1851); RG09/4358 fos 46–48 (1861).
6. Hubbard, *Buildings of Wales*, 193–94.
7. Home Office: Domestic Correspondence, George III: TNA, HO 42/40/148 fos 318–319.
8. *Reprint of the 1st edn one-inch Ordnance Survey of England and Wales: sheet 25, Denbigh, with notes by J.B. Harley* (Newton Abbot, 1970); *OS 6-inch 1st edn maps of Flintshire and Denbighshire 1869–1875* [CD with PDF files] (Warrington, nd.).
9. Report, *Liverpool Mercury*, 30 Sep. 1853: British Library 19th Century British Newspapers collection, <<find.galegroup.com/bncn/>>, accessed 21 Oct. 2015.
10. Board of Trade Harbour Department: Correspondence and papers: TNA, MT 10/665/4.
11. RCAHMW Coflein NPRN 7590 Ebeneser [spelling in source] Welsh Independent Chapel, <<www.coflein.gov.uk>>, accessed 31 Oct. 2015. The chapel was rebuilt in 1848, 1860 and 1881, and has a small burial ground attached.
12. Together with the remnant of Cilgwyn township, most of which had already been transferred to Llanelian-yn-Rhos parish, and small parts of adjoining parishes.
13. *Chester Chronicle*, 8 Nov. 1844, 15 Nov. 1844; *North Wales Chronicle*, 26 Nov. 1844. Unless otherwise noted, these and all subsequent newspaper reports quoted in this chapter are taken from the National Library of Wales's Welsh Newspapers Online <<newspapers.library.wales>>, accessed 1–31 Oct. 2015. Image: Advertisement, *Liverpool Mail*, 16 Aug. 1845: British Library 19th Century British Newspapers collection.
14. Llandrillo-yn-Rhos parish registers, 1693–1921: Conwy Archives Service, CEP32.
15. Advertisement, *Liverpool Mercury*, 18 Jul. 1851: British Library 19th Century British Newspapers collection.
16. H.W. Owen and R. Morgan, *Dictionary of the Place-Names of Wales* (Llandysul, 2007), 95.

When was Colwyn Bay?

17. Report, *Carnarvon and Denbigh Herald*, 24 Aug. 1850: Welsh Newspapers Online, <<newspapers.online.wales>>, accessed 1-31 Oct. 2015.
18. Lease, 1853: FRO, D/KK 894.
19. Bradshaw Timetables: National Railway Museum, York (NRMY), BRAD 12/1.
20. N. Tucker, *Colwyn Bay: Its Origin and Growth* (Colwyn Bay, 1953), 138, 139.
21. I.W. Jones and N. Tucker, *Colwyn Bay: Its History across the Years* (Ashbourne, 2001), 7-8.
22. Obituary for John Porter, *The Weekly News and Visitors' Chronicle for Colwyn Bay, Colwyn, Llandrillo, Conway, Deganwy and Neighbourhood*, 8 Dec. 1899.
23. The sale also included Bodlondeb estate in Conwy.
24. *North Wales Chronicle*, 23 Mar. 1872.
25. For example, *North Wales Chronicle*, 21 Jan. 1865, 25 Feb. 1865, 18 Mar. 1865, 1 Apr. 1865.
26. Tucker, *Colwyn Bay*, between 144 and 145.
27. Tucker, *Colwyn Bay*, 190.
28. Board of Trade records: TNA, BT31/1589/525. The *Hotel 70 Degrees*, built at Penmaenhead in 1972, briefly changed its name to *Colwyn Bay Hotel* before it was closed and then demolished in 2007.
29. This conflict escalated to actual bloodshed, when in 1887 a detachment of police, supported by troops, was sent to Mochdre to seize livestock in payment of tithe. See, for example, D. Richter, 'The Welsh Police, the Home Office, and the Welsh Tithe War of 1886-91', *Welsh History Review*, XII (1984-85), 1, 5-75 (at 60-63).
30. Obituary for John Porter, *Weekly News*.
31. Census enumerators' returns: TNA, RG10/5738 fos 41-42, 46-48 (1871); RG11/5582 fos 52-73 (1881).
32. Owen and Morgan, *Dictionary*, 95.
33. Bradshaw Timetables: NRMY BRAD 37/12; BRAD 38/1.
34. D.T. Hawkings, *Railway Ancestors* (Stroud, 1995), 205.

35. Bradshaw Timetables: NRMY, BRAD 58/7, page 607. The advertising copy will have been carried over from previous editions.
36. Renamed *Colwyn Bay Urban District Council* in 1926.
37. Owen and Morgan, *Dictionary*, 416.
38. Obituary for John Porter, *Weekly News*.w

7

CHESHIRE AIRFIELDS:
A LEGACY IN THE LANDSCAPE

Antony Barratt

It is difficult to comprehend the simplicity of early airfields. Today we are used to huge terminals and acres of concrete. Early airfields were just flat areas of firm ground. Even as late as the end of the 1920s the Director of Civil Aviation issued an advice note to local authorities on the criteria for providing municipal airports, which included the following:

> The airfield should be close to the town centre to reduce travelling time on the ground;
> It should be sited on the side of the town from which the bulk of the flights are expected, so as to avoid over-flying the town centre, but it should be upwind of any industrial air polluters;
> The surface should be smooth enough to drive a car over it at 20 miles per hour, 'without any inconvenience to the occupants',
> As regards ground support if the land could hold a loaded three ton lorry then it should be capable of receiving planes [of that period].[1]

Whether it was a lack of interest, or the financial difficulties of the time, no authority in Cheshire actually built a municipal airport, although several considered it, including Bebington and Chester. There were one or two isolated places where a flurry of aeronautical enthusiasm flowered, but then faded leaving no marks in the landscape, for example Bidston on Wirral in 1919–20.

Military aviation was originally concentrated in existing army establishments, or near naval bases. Cheshire did not feature in any of these developments. RAF Sealand (a base for the Royal Flying Corps from 1916) was initially intended to be sited on the English side of the border and for about the first ten years of its existence was known as RAF Shotwick, but it was in fact eventually built in Wales.[2] The expansion in Cheshire was most significant in the Second World War. During the conflict about 600 airfields were built nationally, but only seven of these were in Cheshire. Most were in the eastern and southern counties of England. In Cheshire the emphasis was on training, although aircraft manufacturing and assembly also became important. As concrete runways were provided, this led to distinctive patterns of airfield, in that predominantly training airfields received three runways in a triangular layout, whilst production airfields had two runways in a simple cross format. As the war developed some airfields fulfilled both roles.[3]

At locations in Cheshire, airfields were built in the following places:

> Hooton 1917
> Woodford 1926 (developed privately by AVRO Ltd)
> Combermere 1931 (built for private use, grass runways only)
> Ringway 1938 (now Manchester International Airport)
> Burtonwood 1940
> Cranage 1940 (perforated steel plate runways, now taken up)
> Little Sutton 1940 (grass landing strip only)
> Tatton Park 1940 (grass landing strip only)
> Calveley 1942
> Stretton 1942
> Poulton 1943

Additionally some of the army camps had a grass landing strip for light communications aircraft to use. The American Army under General Patton used such planes, and operated a small number at Cranage while the General was based at Knutsford.

Cheshire Airfields

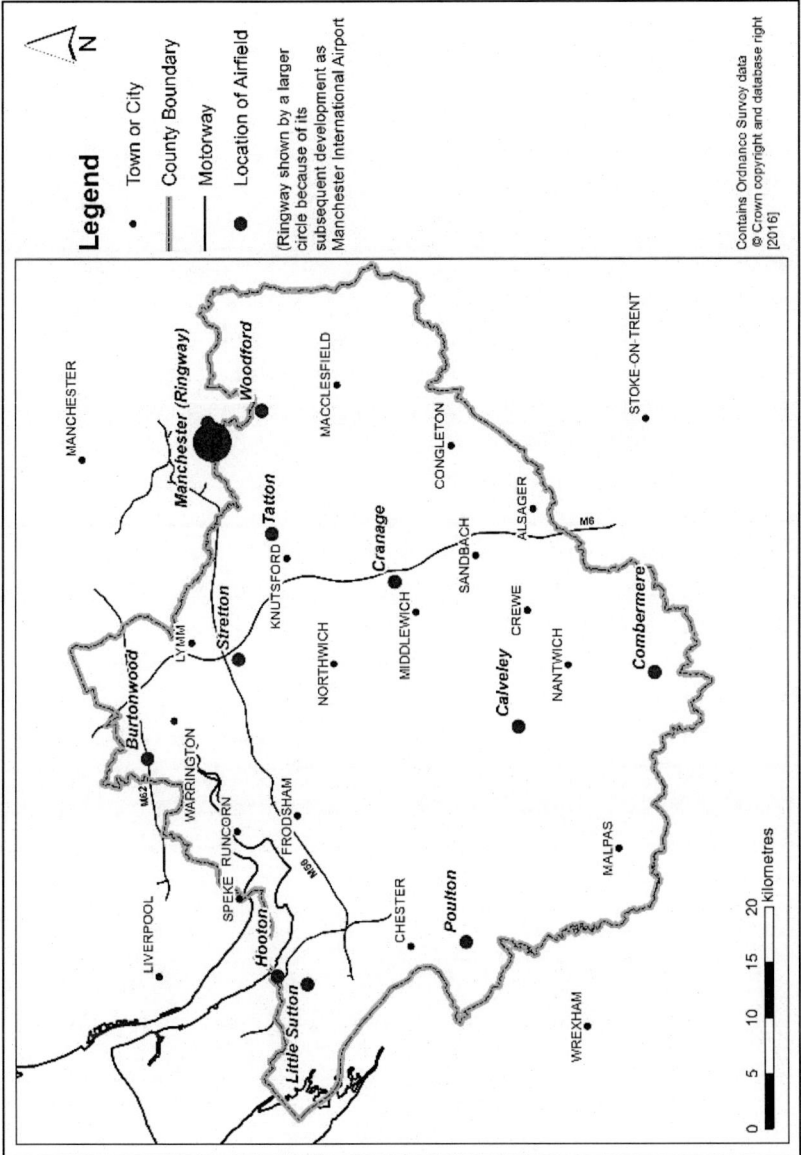

Figure 1: Map showing the location of the Cheshire airfields mentioned in the text. Redrawn by Gary Duckers.

Landscapes Past and Present

This paper will discuss some of the impacts the airfields have had on the landscape of the county. In all cases it meant the eradication of hedges, trees, fields and ditches. Existing buildings were demolished. A chain dragged behind a pair of traction engines was often used to demolish less substantial structures.

Hooton

The oldest airfield in the county, dating from the time of the Royal Flying Corps, is Hooton. Initially it was intended to be a satellite of Sealand airfield. It opened in 1917 as a training station and occupied the polo ground and open land inside the horse racing track, utilising Hooton Hall and outbuildings as the camp. The original hangars were almost certainly canvas ones, although some aircraft were stored under the racecourse grandstand. Four permanent hangars were built, not for the RFC/RAF, but for the assembly of planes imported through Liverpool. No planes came.

With the coming of peace Hooton closed, the land was sold off to local investors and the dilapidated hall was demolished. The new owners aspired to convert the airfield into a civil airfield which at various times was described as the airport for the North West of England and later for Liverpool. It quickly became apparent that it was on the wrong side of the river for Liverpool (the Mersey Tunnel had yet to open), so the City Council, which had acquired the Speke Hall Estate, developed part of it as Speke Airport; this fully complied with the Government's advice. The fourth hangar at Hooton (the smallest) was demolished in about 1920 and the remaining three were sublet as industrial units, to amongst others, the Comper Aircraft Company (which built about 40 aircraft) and Pobjoy Airmotors Ltd, makers of aero engines. For a few months in 1937 there was a passenger service between the Hooton and Speke airfields!

As the prospect of another war began to loom, a Royal Auxiliary Air Force Squadron, 610, the County of Chester Squadron, was based at Hooton and the station was reactivated as a training station. In the early months of the war, anti-submarine patrols were also carried out by requisitioned civil biplanes based at Hooton, some of which had to use pigeons to communicate with base, due to lack of radios. Just prior to the war a group of hangars were constructed at the south-east corner of the airfield for the repair and assembly of aircraft, some of which were to be imported through Liverpool. This time around 10,000 aircraft were assembled or repaired during the course of the war. It was to serve this plant that the concrete runway was laid from 1942 to 1943. A shorter cross runway was also installed.

After the war 610 Squadron returned to Hooton and eventually graduated to jet fighters, but along with the rest of the Royal Auxiliary Air Force it was disbanded as a result of the 1957 Defence Review. Most of the site was quickly sold to

Figure 2: The 1917-built hangars at Hooton (now listed), will hopefully undergo further restoration by the Hooton Park Trust in the future. (Photograph: Martin Barratt.)

Landscapes Past and Present

Figure 3: The remains of Hooton's Second World War main runway in 2015. Note the post-war encroachment of industry in the distance. (Photograph: Martin Barratt.)

Figure 4: The Second World War hangar at Hooton, now used for storage. (Photograph: Martin Barratt.)

Vauxhall Motors for the construction of a car assembly plant. Over the ensuing decades the car plant has gradually expanded. Indeed it looked at one time that the site of old hangars would be required for further construction, but some of the hangars have been given listed status. They are currently in a poor condition, although work is being undertaken which hopefully will arrest further deterioration. The northern portion of the airfield was not sold to Vauxhall; here, a Second World War hangar has subsequently been used for storage and a section of the main runway remains. Interestingly, it appears that the alignment of the runways may have influenced the layout of the car plant in that the line of the main runway and possibly the cross runway seem to be reflected by roadways between the principal buildings of the car plant.[4]

Woodford
During the First World War, A.V. Roe & Co. Ltd (Avro) had numerous manufacturing plants spread throughout various locations in what is now Greater Manchester, and their aircraft flew from one of several airfields across the conurbation. In 1924 the Company decided to rationalise their arrangements and leased New Hall Farm, Woodford to construct an assembly plant. They also built a manufacturing plant at Chadderton, in Greater Manchester.

It was from this assembly plant that thousands of aircraft emerged, including over 4,000 Lancasters, several types of airliners and the famous Vulcan V bomber. The last aircraft to be built was the Nimrod which was cancelled in 2010. Following the cancellation of the Nimrod the plant was closed. Various plans have been aired for the future use of the airfield, including its continued use as an executive aviation centre, with the former assembly building becoming a film studio. However, as time drags on a future aeronautical use becomes more and more remote, and the future increasingly appears to be housing. The existence of the airfield has prevented a large amount of the surrounding land being developed. However, if flying ceases altogether, a built-up area much larger than the airfield will become available for development.[5]

Landscapes Past and Present

Combermere
This site was a private airfield for the use of Sir Kenneth Crossley, the carpet manufacturer, who used to fly to meetings from his home nearby as well as competing in air races. During the war the RAF used it as a relief (emergency) landing ground: the ground conditions were known and so were the alignments of the prepared grass runways. The southern boundary of the airfield is still reflected by field boundaries and the remnants of Sir Kenneth's personal hangar are still on site. Flying does not appear to have resumed after the war and the flying area has been reduced by the insertion of separate field boundaries with accompanying hedges on the northern part of the airfield.

Ringway (now Manchester International Airport)
Ringway, which was then in Cheshire, was one of a number of airfields Manchester Corporation had developed in a little over twenty years. It directly replaced the Municipal Airfield at Barton, which had proved hazardous, particularly as planes got larger. The Fairy Aircraft Company had simultaneously started assembling aircraft manufactured at its Heaton Chapel Works on a portion of the Ringway site.

With the descent to war A.V. Roe & Co. Ltd also started to test and develop aircraft at Ringway, eventually occupying three massive hangars on the south side of the airfield. However, the main role of Ringway was in the training of paratroopers. Initially the plan was to train about 5,000 paratroopers; by the coming of peace more than 70,000 had passed through, including secret agents and resistance fighters.

Almost immediately after the war the airfield was returned to the control of Manchester Corporation and since about 1960 the airport has been constantly developing, which has meant the almost complete disappearance of the wartime structures. Most of the original Fairy site is now in the cargo handling and maintenance areas, while the 1960s terminal was located roughly where the western pier of Terminal 1 is now; the Avro site is now under the second runway and the RAF buildings are under Terminal 3 and car parks. In 2015 further massive development plans were announced, mainly concerning terminals and the concreted aprons for aircraft loading.

The site was placed in the Greater Manchester County in 1974, but part of the second runway extends into what is now the Cheshire East Council area.[6]

Burtonwood
In 1974 Burtonwood was transferred from Lancashire to Cheshire and so is included in this review.

As the demand for aircraft and their production was difficult to co-ordinate, aircraft produced in excess of immediate requirements were stored in wooded areas until needed, or, in the case of Burtonwood, in hangars, if available. This storage role commenced with the initial completion of the airfield in April 1940 and quickly expanded to include the finishing off of aircraft brought through the Mersey ports from overseas for the RAF and Royal Navy. Following the attack on Pearl Harbor and the USA's entry into the war, Burtonwood was selected to assemble and repair aircraft for the American forces, including further aircraft brought in via Liverpool. The site quickly expanded so that within two years it was producing over 400 planes per month. This tempo was maintained, but after VE Day the process went into reverse, with aircraft being dismantled for transfer back to the States, or scrapped. In most cases if the planes had any useful equipment this was salvaged and many of the rest were eventually jettisoned in the North Atlantic.

In due course, as a result of the onset of the Cold War, it was decided that the US Air Force would base bombers in

Europe and they would be maintained at Burtonwood. Before this could happen the base was very heavily involved with maintaining the aircraft involved in the year-long Berlin Airlift. In the early 1950s the Americans started to carry their troops by air rather than by sea, and most of those transited through Burtonwood, for which a passenger terminal was built. By 1958 both the passenger and maintenance functions had been transferred to other stations whilst Burtonwood was placed on a care and maintenance basis. When France left NATO in 1967 the American Army took over the site as a stores depot, but only helicopters used the airfield proper. This arrangement lasted until 1993 when, following the fall of the Berlin Wall, the base was closed. Most of the stores were transferred for use in the first Gulf War.

Virtually all of the 1,800-plus buildings have been demolished and millions of square feet of concrete ripped up and the site is disappearing under residential and commercial development. The main runway after being retained as a V Bomber dispersal site eventually became part of the M62 motorway. Large commercial and retail developers have moved onto the airfield site, including Marks & Spencer and Ikea. But surprises do occur: whilst developing one of the housing areas a wartime retractable pill box was discovered and has been preserved! This type of pill box was used on large airfields and retracted whilst flying operations were underway. Worryingly they were usually provided in groups of three, so the conundrum is: were the other two removed after the war or are they still to be found?

The idea of developing Burtonwood as a replacement for both Ringway and Speke was considered but not pursued, possibly as mining in the area had made intensive use of the runway problematical.[7]

Cranage (sometimes called Byley)

Cranage was always intended to be an Air Navigation School, and this was the role when it opened in the late summer of 1940. However, within weeks it also became a night fighter station, when Hurricane and Defiant fighters moved into the copse on the eastern fringe of the site. When they arrived they had little equipment and indeed had to 'acquire', by fair means and possibly foul, equipment to enable operations to commence. The ground crews utilised tents near the aircraft while flying staff were billeted in nearby properties.

At Cranage the fighters had no sophisticated control rooms – just the eyes and ears of the local Observer Corps. The planes patrolled lines roughly from Farndon to Tabley and Tabley to

Figure 5: This cottage at Cranage is a survivor. There are reports of similar buildings being cleared by dragging a chain between two traction engines and so cutting off the structure at ground level. (Photograph: Martin Barratt.)

Figure 6: One of several pillboxes which have resisted demolition at Cranage. (Photograph: Martin Barratt.)

Congleton, which were thought to be the most likely lines of attacks targeted on Liverpool and Manchester or other northwestern towns. On occasions the aircraft were also used for the defence of Birmingham.

The part of Cranage which had been a navigation school continued in that role until 1945. It never received concrete runways but the grass strips were covered in perforated steel plate mats. These were interlocking steel sections to spread the weight of the plane more evenly over the ground, so preventing the wheels digging into the soft ground. After the war hundreds of the individual sections were rammed vertically into the ground and used as fence posts, barbed wire being strung through the perforations. These fence posts seem to have succumbed to the ravages of nature and have now disappeared.

Cheshire Airfields

The RAF concluded that arrangements for the fighter aircraft at Cranage were not satisfactory, so planned to build three purpose-designed airfields for fighter operations. Two of these were in Cheshire, at Calveley and Stretton, the other was at Wrexham.

After the war the camp became a holding camp for men about to be demobbed and then became a satellite storage area for the US Air Force base at Burtonwood. Once the Americans had left, it served as an unofficial training area for the learner drivers of mid-Cheshire!

On part of the camp area a prefabricated concrete structures factory has been erected along with other industrial buildings. Meanwhile, to the south at Byley, a very large logistics depot has emerged. This is on the site of a shadow aircraft production site where aircraft were built from parts manufactured as part of the Vickers operation at Chester. When completed the aircraft were towed across to the airfield for checking and then delivery.

Both the post-war industrial developments help to show how an emergency wartime requirement can affect the landscape, as it is doubtful if either the concrete plant or the logistics centre would have been approved if it were not for the wartime activity. A more subtle landscape legacy is the fact that the post-war fields on the old airfield are much larger than those around them and do not have substantial hedges or trees, making the old airfield look more like the remains of an open field agricultural system![8]

Little Sutton

The airfield at Little Sutton was primarily a relief landing ground for Sealand and sometimes Hooton. For this reason it never received permanent runways or buildings. This secondary role does not mean it was a sleepy backwater;

Figure 7: Little Sutton airfield *c*.2009. (Photograph: Tony Barratt.)

aircraft using the airfield at any one time could and did exceed 100 in number, usually of the Tiger Moth type. Flying ended in 1945 and the land was returned to agriculture, but the landowner retained the single hangar as a barn and equipment store.

It appears that a few hedges were removed to allow sufficient space for landing and some of them have not been replaced but the old field boundaries, apparent from the 1910 OS map, still appear to be respected in the farming operations.

The site and adjoining land is to be developed for housing and, although the developers indicated an intention to retain the hangar temporarily for storage purposes, it was demolished in December 2015.

Tatton Park
Tatton Park was not a normal RAF airfield, but it did have a grass landing strip and part of the Park was designated as an Emergency Landing Ground. The landing strip was however for aircraft arriving for storage. These were often planes produced at Broughton, near Chester, and later Cranage. The only infrastructure put in place was a track from the grass landing strip to what is now the main park entrance road along

Figure 8: The taxiway built at Tatton for use by aircraft being flown in for storage around the estate. This track is now used by exhibitors at events such as the Royal Horticultural Society show. (Photograph: Tony Barratt.)

which the aircraft would be taken to 'spare spaces' in the trees. This taxiway is now used by the Royal Horticultural Society as the works access to their show ground.

Tatton Park was the principal parachute training centre in the UK. Paratroopers came by aircraft and after descending, they were given a cup of tea before they returned to Ringway by a Manchester Corporation double-decker bus. Those expecting to parachute into water did not use Tatton Mere but Rostherne Mere which is deeper and colder. Nearly 450,000 parachute jumps had been made over the park and the mere, by 1945.[9]

Calveley

Calveley was one of the three stations, planned in 1941, to take over the fighter role from Cranage. However, during the construction phase, Hitler attacked the Soviet Union and large portions of the German bomber fleet were transferred to the Eastern Front, thus reducing the threat of bombing of the northern cities. The fighters were moved to Wrexham whilst Calveley, when it opened on 14 March 1942, became a training station, although retaining the standard triangular layout of a fighter station. At times there could be 170 aircraft based on the station. Flying ceased at the end of May 1945 and the station closed, only to reopen five months later. Upgraded, it closed finally in May 1946.

In 1947 it was suggested that Calveley should be used as a municipal airport for south Cheshire/north Staffordshire, but nothing came of the proposal. The technical areas became light industrial areas and the grassed areas were returned to agriculture. Unusually, a large commercial area developed next to the A51, where no airfield installations had been; this was presumably to benefit from access to the main road. This area has recently undergone further expansion. The runways survived until the early 1960s when they were radically reduced to road width with the excavated material being used as hardcore for the M6. The surviving 'roadways' were used for car testing and police driver training.

More recently the airfield with other adjoining land was proposed as the site for a new eco-town. This proposal seemed to rely heavily on the planning status of the airfield as 'brown land'. It was a suggestion that appeared to meet few of the other criteria for an eco-town and so received little support and soon died. However in 2015, the site was given planning permission for development as the South Cheshire Employment Park. This should see the bulk of the airfield redeveloped, including a new spine road joining the A51 just to the east of it crossing the canal. The plans approved provide for substantial landscaping between the site and the adjoining fields.[10]

Stretton

Stretton was the third fighter station intended to take over from Cranage. When completed, in 1942, like Calveley, the RAF found that they did not need it so they agreed to swap it for a naval airfield in the Hebrides. The Naval Air Station Stretton was named HMS Blackcap. Its role was to accommodate carrier based aircraft while the aircraft carriers were in a west coast port. Naval aircraft are not left on carriers in port because of the fire risks and other possible problems. During the remaining 36 months of war the station hosted 44 naval squadrons.

Stretton was unusual for a naval airfield in having extra wide runways and some hangars with vertically straight walls.[11]

As well as accommodating visiting squadrons Stretton became home to a naval air yard – like a dockyard but working on aircraft. Here aircraft would be repaired or adapted for overseas service. The yard eventually consisted of eleven hangars. Because of congestion at Manchester, a further two hangars were built and can still be seen by westbound drivers transferring from the M6 to the M56. They were built for occupation by the Fairy Aviation Company.

When the war ended Stretton became the home of the Royal Navy, Fleet Air Arm, Volunteer Reserve, Northern Air Division. These were the weekend flyers of the Navy and like their RAF counterpart they were disbanded by the 1957 Defence Review, whereupon Stretton closed. The technical areas became industrial estates, with the camp area becoming a prison.

The main runway was however kept in pristine condition for about fifteen years. This was because, like Burtonwood, Stretton was designated as a V Bomber dispersal site. These sites were intended to disperse the V Bomber fleet. In the event

Landscapes Past and Present

Figure 9: HMS Blackcap, Stretton, photographed from the air on 10 August 1945. The airyard, to the north of the picture, shows extensive development, but much of the rest of the site is sparsely developed. Reproduced by permission of Historic England (RAF Photography). Compare Plate 11 on page 97 (with which this image is deliberately aligned).

of a deterioration of diplomatic relations three or four V Bombers would go to their pre-designated site and await the order to launch a nuclear attack. By this method of dispersal it was hoped that some at least of the V Bombers would survive a pre-emptive strike. It is not known whether the airfield was used in this way; it certainly was not during the Cuban Missile Crisis, as Prime Minister Macmillan felt that to do so would alarm the Soviet Union.

The main runway is still occasionally used by small private aircraft and it has been suggested that this use could be expanded. The part of the airfield to the north of the M56 continues to develop at a significant rate and this is obliterating the remaining evidence of its former military role. The area to the south of the motorway remains undeveloped.[12] (See Plate 11.)

Poulton
Built by Wimpey in 1943, this airfield was required to reduce the workload of RAF Hawarden. Some thought was given to expanding Sealand, but because of the already intensive use in packing aircraft for transport overseas via the Mersey ports, and also the poor ground conditions, it was decided to build an entirely new airfield at Poulton. This site was selected possibly due to the land being in single ownership. From the outset, despite it having the fighter triangular layout, it was always intended to be a training station mainly for ground attack pilots. The pilots after training in Canada would come to Poulton to practise firing on the gun ranges off Prestatyn and practise bombing on Fens Moss, near Wrexham.

Although the station complement was about 1,000 in 1945 they have left little obvious evidence in the landscape beyond that shown in the photograph (Plate 12). Thirteen of the fourteen temporary hangars were removed soon after the

Landscapes Past and Present

Figure 10: RAF Poulton, photographed from the air on 10 January 1947. Just off the top left of this picture is the future site of the Grosvenor Garden Centre and in the right hand corner is Eaton Hall. By the time the photograph was taken almost all the blister hangars had been removed, although it appears one has remained on the third dispersal point from the bottom. Reproduced by permission of Historic England (RAF Photography). Compare Plate 12.

station closed in 1945. For a period after the war the Grosvenor family used the runways for their own flying needs, but now it seems to be used only for the Grosvenors' First World War Rolls Royce armoured car to be given a periodic outing along one of the runways.[13]

The Unexpected Legacy
The intensity of flying training from the airfields of Cheshire, such as Poulton, Cranage, Ringway and Calveley, was so great that it has left a further legacy. Across the county there are memorials to the many personnel who died while on operations or training.

The terminals at Manchester Airport have several memorials, including to the Parachutists, and to the civilian Air Transport Auxiliary, who would deliver any aircraft anywhere in the UK and later Western Europe. At various other locations in the county, for example Greasby and Nantwich, can be found memorials dedicated to individual pilots who stayed with their planes to save civilian lives at the cost of their own.

At Blacon, Chester, there are the graves of 461 members of the British and Commonwealth air forces – many of whom were killed while training. A few German aircrew were buried in Cheshire but most if not all were re-interred at the German War Cemetery at Cannock, in Staffordshire, after the war.

Given that landscape history is necessarily about change, in the main Cheshire has survived the imposition of airfields on to its farmland quite well. At Hooton, Burtonwood, Stretton and now Calveley, extensive industrial and commercial developments are leading to a total obliteration of their former roles, but the 'new' landscapes here are not without interest. Manchester, Ringway, has undergone incredible expansion, eliminating both its agricultural and its earlier aviation history, but it is now the site of a major contributor to the regional and national economy. Little Sutton is soon to be consumed by houses, and Woodford will probably follow suit. Tatton and

Poulton have slipped back into their former parkland roles albeit Poulton carries some scars. Only Cranage has not fared too well. Most of Cranage has succeeded in returning to agriculture and the administrative and technical areas that have been abandoned are reverting to brush and scrub, perhaps harking back to the heathland of former centuries. However, the concrete plant does undermine this return to a rustic landscape. Cheshire has, however, managed to avoid suffering the indignity of some sites in East Anglia whose runways have become storage sites for hundreds of containers.

There are also several examples of 'a legacy in the landscape', as alluded to in the title of this paper. Where the airfields have been redeveloped, most of the traces of an earlier use have largely disappeared, but the Plates show that at Stretton and Poulton the footprint of the former runways can still be seen on the ground. Many of the road names on the new developments have aeronautical connections and no doubt a redeveloped Woodford will have a Lancaster Close or a Nimrod Drive. Some of the hangars have been re-clad, with a reduction in the size of the doors, so making their previous use less obvious but preserving them nonetheless. The recent grant successes of the Hooton Park Trust may mean that some of the aviation architecture here will survive. Let us appreciate the landscape of our aeronautical history while we can!

Endnotes
1. *Report of the Mid-Cheshire Joint Town Planning Advisory Committee* (Chester, 1929), 132–33 (Criteria for selecting sites for airfields).
2. The airfield at Sealand was originally called North Shotwick, as Shotwick had been the preferred location for the airfield. It would therefore have been in Cheshire. When the airfield was expanded the new part was called RAF Queensferry. The name RAF Sealand was adopted in 1924 to avoid confusion with RAF Scopwick in Lincolnshire. North Shotwick was actually

Cheshire Airfields

designated in a Civil Aviation Department report in 1919 as one of a possible national chain of airfields. But little activity resulted from the report, although the airfield figured in some notable experimental flights.

3. A. Ferguson, *Cheshire Airfields in the Second World War* (Newbury, 2008); D.J. Smith, *Action Stations* (Cambridge, 1981); R. Smith, *British Built Aircraft Volume 5: Northern England, Scotland, Wales and Northern Ireland* (Stroud, 2005).
4. P. Richardson, *Hooton Park, A Thousand Years of History* (n.d.); E. Stuart and M. Lewis, *What did you do in the War, Deva?* (Chester 2005); <<http://controltowers.co.uk/H-K/Hooton_Park.htm>>.
5. H. Holmes, *AVRO: The History of an Aircraft Company* (Marlborough, 1994).
6. B. Abraham and L. Jones, *Manchester Airport – Ringway Remembered* (Stroud, 2004).
7. A. Ferguson, *RAF Burtonwood* (Wargrave, 1989); <<http://controltowers.co.uk/B/Burtonwood.htm>>.
8. J. Bamford and R. Collier, *Eyes of the Night – Air Defence of NW England 1940–43*, (Barnsley, 2005); <<www.rafcranage.org.uk_RAF_Cranagewelcome to_RAF_Cranage.html>>.
9. J. Chartres, *The Training of World War Two Secret Agents in Cheshire* (privately published, 1991); Anon, *Wartime Tatton 1939–45* (Chester, 1995).
10. <<http://controltowers.co.uk/C/Calveley.htm>>.
11. As an aircraft carrier was usually less than 80 feet wide the Admiralty only provide 100 feet wide runways. RAF runways were 150 feet wide. With regard to hangars, most naval planes had folding wings so could be housed in hangars with angled walls which required smaller roof spans; these often shed less of a shadow, so making photo reconnaissance by an enemy more difficult.
12. <<http://controltowers.co.uk/S/Stretton.htm>>. Is it worth asking how advisable it would be for light aircraft to land at Stretton so close to the westbound carriageway of the M56?

Landscapes Past and Present

13. Stuart and Lewis, *What did you do in the War, Deva?* Although mainly about Welsh airfields, there is also coverage of several Cheshire airfields, in some depth, in D. Pratt and M. Grant, *Wings Across the Border* (Wrexham, 1998–2005), 3 volumes.

8

LANDSCAPE AS HISTORY – PROBING ITS PUBLIC INTERFACE

Julie Elizabeth Smalley

Abstract
This paper outlines extensive practitioner research involving a variety of adult learning in six communities across and beyond Cheshire. In experimental spirit, a 'landscape based' approach to exploring pasts was tried – and with very positive effect. Consequently the discipline of Landscape History is further considered, but from a business angle, asking **what is its public interface and does it have a competitive edge?** Provision and demand are gauged using sources and methods. Also a range of analytical tools from the commercial world is applied, some exposing weaknesses and threats, but especially ones suggesting strengths and opportunities. It is concluded that as landscape historians, we are indeed reaching some of our markets but evidence indicates we may have plenty more yet to meet.

Conundrum and Quest
I am ardent about Landscape History. It is a joy to be a constant learner and to exchange insights. Many of us feel just the same! Some things frequently puzzle me though, particularly following casual conversations or searches for both reading material and like minds.

> How _do_ people understand the term 'Landscape History', or even see landscape _as_ history? Can the subject be distinguished amongst a rich range competing for

attention? Does the pursuit actually matter to anyone except its already signed-up enthusiasts?

That said I decided to probe a little deeper and put the questions on a firmer footing, not least because they have quite widespread application. The exercise proved timely. Sixty years before this paper was delivered came the publication of *The Making of the English Landscape* (1955), for which W.G. Hoskins later gained the moniker of the Father of Landscape History. Of course, other figures were highly influential. Nonetheless both this notable year and 2016 which marks the 30th anniversary of the Chester Society for Landscape History (CSLH) create an excellent punctuation point.

What really sparked this research however was a conundrum. In the popular domain, both home and abroad, informal lectures and guided tours are offered just about everywhere. I am an avid listener. Too often though I have found myself on the receiving end of surprisingly date-loaded and monochrome views of the past, delivered usually with little context – a 'yesteryear' in greyscale. Rarely did this bring anything closer as much as push it further away, and it is harder to retain. The sense lingered, with dismay, that other audience members did not always embrace this style of account either.

It occurred to me that the essence of landscape *as* history is surely both 'out-there' and 'right-here'. Therefore it seems the most immediate, visible and tactile form that an interest in the past can take, for anyone. Yet somehow it manages to be less recognised and understood and probably less used as historical evidence than it rightfully deserves. So, touching on this (admittedly expansive) interface seemed a worthy area to investigate. After all, Hoskins himself said the English landscape was the richest historical record we possess.[1]

Matters for Investigation

My double question of interest can be expressed as: what is the public interface with Landscape History and does it have a competitive edge to exploit?

First, a quick rear view glance is necessary because it has curious resonance with today. Besides Hoskins's groundwork, things were happening in the sky during that same decade which gave brave new perspectives: in the 1950s came an increase in aerial surveys. This followed the RAF reconnaissance sorties of 1947. Startling overviews of the ground surface enabled recognition of *pattern*. In turn this caused a shift to realising that functional zones existed in a spatial sense rather than as separated sites and monuments. Now this is quite intriguing because it appears the latest technology in airborne surveying is helping to win over possible new 'converts'. What and who will be revealed later in this paper. The next section now turns to sources and methods.

Practitioner Research 1 – Experiential Evidence

During my postgraduate studies to qualify as tutor in Post-compulsory Education and Training, I made a lightbulb decision. I would combine elements of English language teaching with historic environment. This meant cue-and-response, elicitation and above all 'personalise and localise'. I set up a scheme to develop the concept. For five years I based my research primarily in the towns of Crewe, Nantwich, Middlewich, Winsford, and Congleton but also Hazel Grove and even further afield in Painswick (Glos) and Letcombe Regis (Oxon).

Qualitative data was gathered from a variety of field experience which was pleasingly eclectic. It comprised

Figure 1: The Nantwich townscape

delivering my own ongoing programme which I named 'Vital Minds Lifelong Learning' (VMLL for convenience), currently numbering almost 250 sessions. I also included around a dozen occasional talks in contexts ranging from historical and heritage societies, to museums and women's groups. Three CSLH Discovery Days were facilitated plus two map workshops for the annual CBA[2] Festival of Archaeology. These innovative Discovery Days were conceived specifically for CSLH. I held them in compact towns which I considered offered the most for members to 'do' practical landscape history. Combining printed source material with carefully prepared self-guided circuits to walk and then open discussion to share findings was a popular formula. Text for museum exhibition panels which I co-researched and wrote sparked later discussions with visiting members of the public. Some experience did in fact overlap

Landscape as History

with ten years of earlier work, in particular leading scores of guided walking tours.

The original objective was to see if, instead of 'date and detail', I put 'landscape and looker' at the heart of historical enquiry could it work, even for the non-historically minded? With 'context at the core' (a curious inversion!) would engagement – and recall – be better? In each case, we plunged back in time by looking at localities and settlement very much from where we were – either standing in the open air or walking or even sitting inside: ambient, virtual, real or re-imagined. This flexibility both in mind and body gave far greater chance of input from those present because it started from a common point of familiarity. It should be made plain that prior to introducing any session, thorough work on physical and documentary sources was in place to ensure diligent standards. *Evidential* interpretation was always stressed.

A natural kind of market segmentation occurred arising from (a) age bands, (b) interest groups, and (c) contact frequency. For example, some of the guided walks were for French twin-town citizens (Nantwich) and some for local children (Middlewich). The 'Vital Minds Lifelong Learning' programme (numerous locations) and the Festival of Archaeology event (Crewe) were held for retired people. Others were convened more as social clubs which anticipated a range of topics to hear, not necessarily history-related. Yet others were for specialist societies, for example those devoted to Family History with members attending who were experienced in aspects of historical research (Hazel Grove). For CSLH the Discovery Days were (and still are) for interested members to acquire practical skills. Some were single contact whilst others were regular meetings held over a period of years, with loyal 'repeat attenders'.

Figure 2: A map workshop for all ages.

As for method, empirical evidence focused mainly on attitudes and knowledge and to a lesser extent skills. It was collected via interaction at the time plus comments and testimonials afterwards. Although plainly subjective this was direct and honest. Quantitative data was harder to collect, chiefly due to not wishing to spoil the experience in order to press for information! Attempts were made, though, by way of questionnaire. Perhaps this is a potential future direction should greater hard evidence ever be required. So then, hundreds of individuals from all sorts of groups effectively comprised one batch of sources. The derived methodology is known as 'wisdom of crowds'.

Landscape as History

Practitioner Research 2 – Product and Package
The other source was of course the archaeology of the landscape itself: how portions formed, survived and how its very incompleteness – yet still visual presence – may be read as a record. 'New' content, via fresh appraisal of urban areas and their surroundings, was exciting to research and present. On the whole, for these people, usually the less experienced 'lifelong learners', such bundling of material was a major departure – and eagerly taken up. Nothing similar appeared to be on offer.

To aid analysis and interpretation I developed a bespoke formula. Assembling, and testing, this template proved enormously practical and is one which this author uses in almost every instance. The five key elements are: **maps; terrain** (in urban as well as rural areas); **settlement** (including empty spaces, buildings and architectural character); **place-names** (especially streets, lanes, parts of towns); and **route-ways** (all modes of transport and their networks). Reference to **boundaries** and the working heart of any given community, its 'economic lifelines', underpinned these five.

Concepts were introduced by bringing in a thoughtful mix of these elements. Winsford's oldest thoroughfare (Delamere Street) is sited on a ridgeway atop a glacial moraine. Railway town Crewe's maps and roads reveal its relatively recent dispersed rural settlement. Middlewich and Nantwich street names such as Leadsmithy Street (Middlewich), Waterlode (Nantwich) and Pepper Street (both) are measures of earlier commerce and connections, once simple 'translations' are pointed out. Of course the sheer stretch of the 'diachronic' (i.e. 'through time') factor is relished to give glimpses of *process*. This pattern/process pairing is critical for understanding landscape and settlement change which in turn helps explain why our towns and countryside look as they do. Imprints of language on the land are absolutely everywhere. Hence, and by popular request, 'linguistic legacies' have come to form a prominent strand. An everyday example of sources was the humble street sign.

When appropriate to theme or location, this kind of indicator gave us tremendous scope to deconstruct meanings. Taking the names on the right, there are the *chester, ton* and *ford* as ubiquitous starting-points for relating words to settlements. The emphasis here lies on starting-point as it is always stressed that earliest possible spellings of any name must be sought when attempting to establish meaning. Dodgson's *Place-Names* volumes[3] are instrumental. Again people readily drew on what they knew as a platform for adding more – knowledge acquisition known as constructivist learning. Furthermore the rigour of this essential process just outlined is usually well accepted. Because social values are encoded within any designed landscape, we had endless scope again to examine the thinking behind why places appear as they do. Confident remarks were put forward because of more ownership of understandings. For *non-specialists* this is a heartening aspect of beginning what could be termed the 'curiosity cycle' and integrating thinking with environment.

Figure 3: A Cheshire street sign.

Whilst giving obvious pre-eminence to the landscape and its diverse physical and historic features, clearly this is a stepping-stone – a stepping-stone to engagement with the sources. In consequence, attempts at valid historical conclusions can start to be drawn.

Literary Supplement
A supporting survey on publicly available printed output was felt to be necessary. This I did in tandem with my oral presentations. As ever, it was to determine if and how anything for official dissemination acknowledged broader historic landscapes. Information points were scrutinised for leaflet or booklet offerings. I also incorporated observations from my previous PGCE Study.[4] These semi-casual observations are regularly updated. Put simply though, very little material strayed away from a chronological narrative and monument-driven format.

In a 'straw poll' of bookstores, periodic checks were made on titling and positioning of bookshelves and their categories. Of special interest of course were those dealing in history, archaeology, heritage and the historic environment. Amazon's online store also received a brief audit. It was revealing. Basically there is little if any separate gathering of landscape titles. Instead labels are for British, World, Military, Political, Medieval, a little Ancient and Archaeology (and sometimes Outdoors or Travel can encompass Landscape History). This replies to the second question of the trio of puzzles posed at the outset. The subject is not clearly distinguished, although some crossover occurs. However, the fact that it does embrace so many disciplines is actually what gives the appeal. It should be noted that Hoskins's seminal book is still available. Indeed Amazon show this as a bestseller – in 'Geographical History'. Conversely, the Taylor revision of Hoskins (1988) is under 'Historical Geography'! Fluid boundaries are to be expected. Luminaries in the field are present and publishing and a select number of excellent academic volumes can be sought out, especially on online stores. But this literature review concerns itself with the *readily accessible* public interface.

Findings From Real World Research
Outcomes were extremely encouraging. Here is a set of observations in no particular order.

- Perceptions of the discipline are disappointingly fuzzy. Few realised it existed *per se*.
- People found that engagement with the landscape through walks, maps, discussion and looking at other historical sources was time very well spent. Initially some were frankly fearful of 'a vision of boring facts and figures of our past'. Post-session comments included, however, 'a fascinating series of revelations' and even, in true interdisciplinary spirit, 'a stimulating discussion about all aspects of social history and human development'! This answers the third puzzle posed at the start. The pursuit *does* matter to a broad and varied range of people.
- Participants readily drew upon their own memory maps and/or made fresh connections. Contact with something physical helped clarify blurry grasps of chronology – and often corrected misapprehensions. With mapwork, or 'fingertip history', many would trace connections on paper and perhaps communicate narratives. What surprised tutor and participants alike was that the fascination of this 'brand of delivery' was for many a welcome way of viewing and understanding bits of the world.
- The essential joint nature of the group activity allowed us to be co-explorers. Repeated encounters demonstrated how easily the landscape avenue to history could be entered and assimilated – and again by widely varying participants, who are in a sense customers of the product.

Landscape as History

- Many individuals realised that landscapes are, in fact, physical AND mental AND emotional in the way that we appreciate them. They spontaneously expressed this notion. This is in fact well attested in archaeological theory with the 'phenomenology' and 'ideational' schools of thought. In these, landscapes are deemed to be constructs of experience, emotion and memory. Quite a few respondents reflected this by mentioning their 'clear visions of former streetscapes' and heightened sense too of soundscape – speech, accents and dialects were recalled.
- Quite a few attendees admired what they called a new-found '3D feeling'. They felt *inside* and *part* of the subject matter. Landscape combines geography with history. I was told by some that this apparently carries connotations of being 'easier' (fewer dates to devour?) and fascinating to explore. One person winningly summed up the landscape approach to the past as – 'a primary sorting key'. I think that is significant.

At this interim point, public interfaces with Landscape History genre showed ample promise. We seemed to be tapping into a vibrant energy. A competitive edge was becoming clear.

Competitive Edge Put to the Test
So what is the business angle and why consider it to be of any use? Certainly it is crucial to know who and where are the markets if the subject and indeed its societies are to survive and thrive. Besides, younger generations of enthusiasts are always needed to carry it on.

Throughout the preceding activities I thought about possible gaps in the market and how they could be filled. Based on real-world experience I compiled an initial SWOT analysis of the discipline of Landscape History and the most outstanding strengths, weaknesses, opportunities and threats that became apparent. This is by no means exhaustive.

Analytical Tools: SWOT ANALYSIS

STRENGTHS
Relatability: This standout quality is possible because of that compulsive air of mystery. Also sensory notions were in play: the feeling that this is *where* events happened or circumstances played out. Participants would readily be co-actors in investigation rather than passive recipients.
Forward looking: 'Learn from the past and look to the future' is a fitting motto of relevance. People are helped to realise that we are in fact custodians of the land and its heritage, so a healthy realisation of stewardship is fostered.
Inclusivity: From expert down to appreciator, being age-friendly, overseas visitor-friendly and family-friendly makes for an inclusive and versatile pursuit. This has important ramifications in today's pluralist communities, for example in helping new arrivals absorb cultural background.
Non-reliance: Provision is not dependent *solely* on textual documents and their skilled interpretation and ready availability, at least in the first instance; nor are dig sites needed. Fuller understanding, naturally, can only come with further reference to sources, but at least initial attention is aroused.
Soft skills: Topical and desirable, so-called soft skills are employed: those of empathy, creativity, critical thinking, groupwork ... things that computers cannot beat us at (yet).

WEAKNESSES
Recognition: In terms of the very first question posed at the outset, ask any cross-section of people what 'landscape history'

means. If a definition is offered at all, it might be restricted to a location's geology; or lovely vistas with strong aesthetic appeal; or perhaps wild places. Worked, humanised landscapes are not seen as a mode of enquiry. Automatically this is something of a weakness in promoting a history session or piquing interest. Enthusiasm is obvious, yet do members of the general public know what they are enjoying is in fact Landscape History? It does not appear so! Would they prefer 'Landscape Detecting'?
Mediation: It is fair to say plenty of general knowledge was always needed, due to its interdisciplinary span. So of course, mediating between landscape and looker is essential – yet part of the fun, allowing knowledgeable individuals to contribute. For popular uptake, focus then is far more likely to be on landscapes which are urban and/or *relatively* modern. Added to this are local settings which constitute the immediate environment of an individual or group or other areas which they know well.

OPPORTUNITIES
All-round workouts for the mind: Being so interdisciplinary in character causes questioners to seek, or see, links. Psychological stimulus is obvious, and thanks to its outdoor, physical nature there is further potential for health and well-being beyond purely historical and investigative motives. For ageing populations in a high-tech world this is undeniably worthy!
Transferable skills/Knowledge: The typically holistic approach transcends any single locality. Thinking is allowed to become comparative and even international in scope. In this way unlimited application exists to delve into certain areas and contrast openly with others.
Converts: One of the newest excitements – 60 years after those early aerial surveys – comes in the shape of flying drones. Remotely piloted, they bring home riveting (if occasionally

controversial) birds-eye views as never seen before. Is this a sudden interest in what we ourselves already know to be 'settlement morphology'? Software too allows map imagery to be compared on a now and then basis, or before and after, using 'swipe' or 'spyglass' options. Memorabilia sites on the internet are taking this up with enthusiasm. Local urban change materialises on the screen and brings in whole new strata of awareness to what *we* have long found enchanting. Attracting new, younger and different enthusiasts seems distinctly possible.

Media appeal: Competition arises from the obvious and high profile pull of TV archaeology. 'Young Archaeology' clubs exist but there is no apparent counterpart for landscape historians. Could this be a *complement* rather than a substitute? An opportunity, not a threat?

THREATS

Convention: Often unproductive! Destructive changes within contemporary environments erode historic traces – and maybe the sense they ever did exist underfoot. Current levels of interpretive skill simply do not appear enough to appreciate and record, and possibly protect from environmental challenge. In an astonishingly fast pace of landscape destruction ('applications flood in to build on greenfield sites'[5]), identification skills are crucial.

Presentation media on site: Despite quite often being top quality, an overload can actually interfere with the chance to do one's own assessment. The imaginative faculty gives way to a fully laid on, multiple, high-tech experience.

Phone apps: Handheld devices and Smartphone apps can assist walkers to 'tread a heritage trail'. Again, they may be a little too closely guided and do it all for you. Yet, is this too not

Landscape as History

Landscape History at its iceberg tip? So, it is a threat but also an opportunity to gleam.

Analytical Tools: from USP to PLC

UNIQUE SELLING POINT (USP). As suggested, Landscape History is the most immediate, visible and tactile form that an interest in the past can take, for anyone.

MARKET GAP. A niche was identified for this defined subject genre both in popular printed output and learning provision. By extension this might involve a variety of market segments besides the familiar profile. Young people especially deserve encouraging.

PRODUCT LIFE CYCLE (PLC). In terms of 'introduction, growth, peak and decline' product life cycle (and it is a realistic analogy) I suspect and hope that we are somewhere on the 'growth' phase.

Sharpening the Business Angle

It is true to say that limitations in an informal study such as this are probably sample size and reliance upon random responses with inherent bias. Those without any interest at all were simply not present. Yet the rest were not 'already signed-up enthusiasts' either! Whether it was parties on civic friendship cultural visits; museum and exhibition-goers; appreciative Americans soaking up their heritage; retired people busy with lifelong learning classes; genealogy enthusiasts; or even children marching like soldiers on a real Roman fort site … the appetite, or demand, was obvious. To deliver and research all this was a joy.

Charting new ways forward is a clear imperative. As suggested in Market Gap above, there could be openings in a number of areas. Five are identified here. Museum outreach is an obvious candidate, not as traditional silent tours but as engaged participants. Interactive walks would need to be pitched at appropriate age/interest/knowledge levels. The all-important youth market could possibly be met not just through schools but via the Scouting and Guiding movement which itself values the outdoor element paired with skills acquisition. Accomplishments are recognised in specific awards such as the Duke of Edinburgh scheme. There are always youth clubs. It is noted that the discipline of archaeology has long supported a nationwide establishment of Young Archaeology Clubs. Perhaps a companion branch might be a useful development. The family leisure sector is a sizeable component but one which does not as yet appear to include landscape detection as a fun introduction to outdoor discovery. Finally, domestic tourism and indeed overseas marketing surely represent two more avenues of potential, and expanding, interest groups. The production of fresh learning materials is an exciting corollary to these openings.

Concluding Matters

So, landscape as history – does it really remain only a theme of local history or instead has it its own special reach to the public? Empirical evidence reinforces a view that our niche can match competition, yet is still under-exploited. What is compelling, I find, as did the majority of participants, is that Landscape History is instrumental in giving us insights into ourselves and society. Almost everyone can contribute. It underscores the urgency of enhancing our research and the education-led nature of the Chester Society for Landscape History.

Celebrating the enthusiasm of those I have worked with was, I felt, quite important but more so was to show ways in which all this might be taken forward. To encourage critical thinking, at any age, at least an elementary appraisal of sources is a positive move. Clearly this can lead to so much more. My probing of this public interface continues. I keep testing the evidence! It inspired me and I hope it might inspire readers too. After all, landscape is possibly the richest historical springboard we possess.

Endnotes:
1. W.G. Hoskins, *The Making of the English Landscape* (London, 1955), 14–15.
2. Council for British Archaeology.
3. J. McN. Dodgson, *The Place-Names of Cheshire*, 5 parts in 7 volumes (Cambridge, 1970–98).
4. PGCE Independent Study (2010) prepared for Manchester Metropolitan University.
5. From the Campaign to Protect Rural England (CPRE) promotional material, Sep. 2015.

Suggestions for Further Reading

Books

M. Headon, *A Landscape History Alphabet: A Guide to Sites and Features in our Area*, Monograph no. 2 (Chester, 2010). [Published by CSLH.]

W.G. Hoskins, *The Making of the English Landscape* (Harmondsworth, 1970), but also available in other editions, including the revision by C. Taylor (London, 1988).

R. Macfarlane, *Landmarks* (London, 2015).

R. Muir, *Be Your Own Landscape Detective – Investigating Where You Are* (Stroud, 2007).

Article

J.E. Smalley, 'Heritage … with humour … as "therapy"? Please explain!', *Journal of Community Archaeology & Heritage*, II (3) (2015), 238–43.

INDEX OF PLACES

All locations are in Cheshire unless prominent towns or cities, or otherwise stated.

Abergele (Conwy) 196, 197, 198, 201
Acton 19,
Adlington 114, 124
Alderley 19, 43
Aldford 74
Althrey Hall (Wrexham) 67, 73, 77, 84
Altrincham 15
Alyn, River (Denbighs. and Flints.) 65
Appleton 6, 19–20, 23, 165, 168, 171, 174
Ashton in/near Tarvin 134, 151, 156
    Ashton Hayes Estate 139
Aston 62

Bache Hall 61, 76, 85
Badger Clough 103, 112, 124
Barnton 15, 16
Barrow 131, 136
Barton 222
Bebington 215
Beeston 23, 130, 151
Belgrave 56, 71, 75, 83
Bersham (Wrexham) 60, 83
Bidston 215
Birgrieve 101
Birkenhead 45

Index of Places

Birmingham 226
Blacon 235
Bollington 41
Borderlands (Ches.–North Wales) 47–79
Bosley 42
Brereton 24
Bretton (Flints.) 65, 83
Brimstage Hall, Wirral 71
Bromborough 61
Bromfield (and Yale, Wrexham) 59, 60, 64, 65, 68
Bronington (Wrexham) 68, 77
Brough (Derb.) 112, 117
Broughton (Flints.) 71, 83, 228
Bruen Stapleford 59
Bruera 58–59, 60, 85
Budworth 23
Burton 60, 66, 75, 77, 83
Burtonwood 4, 216, 223–24, 227, 231, 235
Butley 42, 43
Buxton (Derb.)
    routes/roads to 110, 112, 116, 117, 120, 121, 122
Byley see Cranage

Calveley 216, 227, 229–30, 231, 235
Cannock (Staffs.) 235
Capenhurst 59, 61, 71, 86
Carrington Moss 26, 28–30, 31
Chadderton (Greater Manchester) 221
Chapel-en-le-Frith (Derb.) 115, 116, 117

Chat Moss (Lancs.) 30
Cheadle 19, 41
Checkley cum Wrinehill 15,
Chester 45, 56, 60, 65, 76, 133, 215
　　port of 117
Chirk (Wrexham) 50–51, 77, 83
Cholmondeley 74–75, 84
Chorlton 59, 84
Church Coppenhall 15
Church Lawton 17, 19
Cilgwyn (Conwy) 189
Clotton 43
Clutton 53
Coddington 53–54, 59, 74, 85, 122
Colwyn (Conwy) 96, 189, 190, 194, 204, 205, 206, 209, 211
Colwyn Bay (Conwy) 7, 188–214
Colwyn Bay Hotel 199–201, 204, 206, 211
Colwyn Bay Station 196–99, 201, 204, 205, 208, 209
New Colwyn 202, 210, 211
Old Colwyn 188, 205, 209–10, 211
Combermere 4, 216, 222
　　Abbey 62
Congleton 35–37, 45, 120, 226
　　enclosure 28, 34–37
Cow Worth, Stanney 62, 86
Cranage 216, 225–27, 228, 229, 231, 235, 236
Crewe 245
Cuddington 21

Index of Places

Dane, River 120
Danes Moss 26
Dee
    River 3, 10, 49, 53, 60, 64
    valley 13, 30
Delamere
    Gresty's Waste 46
    see also forests
Denbigh (Denbighs.) 64, 189, 206
Dernhall 43
Dinerth (Conwy) 189, 192, 206
Disley 110, 124
Dodleston 54–55, 59, 65, 72, 73, 83
Duddon 43
Dukinfield 45

Eccleston 51, 56, 72, 83
Edge 77, 85
    Hall 54
Eirias (Conwy) 189, 190, 194, 196
Elton 51, 58, 86
Emral Hall (Wrexham) 49–50, 66, 67, 68, 73, 77, 84
English Maelor (Maelor Saesneg) 3, 47, 49, 59, 63, 64, 65, 66–67, 68, 73, 75, 76, 78
Errwood (Derb.) 117
Esclusham (Wrexham) 60

Farndon 225
Featherbed Moss 26

Flint Castle (Flints.) 56
Foulk Stapleford 49, 59, 73, 85
Frodsham 73
    Lordship 15

Gowy
    River 10, 49, 51, 58
    marshes 59
    valley 49
Goyt, River 117, 125
Grappenhall 43, 164, 165, 183
Greasby 235
Great Budworth 16, 164
Grimsditches 174

Hale 133
Halghton (Hanmer, Wrexham) 69, 84
Halkyn (Flints.) 73
Hampton Heath 72
Hanmer (Wrexham) 49, 63, 68, 84
Haulton Ring (Hanmer, Wrexham) 51, 68, 75, 84
Hawarden RAF (Flints.) 233
High Legh 43
High Peak 109
    see also forests
Holyhead (Gwynedd) 7
Hooton 216, 218–21, 227–28, 235, 236
Horton cum Peel in/near Tarvin 130
Horton near Tilston 15

Index of Places

Huntington 59, 60, 85
    cum Cheaveley 60
Hurleston 15, 19
Hyde 45

Iddinshall 51–52, 61, 73, 85
Ince 58, 61, 63, 86
Irby 61, 63
Is-y-coed (Wrexham) 60, 77, 83

Jordanwall Nook 101–2

Kelsall 15
Kerridge Hill 105–8
Kettleshulme 43, 115
Kinderton 18
Knutsford Heath 46

Lache Eyes 133, 134–35, 159
Latchford 165, 170–71
Lathkill, River 109
Lea Newbold, near Aldford 60, 74, 85
Leighton Moss 28
Lindow Moss 26, 27
Little Sutton 216, 227–28, 235
Liverpool 218, 223, 226
Llandrillo-yn-Rhos (Denbighs.) 188–90, 193, 194, 204, 205
Llay (Wrexham) 60, 83
    Hall 66, 68, 69, 73, 78, 83, 89
Llwydcoed (Conwy) 189, 191

Llyn Tro (Wrexham) 51, 66, 70, 75, 83
Llys Edwin (Northop, Flints.) 70–71, 83
Llys Farm (Prestatyn, Denbighs.) 63
London 134, 154
    routes/roads to 108–9, 117, 166, 167, 170, 172, 186
Lower Burse (Wrexham) 67, 73, 83
Lower Huxley 72, 85
Lower Walton 16
Lyme
    Hall 112
    Park 102, 113
Lyme, Overhanley 43
Lymm 6, 15, 23, 165, 168

Macclesfield 17–18, 45, 116, 120, 121, 124
    routes to 114–16, 118, 120
    see also forests
Maelor Cymraeg see Welsh Maelor
Maelor Saesneg see English Maelor
Maes-y-groes (Wrexham) 76, 84
Malpas 76
Manchester 29–30, 226
    Airport (Ringway) 5, 216, 222–23, 224, 229, 231, 235
    Corporation 29–30, 222, 229
    Ship Canal 29, 31, 164–65, 182, 183
Manley 17
Marbury 20–21
Marchwiel (Wrexham) 75
Marford (and Hoseley, Wrexham) 59, 60, 64, 66

Index of Places

Marlston-cum-Lache 57, 72, 73, 75, 83, 134
Mellor Old Moor 99–100
Mersey, River 73, 175–76, 181, 182
Middlewich 18, 245
Mobberley 15
Mochdre (Conwy) 189, 190, 205
Mossley Moss 29, 35, 87, 88
Mouldsworth 134, 136, 139, 156

Nantwich 235, 242, 245
Nerquis (Nercwys, Flints.) 72
Netherhanley 43
Netherleigh Hall 57, 77, 83
New Hall (Chirk, Wrexham) 50, 51, 77, 83
Newton near Middlewich 18
Northampton 17
Northenden 20
Northop (Flints.) 65, 83
Norton Priory 62

Old Beachin (Coddington) 53, 54, 59, 85
Odd Rode 24–25
Over 15, 16
Overton (Wrexham) 66, 84

Panniers Pool 118–19
Peel Hall Estate 6, 91, 92, 130–63
Penley (Wrexham) 66, 67, 69, 75, 76, 77, 83, 84
Penmaenrhos (Conwy) 189, 192, 197
Penrhyn Bay (Conwy) 203

Peover 17
Plassey (Wrexham) 73, 74
Poulton 17, 83
    Abbey 62, 63, 78
    RAF 98, 216, 233–35, 236
Powys Fadog (Wrexham) 64, 65
Prestbury 114
Prestatyn (Flints.) 63
Puddington 53, 86
Pulford 56, 65
Pwllycrochan Estate (Conwy) 191, 198–99, 203, 206–8
    Halt 196–97

Radnor near Somerford 18–19
Rainow 105, 116, 117
Rhiw (Conwy) 189, 190, 191, 192, 205, 211
Rhos-on-Sea (Conwy) 193, 210
    Rhos Bay 193, 196, 204–5, 211
Ringway see Manchester
Rostherne 16, 43
Rulow Brook 119, 120, 121, 122, 124
Runcorn 23, 41, 171
Ruthin (Denbighs.) 64

Saighton 60
    Grange 72
St Werburgh's Abbey, Chester 17, 60–61, 62, 63
Sealand, RAF (Flints.) 216, 227, 233, 236–37

Index of Places

Shotwick 53, 55, 59, 72, 85
    RAF 216, 236-37
Shrigley Moor 103
Shurlach 16
Shutlingsloe 118, 124
Speke (Merseyside) 218-19, 224
Sproston 19
Stalybridge 45
Stanlow Abbey 62
Stanney 62-63, 86
Statham 165
Stockport 32, 34, 35, 45
    Moor 32-33
Stockton
    Heath 167, 171-72
    Quay 172, 183
    Yate 171-72
Stretton 97, 216, 227, 231-33, 235, 236, 238
Swettenham 15

Tabley 15, 225
Tarvin 130, 151
Tattenhall 15
Tatton Park 216, 228-29, 235
Taxal 43, 115, 117
Tegg's Nose 119
Thelwall 5-6, 95, 164-187
    Eyes 175, 181-182, 185
    Waste 93, 94, 175-179, 183

Thurstaston Common 46
Tranmere 15

Upton
  Grange 61, 78, 85
  Heath 40
  Manor 61

Valle Crucis Abbey (Denbighs.) 62

Wallasey 15
Warrington 167, 169–70
Weaver, River 58
Welsh Maelor (Maelor Cymraeg) 64, 67
Weston near Runcorn 15, 23
Wettenhall 15
Whaley
  Bridge 109–11
  Moor 103
Whitchurch (Shrops.) 65, 76
Wildboarclough 118
Willington (Wrexham) 67, 69, 73, 75, 77, 84
Winsford 245
Wincham 19
Wincle 120, 122, 124
Wirral 10, 13, 30, 53, 61, 71
  see also forests
Witherwings 174, 175
Wolvesacre (Wrexham) 67, 76, 84
Woodford 216, 221, 235

Index of Places

Wrexham (Wrexham) 3, 49, 59, 60, 227, 230, 233
Wybunbury 15

Yale (Wrexham) see Bromfield

References to other regions/counties and countries:

Derbyshire 4, 39, 110, 112
Durham 46
East Anglia 236
Essex 3, 47, 49
Hertfordshire 47
Holland 133
Lancashire 4, 38, 62, 223
Leicestershire 39, 42
Lincolnshire 47
Norfolk 47
Northamptonshire 39
Northumberland 42, 46
Nottinghamshire 39
Shropshire 42, 45, 46, 58, 63, 65, 78
Staffordshire 4, 63
Suffolk 3, 47, 49
Wales 47, 52, 56, 65, 72, 73, 78
West Midlands 47
Yorkshire 46, 47

INDEX OF SUBJECTS

aerial photography
  general 6, 47, 99, 120, 124, 130, 241, 251–52
  specific 51, 77, 87, 94, 97, 98, 121, 150–51, 232, 234
airfields 4–5, 97, 98, 215–38
assarts: see woodland, clearance of

boundary markers 4, 43, 103–8, 120–21, 123–25, 177
bridges 28, 36, 70, 109–10, 151, 173, 181
Burdett's map 26, 166, 171
burgesses 17–18, 32–33
burial mound 103
butts 17–18, 20, 42–43

canals 35–36, 172–73, 183
  see also: Manchester Ship Canal
Cash, S. 144, 148, 161
castles 47, 53, 56, 60, 65, 75, 156–57, 163
champion countryside 5, 9, 11–12, 39–40
chapels 60, 117, 143–44, 194, 205, 212
cheese 117, 170–71
Chester Society for Landscape History xiv, 1–3, 5, 7, 10, 240, 242–43, 254
churches 193–94, 197, 203–5
Civil War (1640s) 75–76, 101
climate 11, 52
closes 9, 12, 15, 18–20
Clwyd-Powys Archaeological Trust 77
common fields 8–9, 16, 40, 42, 137
  see also: open fields
common pasture 5, 6, 9–10, 12, 21–36, 94, 108, 109, 114, 173
crosses 4, 99–104, 110–14, 117–26

Index of Subjects

diaries 6, 133–34, 136, 143–44, 151, 152, 154–55, 173–74, 182
disafforestation 61, 101
doles 17, 20, 137
Domesday Book 13, 30, 64
dry stone walls 101
duck decoy 131–35, 159

Enclosure Awards 12, 21–22, 25, 34, 40, 43, 88, 174, 181
enclosure processes 5, 8–46, 66, 101, 108, 125, 173, 176–79, 183
Enclosure Trusts 34–36, 45–46
estate maps
    Peel Hall 91, 131, 134–35
    Thelwall 6, 93, 95, 164, 168, 176, 179–82

farm buildings 152–53
field-names 47, 75, 114, 124, 131–32, 135–37, 157, 158, 182
    See also: doles, loonts, selions, Town Fields, quillets
First World War 218, 221, 235
flatts 17, 19, 42–43
forests
    Delamere 26, 41
    High Peak 101
    Macclesfield 104, 109, 110, 112, 114, 119–20, 123, 124
    Wirral 61, 69
    other 65, 78
furlongs 17–18, 178

garden mound 149–52, 156–57
gardens 6, 77, 144–53, 156–57, 158
geology of Cheshire 11, 49
glebe terriers 20
granges 60, 62–63, 78, 120
guide stones/stoops 99, 118

hangars 218–23, 228, 233–34, 236, 237
Hearth Tax returns 6, 143
hedges 105, 177, 185, 218, 228
Hoskins, W.G. 1, 3, 39, 47, 49, 131, 240–41, 247
hotels 7, 199–201, 203–4, 206, 208, 209, 211, 213
    see also: inns

inclosure: see enclosure
inns 169–71
Inquisitions Post Mortem 11, 19, 42–43

Landscape History, nature of 1–7, 239–55
Leland, J. 49, 74
Lifelong Learning 2, 242–43
loonts 15–17, 19–20, 179–80

manor houses 53–55, 59, 64, 67
market gardening 29–30, 39, 45
market 167, 182
meadow 6, 9, 12, 181
meresmen 105
milestones 112
mills 32, 137, 150, 170
moated sites 3–4, 47–86, 89, 149, 151
monasteries 62–63, 102
    see also: Combermere Abbey, St Werburgh's Abbey,
    Chester and Stanlow Abbey
moss-rooms 5, 26–28, 32–34, 87–88
mosses 5, 25–28, 87–88, 174
    reclamation of 28–31, 45

new building 18, 30, 32–33, 35–49, 53, 73, 75, 136, 153–54, 156, 200

Index of Subjects

newspapers 195–96, 198–206, 208–10
night-soil 29–30

Ogilby's map 109–11, 124
open fields 5, 8–10, 12–21, 40, 42, 179
    see also: common fields
orchards 20, 73, 150, 152, 155
Ordnance Survey maps 16, 76, 99–101, 105, 107, 193, 202
Ormerod, G. 117, 143, 148, 156

packhorse routes 109, 112, 117–18, 125, 171
parks 60, 64, 72, 120, 182, 228–29, 236
peat 5, 25–28
place-names 7, 66, 103, 112, 115, 117, 120, 124, 155–56, 174, 188–214, 245–46
ponds/pools 51, 71–72, 133, 137–38, 150–52
poor relief 74–75, 186
    see also: workhouses
population 13, 30, 32, 52, 164–65, 182, 187, 205
potatoes 165, 179–81
probate inventories 6, 154, 155, 168

quarries 107, 193
quillets 15

railway stations 7, 192, 196–98, 201, 208–9, 211
railways 7, 29, 31, 35–36, 39, 190, 192, 196–98, 209
roads
    in Peak District 99, 109–12, 114–17, 120–23
    other 17, 35–36, 74, 166, 170–72, 173, 175, 178, 201, 203
    see also: turnpikes
Royal Air Force (RAF) 216, 218, 222, 223, 227, 228, 231–34, 237, 241
Royal Auxiliary Air Force 219

Royal Flying Corps 216, 218
runways 216, 219–21, 222, 223, 224, 226, 227, 231, 231–35, 236, 237

salt 117
Saxton's map 155–56
seaside resort 7, 188–214
Second World War 30, 219–35
selions 17, 43
settlement patterns 3, 52, 59, 79, 190, 192, 205, 245
stagecoaches 167, 169–71
standing stones 102–3, 118–19, 124–25
Statute (Provision) of Merton 23–25

Tithe Awards 13–16, 21, 28, 41–43, 76, 131, 176, 179, 185, 189–90, 193, 195
tower houses 71–72, 156–57
Town Fields 13–16, 19–20, 41, 43, 179
trees 105, 112, 177, 218
turbary 21–25, 28
    see also: peat
turnpikes 35, 104, 115–16, 119, 201–2

under-drainage 37–38
US Air Force 223–24, 227

vineyard 152

War Memorials 235
waste 6, 23–24, 61, 78, 94, 101, 108, 109–10, 112, 175–79, 183
Wedge, T. 16, 37
woodland 9–10, 12, 23, 53, 174
    clearance of 49, 58, 61, 65–67, 78
workhouses 33, 35, 37